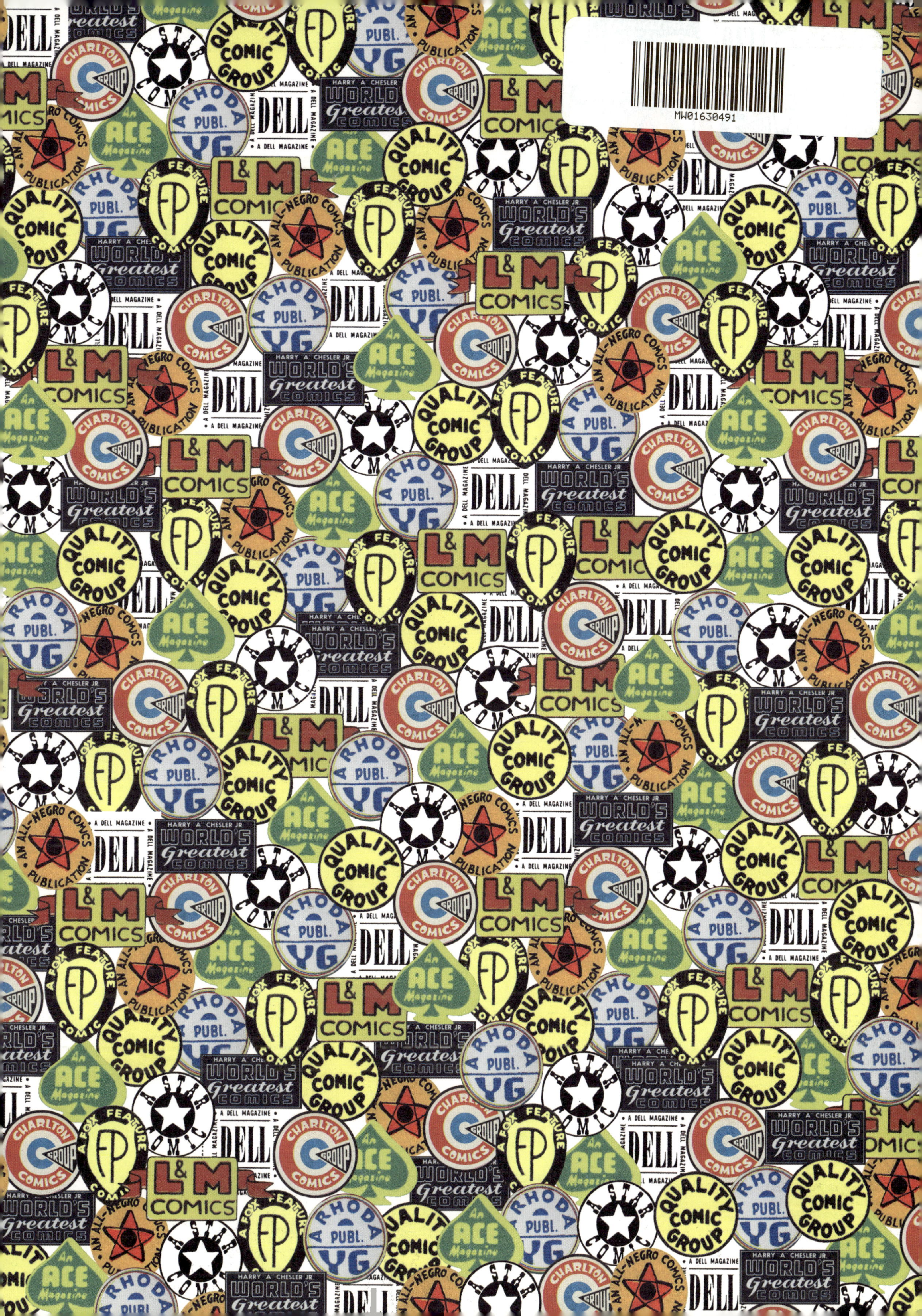

MW01630491
DELL
A DELL MAGAZINE
CHARLTON COMICS GROUP
QUALITY COMIC GROUP
FP
A FOX FEATURE
PUBL. YG
ARHODA
AN ALL-NEGRO COMICS PUBLICATION
An ACE Magazine
L&M COMICS
HARRY A CHESLER JR.
WORLD'S Greatest COMICS
A STAR COMIC

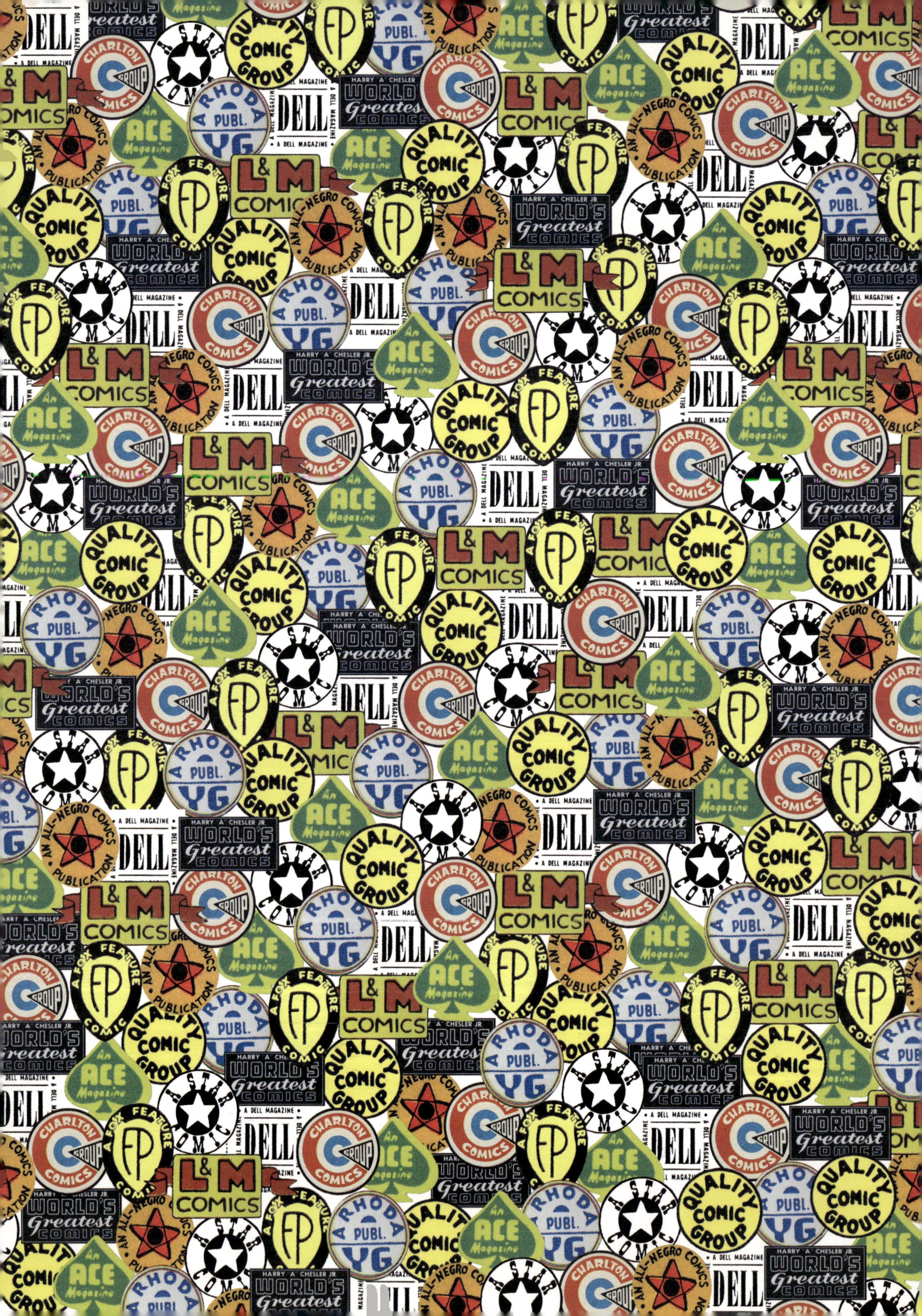
DELL
A DELL MAGAZINE
CHARLTON COMICS GROUP
QUALITY COMIC GROUP
FP
A FOX FEATURE
A RHODA PUBL. YG
An ACE Magazine
L&M COMICS
AN ALL-NEGRO COMICS PUBLICATION
A STAR COMIC
HARRY A CHESLER JR.
WORLD'S Greatest COMICS

MORE HEROES OF THE COMICS

FANTAGRAPHICS BOOKS, INC.

Editor and Associate Publisher: Eric Reynolds
Research Consultant: Kevin Dougherty
Book Design: Keeli McCarthy
Jacket Design: Jesse Reyes
Production: Paul Baresh
Publisher: Gary Groth

FANTAGRAPHICS BOOKS INC.
7563 Lake City Way NE
Seattle, Washington, 98115
www.fantagraphics.com

ISBN 978-1-60699-960-8
Library of Congress Control Number:
2016944765
First printing: October 2016
Printed in China

MORE HEROES OF THE COMICS

by Drew Friedman

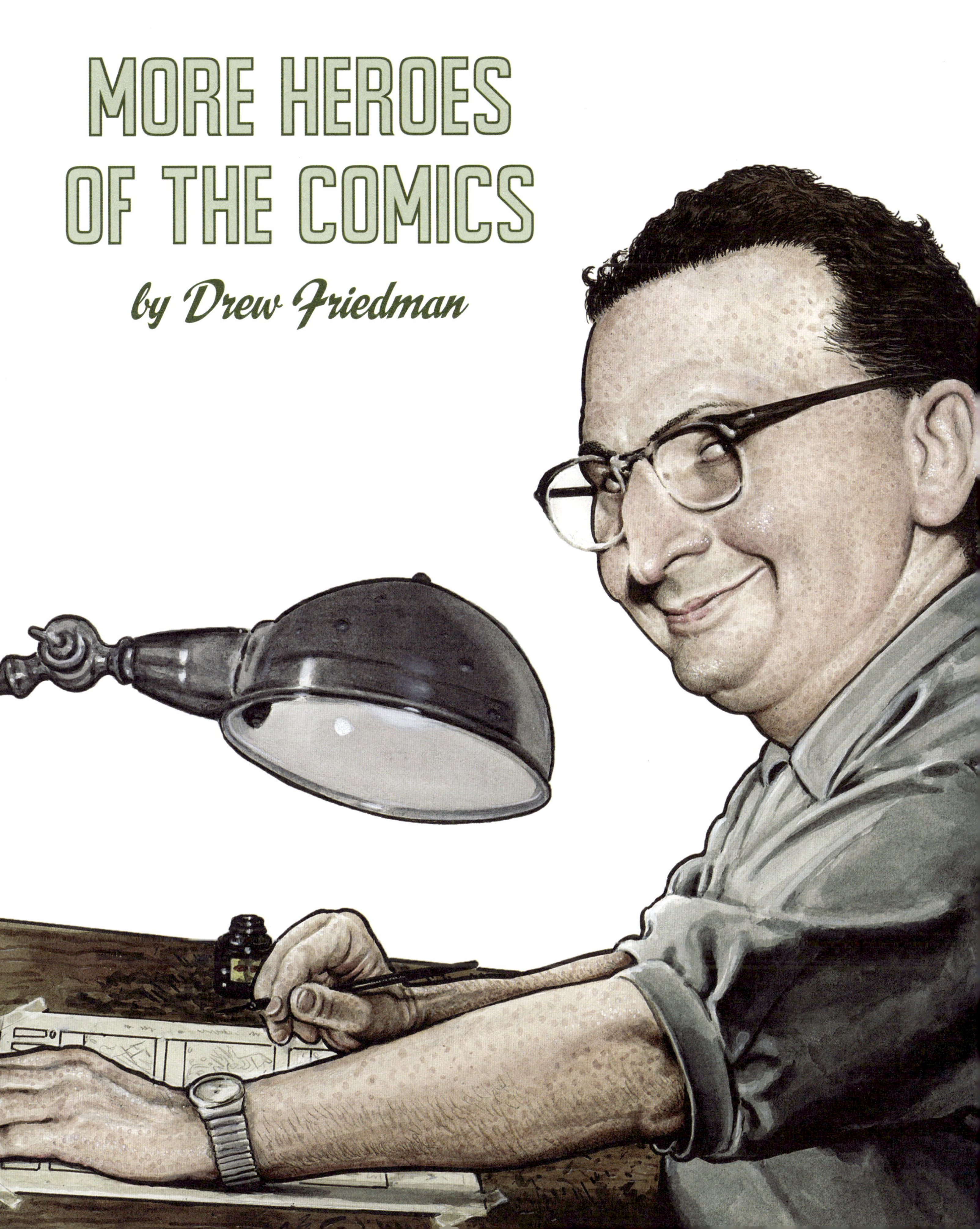

More Heroes of the Comics

I'd like to thank the following people who helped me in the creation of *More Heroes of the Comics*:

Kevin Dougherty, my research consultant. Kevin went above and beyond the call of duty in unearthing rare facts and information about the creators depicted. I can't thank him enough for his help.

My wife Kathy for her support, patience, and most importantly, copy editing.

Thanks to the following for their suggestions, assistance, and positive support:

Todd Klein, John F. Kelly, David Burd, Ron Zoni, Chris Boyle, John Wendler, Carol Fuchs Vigoda, Ashley Vigoda, Frank Santopadre, Bill Schelly, Mike Catron, Paul Levitz, Danny Fingeroth, Joe Frank, William Stout, Daniel Clowes, Marc Maron, and James Warren.

Jackie Estrada's two books of photographs *Comic Book People* were very helpful with reference for several of the more obscure subjects in both my books. The Grand Comics Database and the Digital Comics Museum are both essential sites celebrating the history of comic books. Check 'em out.

Thanks to Karen Green for her wonderful foreword.

Title page portrait: Myron Fass. The Superman image on the back cover is based on a painting by H.J. Ward.

Thanks once again to Jesse Marinoff Reyes for his cover and back cover design. Just when I thought he couldn't improve on his cover design for *Heroes of the Comics*, he proves me wrong. Thanks again to Keeli McCarthy for her magnificent interior design. Thanks to my editor Eric Reynolds and to Gary Groth and everyone at Fantagraphics, this year celebrating their 40th anniversary. I'm proud to be a part of their history.

More Heroes of the Comics is dedicated to Mark G. Parker.

—Drew Friedman, June 2016

FOREWORD

Deep in the archives of Columbia University's Rare Book & Manuscript Library, a researcher may find several envelopes filled with images of distinguished-looking faces. These constitute the *Imagines Philologorum* of Alfred A. Gudeman, a German-Jewish classics scholar, who got his Bachelor of Arts at Columbia in 1883. Gudeman gathered more than five hundred portraits of Greek and Latin scholars: some are copied from the lithographed frontispieces of incunabula, some are formal photographs, and many are the only image ever made of these men (because *of course* they're all men). In 1911, Gudeman published an edition of fewer than one-third of his total cache, after returning to Germany in search of academic work. Just before falling victim to the Holocaust, Gudeman gave the collection to his lawyer, and instructed him to send the images to Columbia, where they sit, still in the envelopes from 1940.

How unfortunate it would be if the faces of the stars of comics were likewise hidden away, unknown to the general public! Many of them were and have been photographed to a fare-thee-well during their lives, to be sure, and a simple Google search will turn up more images of, say, Jack Kirby, than anyone might know what to do with. Some, however, are more elusive—Hy Vigoda, anyone?—and the comics reader may find him- or herself trying to extrapolate the visage of the creators from the personae of the characters on their pages.

Isn't it fortunate, then, that the Golden Age of comics has found its own Gudeman, the phenomenally talented Drew Friedman. Friedman's attention to detail is compulsive in all the best ways, and his portraits reward close and continuous examination. Note, for example, the way the wavy lines in Murphy Anderson's hair echo the motion lines on the page beneath his pen. In a subtle touch of editorial commentary, logo letterer supreme Ira Schnapp sits before his *World's Finest* creation. Curt Swan's generous profile is in dialogue with Superman's elegant one. John Romita Sr., who brought the city to such vibrant life, is shown drawing a building, with Spider-Man barely in the frame. Compare these portraits to the photo reference available in Google Images—Bob Haney's is a good example—and you'll often see the subtle transformation wrought on their features, turning representation into perception . . . and, from there, into art.

Friedman's personal comics history has a long pedigree, dating back to an adolescence spent visiting his father at Magazine Management, where he hung out with Stan Lee. (As you do.) My own familiarity with his work began in the 1980s, with his B-actor comics in *Heavy Metal*, and continued on to his portraits of old Jewish comedians. And, while a world without William Frawley comics is truly a dreary world to be in, Friedman makes it a little brighter by bringing us the faces of the renowned and the obscure, with an almost obsessive care. Cartoonists whose identities often had to be teased out by fans, due to the early industry's widespread resistance to including credits, are not only identified but restored, lovingly. It's said that some cultures believe portraiture steals the soul—with his portraits, Friedman instills the soul. Enjoy.

—**KAREN GREEN:** *Graphic Novels and Ancient History Librarian, Columbia University.*

JACK ADLER

1917-2011

plate 1

Jack Adler was born in Manhattan and attended the High School of Art and Design and Brooklyn College. In the late '30s, Adler worked on color separations for King Feature's *Prince Valiant* Sunday comic. Adler was an inveterate tinkerer and an avid photographer, skills that served him well in taking black-and-white artwork through the numerous steps involved in producing a four-color newsprint comic with a glossy cover. Some sources credit Adler with creating the color separations for *Action Comics* #1 in 1938, and *Superman* #1 a year later. Adler joined DC's staff in 1946 doing production and coloring with his high school friend Sol Harrison.

Adler was especially skilled at using advanced techniques to create compelling and vibrant covers. Comic books were cheaply printed and typically rushed through production, but he created full-color covers featuring photographic enhancements and painterly effects, achieved through a complex series of overlays and washes. His technical expertise led DC through their brief flirtation with 3-D comics in 1953, resulting in the one-shots *Batman 3-D* and *Superman 3-D.*

In 1965, Adler was called on to help reproduce the comic book excerpts featured in Jules Feiffer's seminal *The Great Comic Book Heroes*. Having little to work with, as none of the original art or negatives could be found, he shot Photostats of printed comics through a series of different lights and filters, painstakingly removing the color and generating a workable approximation of the original black-and-white line art that was then recolored.

In 1975, Adler became production manager and vice president at DC Comics, a position he held until his 1981 retirement.

Howard Stern credits his mother Rae's cousin, Jack Adler, as the reason he was able to graduate high school, for his assistance on his senior project. Stern has affectionately discussed his mother's late cousin over the years on his radio show.

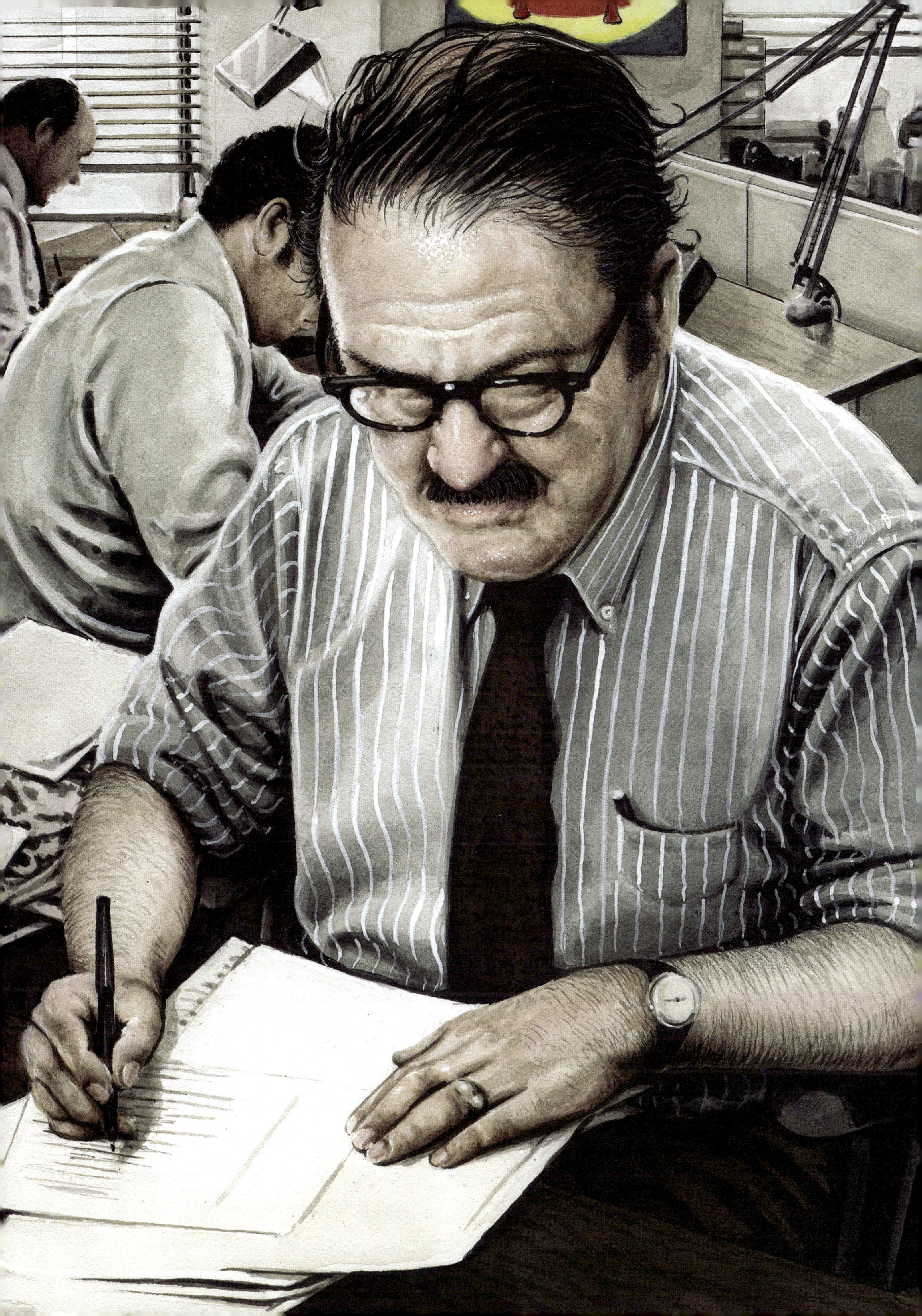

MURPHY ANDERSON

1928-2012

plate
2

Born in Asheville, North Carolina, Murphy Anderson graduated high school in 1943 and spent less than a year at the University of North Carolina before leaving for New York to try his hand at drawing comic books. Murphy quickly landed a bullpen job at Fiction House and published his first comic book work: a two-page, nonfiction filler, "Jet Propulsion," in *Wings Comics* #48. Two months later, he published his first comic book story, "Suicide Smith and the Air Commanders" in *Wings Comics* #50. He entered the US Navy in 1945 and continued comic book and illustration work while stationed in Chicago. In 1947, he returned to civilian life and began a two-year run drawing the *Buck Rogers in the 25th Century* daily comic strip for the National Newspaper Syndicate. He left the strip after two years, and freelanced for Atlas Comics, Ziff-Davis, and DC Comics, where he would soon become a regular presence as an inker and penciler. His first work at DC was published in *Strange Adventures* #12 in 1951.

At DC, Anderson helped revive Golden Age heroes like Hawkman (1964), and, two years later, gave the same treatment to The Spectre. As the '60s turned into the '70s, he joined forces with penciler Curt Swan, and helped define that era's Superman.

Anderson would draw Wonder Woman for the cover of the debut issue of Gloria Steinem's *Ms.* magazine in December 1971.

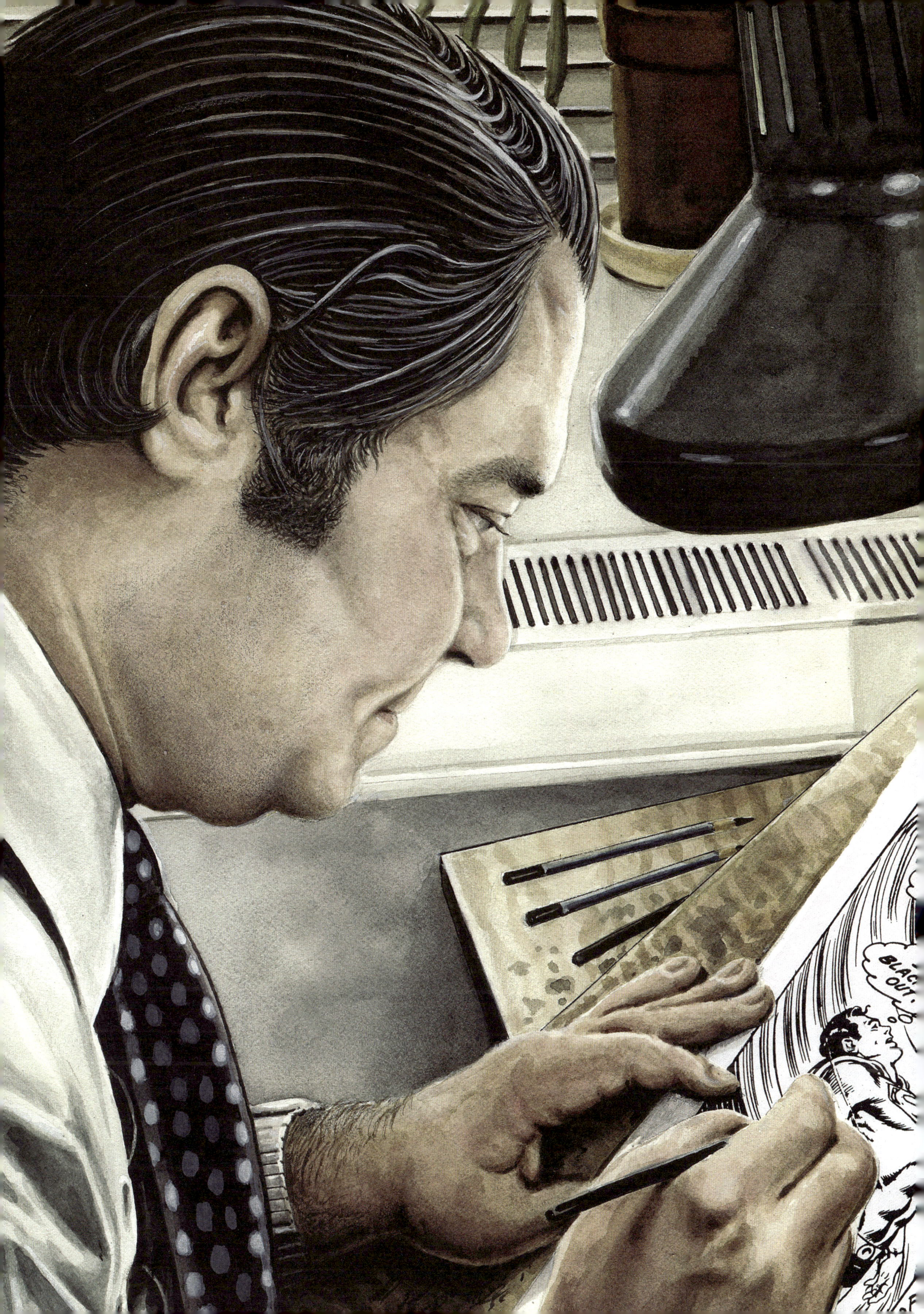

ROSS ANDRU

1927–1993

plate 3

Rossolav Andruskevitch was born in Cleveland, Ohio, and moved to New York as a child where he attended the High School of Music & Art. Soon after serving in the US Army, he changed his name to Ross Andru and began studying under *Tarzan* artist Burne Hogarth at the Cartoonists and Illustrators School in 1946.

Andru so impressed Hogarth that his teacher offered him a job assisting him on the complex Sunday *Tarzan* page. A few years later, he teamed up with inker and high school friend, Mike Esposito, a relationship that would endure for four decades. The team's first published work was in 1950, on the six-page story "Wylie's Wild Horses" for Hillman Periodicals *Western Fighters* Vol. 2 #12. The team's next major step was a long association with DC Comics war titles like *All-American Men of War, Star Spangled War Stories,* and *Our Army at War.* In 1958, they took over *Wonder Woman* and spent nine years on the title, before moving to *The Flash* in 1967.

In 1972, Andru and Esposito briefly published their own *Mad*-influenced humor magazine, with the unlikely title *Up Your Nose (and Out Your Ear).* Soon, Andru found his way to Marvel Comics. He first worked on the Spider-Man-starring *Marvel Team-Up*, but soon began a five-year association with the company's best-selling *The Amazing Spider-Man.* Esposito would eventually join him on the title.

In 1976, he penciled the first-ever DC/Marvel crossover, *Superman vs. the Amazing Spider-Man.*

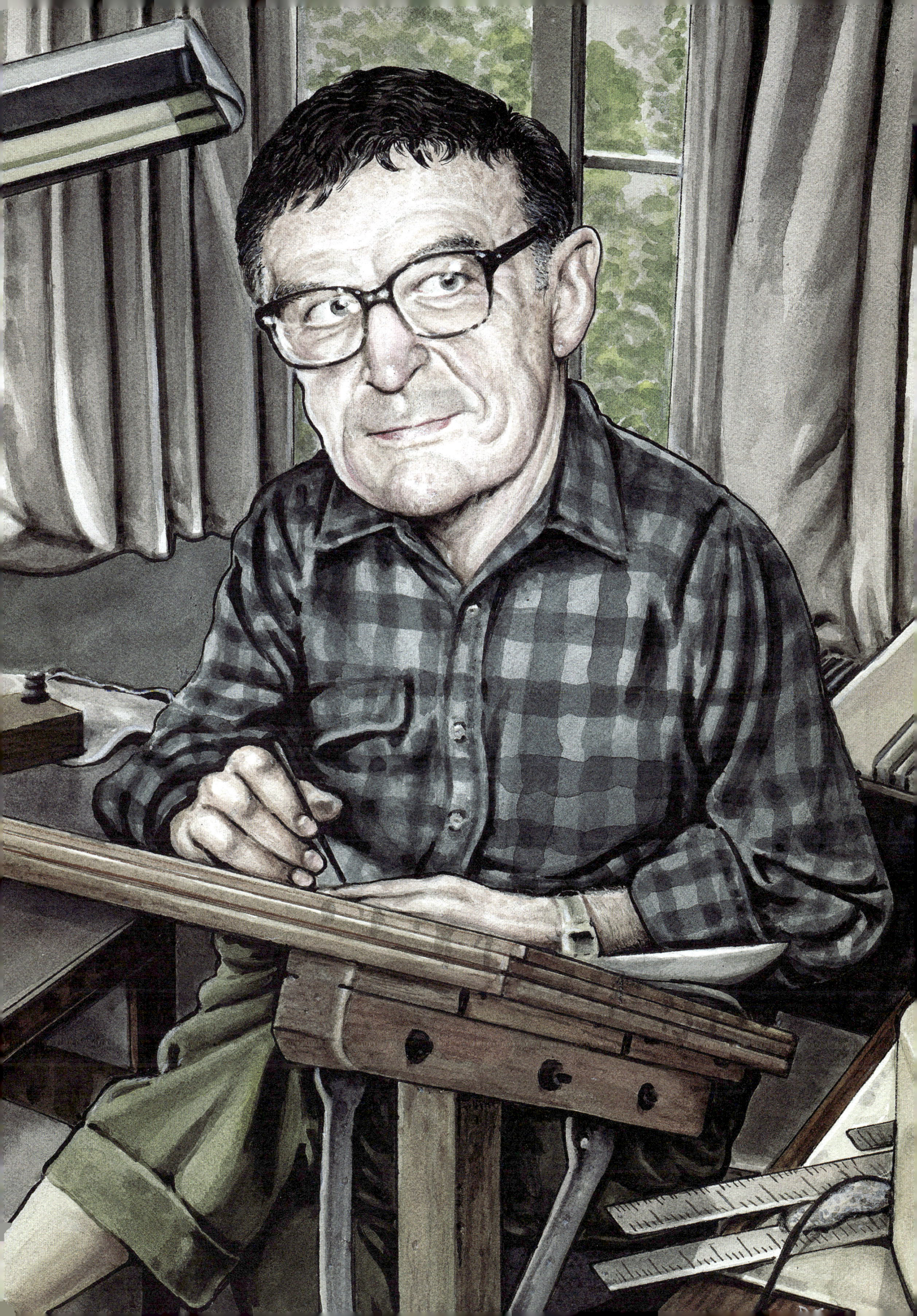

EVERETT M. "BUSY" ARNOLD

1899–1974

plate 4

As a young boy in Rhode Island, Everett Arnold's disruptive classroom behavior earned him the nickname "Busy" from his teachers. Arnold graduated from Brown University in 1921 and embarked on a career in sales, working for a succession of New York printing press manufacturers. In the early '30s, Arnold became vice president of Greater Buffalo Press, a company that specialized in four-color printing of advertising circulars and Sunday comics sections.

In 1937, Arnold started Comic Favorites, Inc., collaborating with several newspaper syndicates to publish *Feature Funnies*, a mixture of reprinted newspaper comics and new material supplied by comic book suppliers like Harry "A" Chesler and the Eisner & Iger shop. By 1939, he bought out his partners, and the company became known as Comic Magazines, Inc. Under the imprint Quality Comics, he released *Smash Comics* #1, their first book of entirely original material. Later that year, Arnold convinced Will Eisner to leave his partner Jerry Iger and join the Quality Comics staff.

Arnold and Eisner met with Henry Martin, sales manager of the Register and Tribune Syndicate, who wanted to create a comic book insert for Sunday newspapers. Arnold launched the project with newspapers in Philadelphia, Baltimore, and Washington DC, and Eisner's sixteen-page comic section featuring *The Spirit* made its debut on June 2, 1940. "The Spirit Section" would would eventually be a weekly insert in twenty newspapers for the next twelve years. At its height, *The Spirit* had a combined circulation of five million copies.

Arnold's comic book business thrived during World War II, as titles that originated prior to the war were allocated a more generous quota of scarce paper. In addition to war, western, and romance titles, Quality Comics published superhero comics, including *Plastic Man* and *Kid Eternity,* as well as the aviation-themed *Blackhawk.*

Quality Comics, Quality Romance Group, and E.M. Arnold Publications were just some of the names Arnold would publish under for the next two decades. He left the comic book business in 1956, choosing instead to concentrate on digest-sized magazines with titles like *Homicide Detective Story Magazine* and *Killers Mystery Story Magazine.*

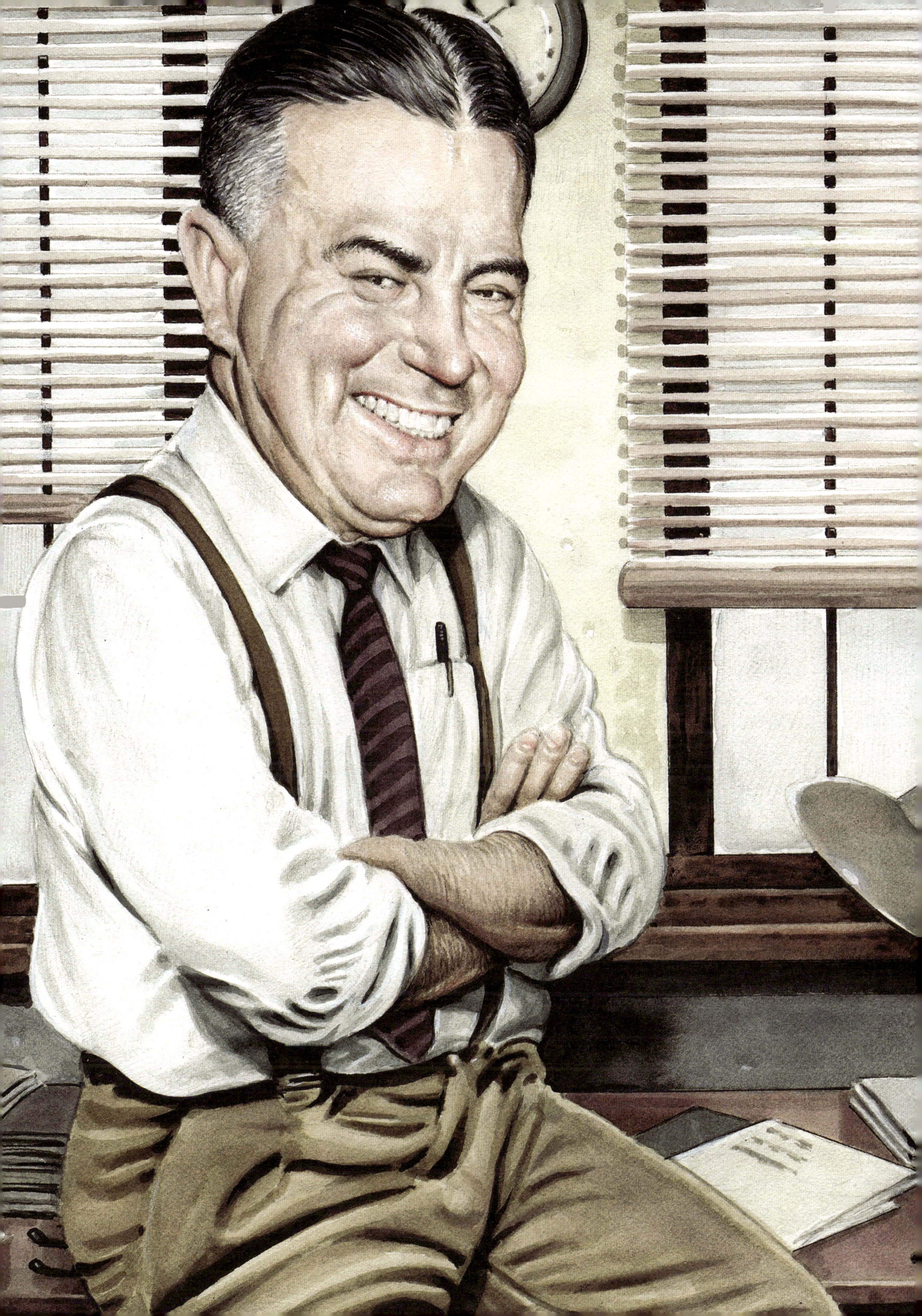

DICK AYERS

1924-2014

plate
5

Richard "Dick" Bache Ayers's first professional work was the comic strip *Radio Ray*, for the military newspaper *Radio Post*, in 1942. After being discharged from the Army Air Corps, Ayers wrote and drew an adventure story for Dell Comics that was never published.

In 1947, Ayers studied under Tarzan artist Burne Hogarth at New York's Cartoonists and Illustrators School (later, the School of Visual Arts). Superman co-creator Joe Shuster visited the class and gave Ayers work at his shop, penciling the short-lived *Funnyman* for Vin Sullivan's Magazine Enterprises. Ayers soon found himself inking and penciling westerns for the publisher, which lead to his creation of the the western/horror hybrid character, Ghost Rider.

Ayers freelanced extensively during the 1950s for Atlas Comics, drawing horror stories for the titles *Strange Tales* and *Tales to Astonish* in the years before the company became Marvel. Ayers was one of Jack Kirby's inkers on the early Marvel superhero titles *Thor*, *Fantastic Four*, and *Incredible Hulk*. In 1964, he replaced Kirby on *Sgt. Fury and his Howling Commandos* and spent the next ten years drawing the World War II title, missing only a single issue.

In 1967, Marvel published Ayers's revamped *Ghost Rider*, toning down the more horrific elements for the Comics Code while keeping the appearance of the character almost identical to the version previously published by the then-defunct Magazine Enterprises.

His later work included promotional comics for RadioShack, like *The Computer That Said No to Drugs*.

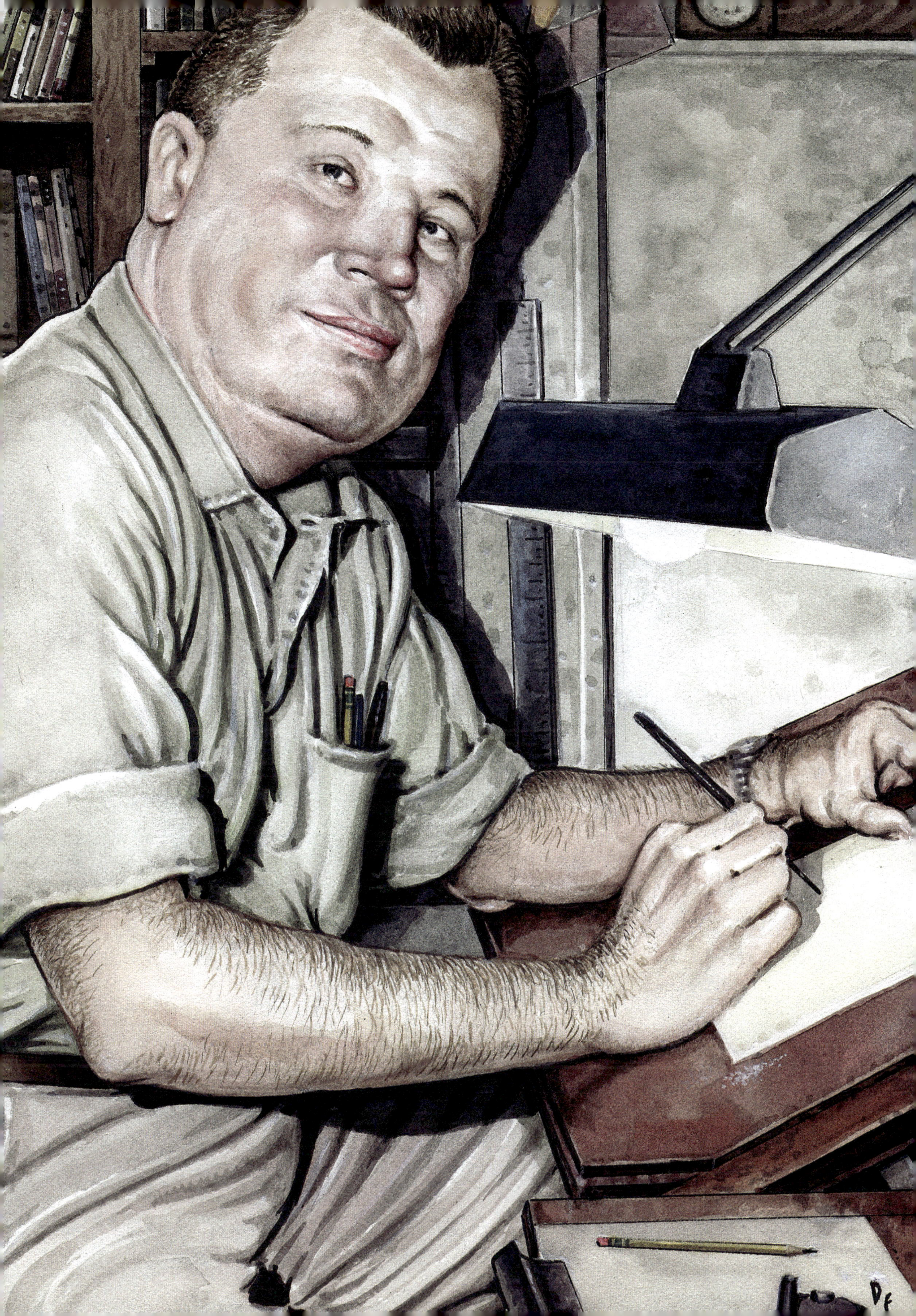

OLIVE BAILEY

1904-1994

plate 6

Born in Dayton, Ohio, Olive Bailey learned to draw from her mother as she and her family crisscrossed the West while she was still a child. Bailey later studied painting at the University of Detroit. She illustrated the 1945 children's fantasy novel, *Shadow Castle*, by Marian Cockrell.

Isabel Manning Hewson wrote and narrated the popular radio fantasy-adventure series, *Land of the Lost,* which aired on the Mutual Broadcasting System from 1943 to 1948. It revolved around the adventures of a young boy and his little sister, who, because of their kindness to a very special fish named Red Lantern (voiced by Art Carney, among others), are granted the privilege of visiting the undersea Land of the Lost. In 1945, Olive Bailey illustrated a popular *Land of the Lost* children's book written by Hewson and published by McGraw-Hill.

In 1946, Max Gaines's Educational Comics, (EC), published the first issue of *Land of the Lost Comics,* written by Hewson and again illustrated by Bailey. The child-friendly series ended in 1948, after nine issues, following Max Gaines untimely death and son Bill Gaines shifting the focus of the company to the more adult-oriented Entertaining Comics. Paramount's Famous Studios also produced three *Land of the Lost* "Noveltoons" shorts starting in 1948, which Bailey was not involved with.

Olive Bailey never worked in comics again; she focused on painting. She settled in Darien, Connecticut with her husband, industrial designer Arno Scheiding.

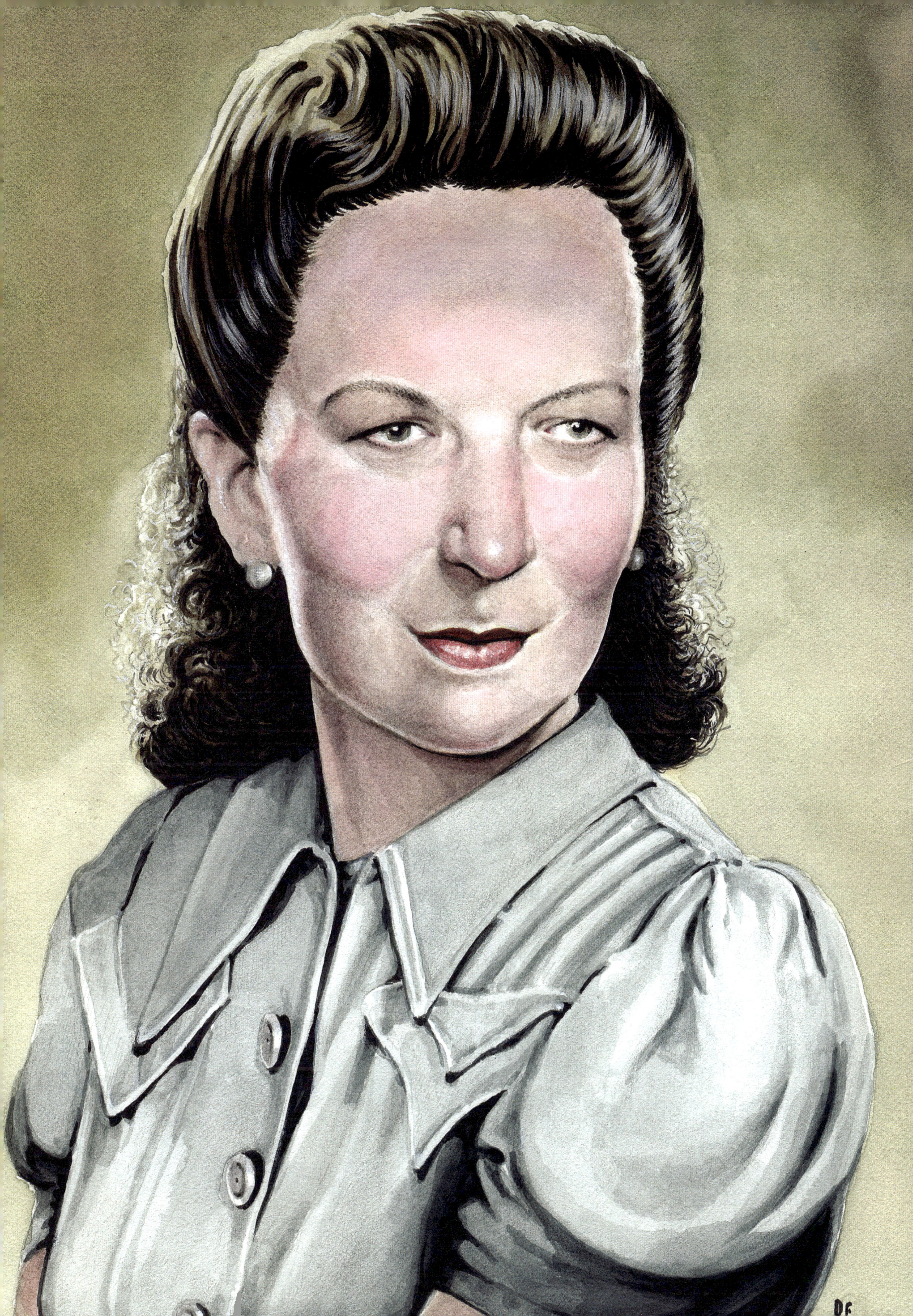

BERNARD BAILY

1916-1996

plate
7

A pioneering comic book artist, Bernard Baily was born in the Bronx and graduated from James Monroe High School in 1934. After an unsuccessful year in college, Baily found himself working for editor Jerry Iger, alongside Will Eisner and Bob Kane, for *Wow, What A Magazine!* He contributed two one-page features: *Smoothie* and *Stars on Parade*. *Wow, What A Magazine!* folded after four issues, prompting Eisner and Iger to start their own comic book production line. Baily joined the first iteration of the Eisner & Iger shop, revamping his *Stars on Parade* into *Screen Snapshots* for 1937's *Feature Funnies*. He also drew a daily comic strip, *Phyllis*, for the Phoenix Features Syndicate.

In March 1938, Baily contributed "Tex Thomson" for *Action Comics* #1, sharing the first issue with the debut of Superman. Tex Thomson lasted thirty-two issues in *Action Comics*. He later teamed up with Superman co-creator Jerry Siegel to introduce the Spectre in *More Fun Comics* #52 (1940).

Baily continued working throughout the '70s at various comic book companies, including Atlas, Marvel, Fawcett, etc., creating cover and interior art. His last published work was a story for DC Comics' *House of Mystery* in 1980.

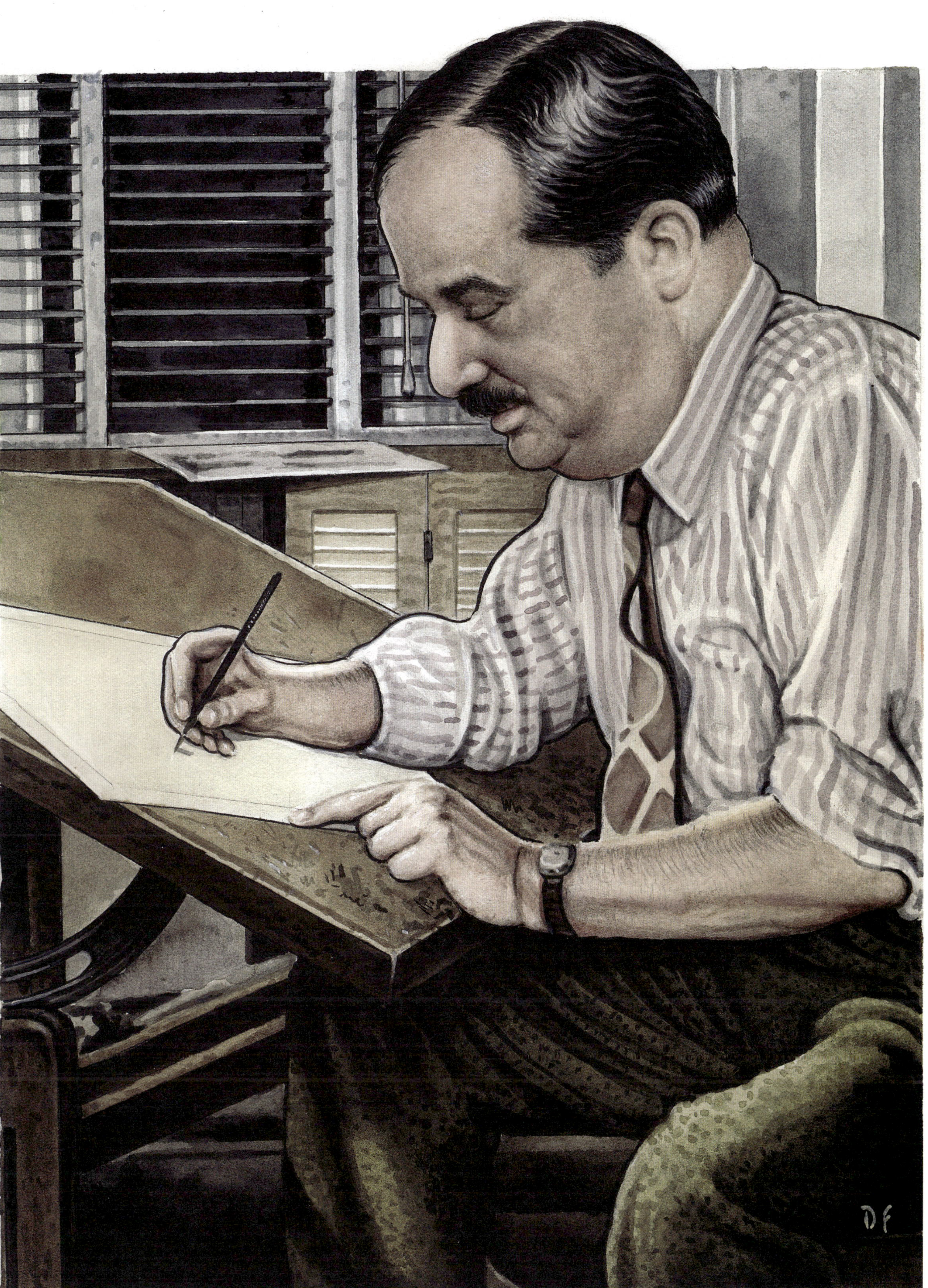
DF

KEN BALD

b. 1920

plate **8**

Born in New York City and raised in Mount Vernon, Kenneth Bruce Bald spent three years studying art at Pratt Institute in Brooklyn. Bald began his comic book career working for Jack Binder's comics production shop. Bald's earliest confirmed work is a sixteen-page story, published in 1942: "Ali Baba and His Forty Nazis," featured in Timely's *Captain America Comics* #42.

Bald's art career was put on hold when he enlisted in the Marines in 1942. He returned to the States in 1946 and went to work for Stan Lee at Timely. His first postwar work at Timely was penciling and inking an eight-page backup story in *Millie the Model* #2, and, in the same month, a seven-page "Miss America" story in *Marvel Mystery Comics* #76. During the same period, he also contributed to Fawcett's *Whiz Comics* and American Comics Group's *Adventures into The Unknown.*

In 1957, he switched to comic strips, drawing *Judd Saxon* for King Features. In 1962, Bald commenced a twenty-two-year stint on *Dr. Kildare,* based on the Richard Chamberlin television show of the same name. The newspaper comic strip outlasted its namesake by eighteen years. He also collaborated with TV producer Dan Curtis to bring Curtis's Gothic soap opera *Dark Shadows* to the comics page from 1971 to 1972. Although he officially retired after his *Dr. Kildare* strip was canceled in 1984, he made a brief return to Marvel in 2015 to create a cover for *Contest of Champions* #2. Bald's effort earned the ninety-five-year-old the Guinness World Record title as "Oldest Comics Artist." Al Jaffee claimed the title in 2016.

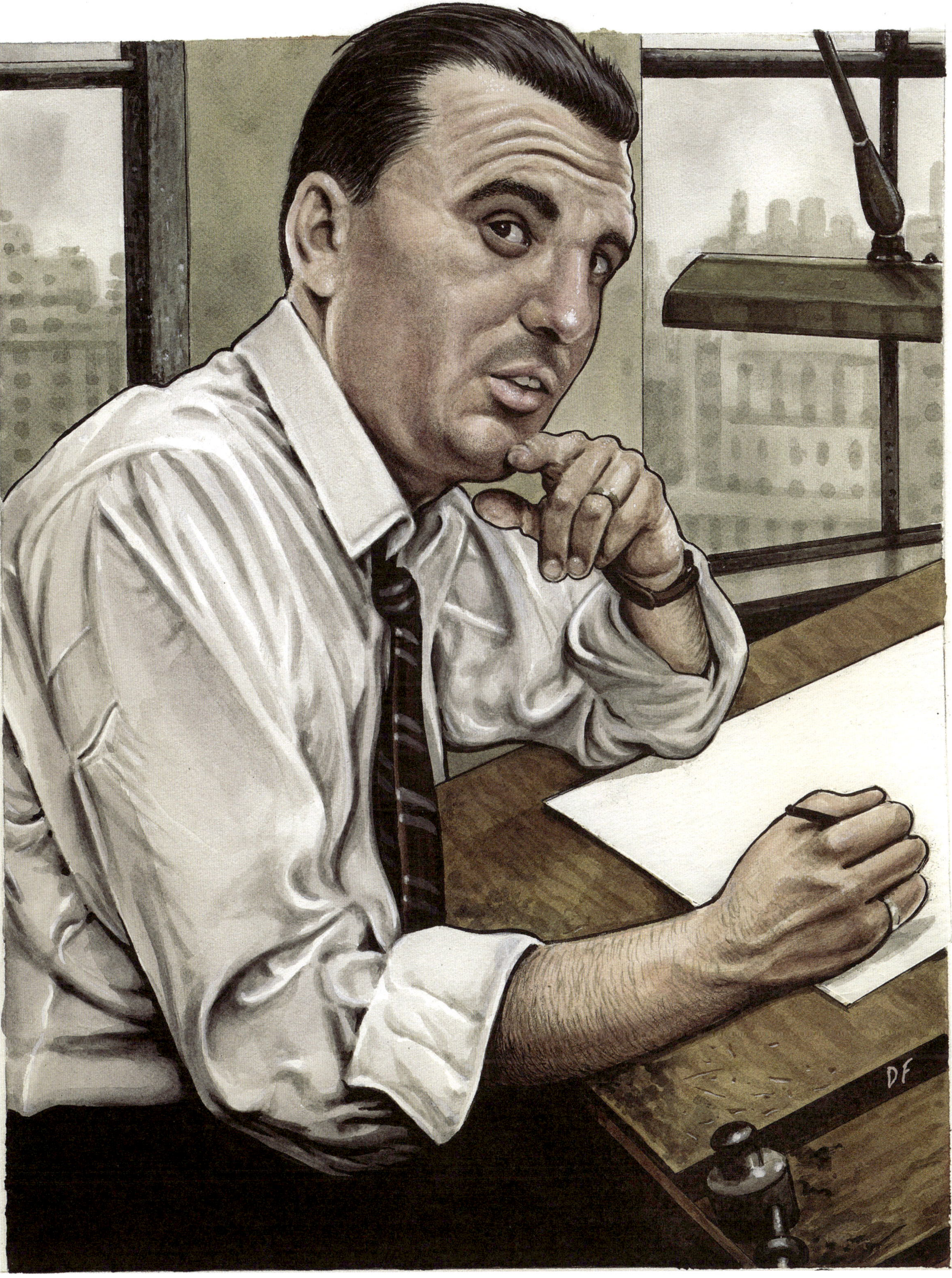
DF

IAN BALLANTINE

1916–1995

plate 9

Ian Keith Ballantine was born in New York City. His father was an actor and his mother was a publicist. After getting his undergraduate degree at New York's Columbia College, Ballantine attended the London School of Economics. In 1939, Ballantine's master's degree thesis on the economics of publishing outlined a loophole in US law that would allow the importation of British books into the United States. Ballantine's idea so impressed Penguin Books founder Allen Lane that he hired the twenty-three-year-old and his wife, Betty, to launch a Penguin office in New York City.

Penguin's paperbacks were largely reprints of British books that had been published in expensive hardcover editions and sold through traditional bookstores. Ballantine thought there was an untapped market for inexpensive titles featuring works by American authors. Ballantine left Penguin in 1945 and launched Bantam Books Inc. Bantam published 4"x7" paperback editions of American authors like F. Scott Fitzgerald, Mark Twain, and Zane Grey. Bantam's reprint of *The Great Gatsby* featured a sexy painted cover that resembled a pulp magazine, accompanied by a blurb promising "The great novel of the sinful twenties."

Along with his wife, Betty, Ballantine brainstormed his next publishing venture, Ballantine Books, while recuperating from a skiing injury. His new imprint would mainly publish paperback originals, with a strong emphasis on new fantasy and science fiction authors like Ray Bradbury, Philip K. Dick, and Anthony Burgess. In 1954, Ballantine Books published *The MAD Reader*, an anthology of stories from the early issues of William M. Gaines's *Mad*, written and edited by Harvey Kurtzman, which was essentially the first book to reprint material from comic books. *The MAD Reader* and the four sequels that followed remained in print for almost fifty years. Ballantine books would also publish Kurtzman's *The Humbug Reader* and, later, his original "graphic novel," *Harvey Kurtzman's Jungle Book*.

Beginning in 1964, Ballantine books struck a deal with William M. Gaines to publish paperback reprints of EC comics, which had been out of circulation for a decade. New editions of *Tales from the Crypt*, *The Vault of Horror*, and *Tales from the Incredible* appeared, along with two collections of Ray Bradbury stories: *Tomorrow Midnight* and *The Autumn People*. All five featured cover art by Frank Frazetta.

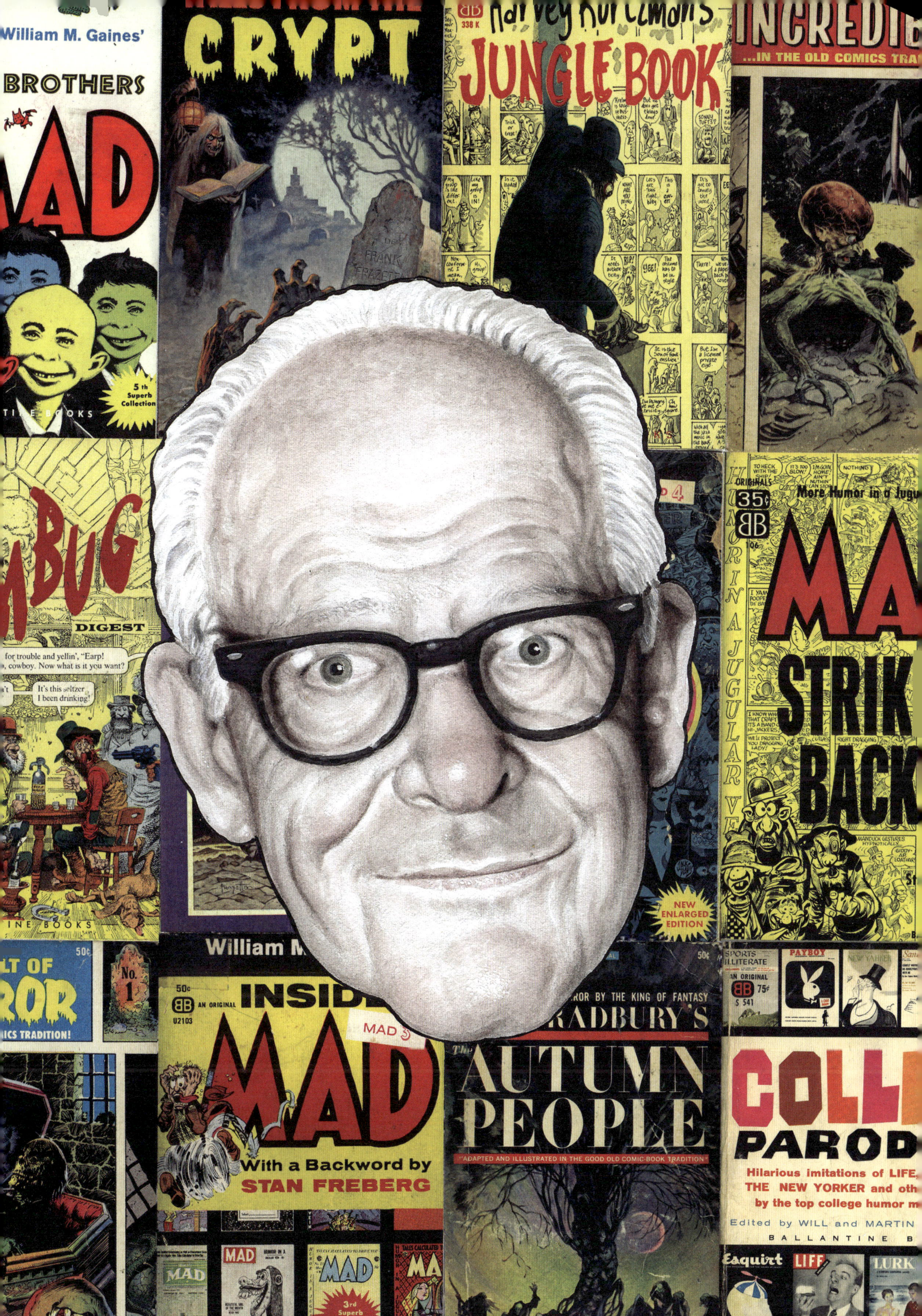

William M. Gaines'
BROTHERS
MAD
5 th Superb Collection
CRYPT
Harvey Kurtzman's
JUNGLE BOOK
INCREDIB
...IN THE OLD COMICS TRA
DIGEST
for trouble and yellin', "Earp! ...cowboy. Now what is it you want?
It's this seltzer I been drinking!
35¢
More Humor in a Jugu
MA
STRIK
BACK
NEW ENLARGED EDITION
William M
50¢
INSIDE
MAD
With a Backword by
STAN FREBERG
ROR BY THE KING OF FANTASY
RADBURY'S
AUTUMN
PEOPLE
"ADAPTED AND ILLUSTRATED IN THE GOOD OLD COMIC-BOOK TRADITION"
COLL
PAROD
Hilarious imitations of LIFE,
THE NEW YORKER and oth
by the top college humor m
Edited by WILL and MARTIN
BALLANTINE B

ALLEN BELLMAN

b. 1924

plate 10

Born in New York, Allen Bellman studied at the High School of Industrial Arts. On Columbus Day 1942, he responded to a help wanted ad in the *New York Times* that led to a job assisting artist Syd Shores on *Captain America*. His earliest credited work appeared the next year, writing and drawing "The Mystery of the Ghost Killer" in *All-Winners Comics* #11.

At Timely, Bellman worked primarily as an inker on Sub-Mariner, Human Torch, and Captain America features for *Marvel Mystery Comics* and *All-Winners Comics*. He also wrote and drew the backup feature, *Let's Play Detective*, that appeared in various Timely titles.

Bellman's last regular comic book work was in 1952, scripting and drawing "The Temptress of Jupiter!" for Atlas Comics' *Space World* #6. He left comics in the early '50s and worked in the art department of a daily newspaper in Florida.

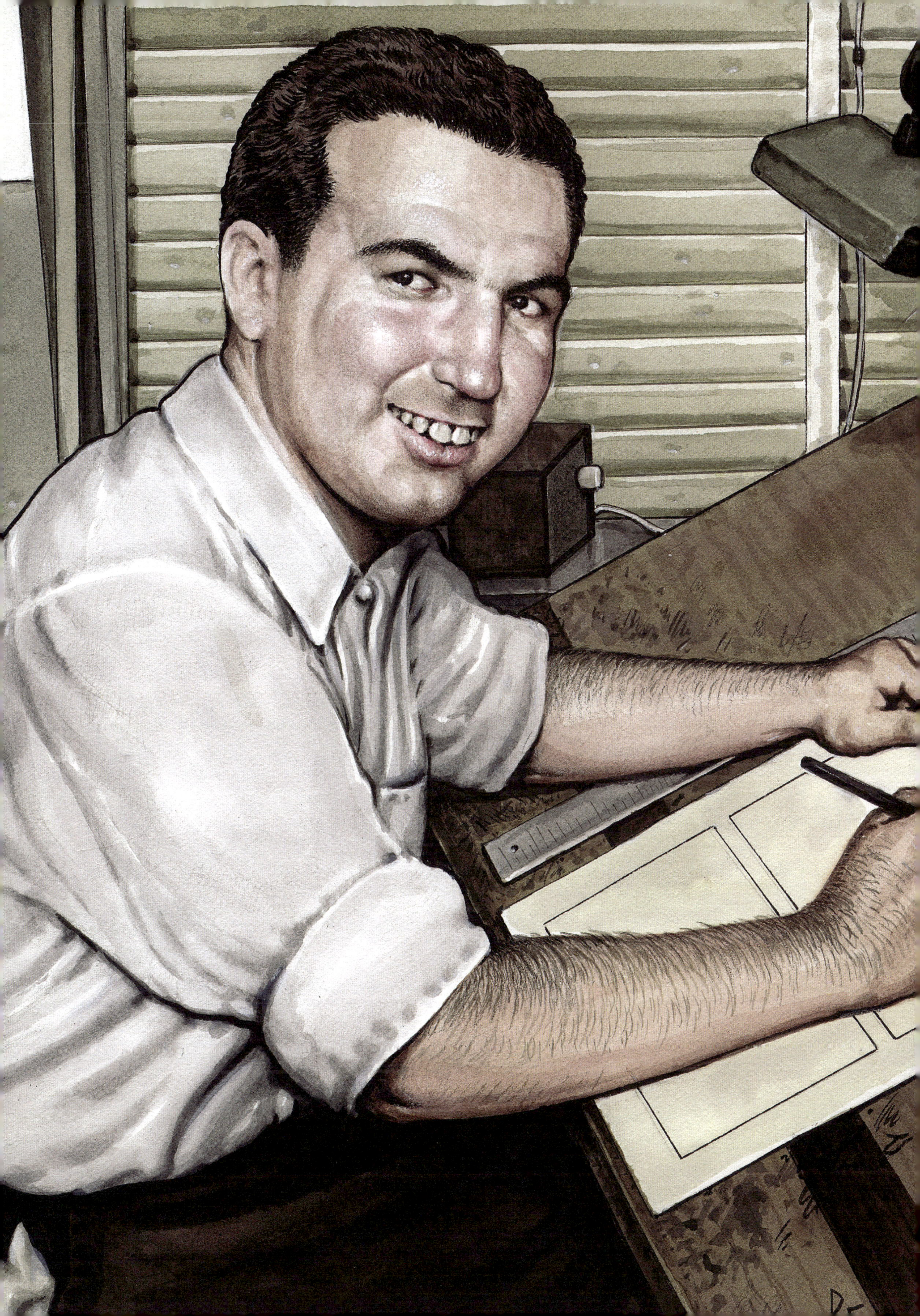

OTTO BINDER

1911–1974

plate 11

By the time he was twenty, Otto Oscar Binder of Bessemer, Michigan, was having a modicum of success collaborating with his older brother Earl on science fiction tales, published in pulp magazines such as *Amazing Stories*. But it was another, older brother, Jack Binder (creator of the original Daredevil), whom Otto followed into the comic book business.

After a year spent, alongside his brother, working for the colorful, cigar-chomping Harry "A" Chesler, Binder made his way to Fawcett Publications. Binder paid his dues working on titles like *Bulletman* before he was assigned to write for the company's flagship Marvel "Family" books: *Captain Marvel, Mary Marvel*, and *Captain Marvel Jr.*

Binder would spend over a decade with Fawcett, penning almost a thousand Marvel-family stories and co-creating (with C.C. Beck and Marc Swayze) a whimsical world of talking tigers and intelligent supervillain worms.

After Fawcett closed its doors in 1953, Binder found a home at DC Comics writing Superman-related titles. He lent his imagination to an outlandish menagerie of super-apes, super-cats, and super-dogs that would rival his Fawcett work for absurdity and originality. He wrote the first published appearance of Supergirl, introduced the Bottle City of Kandor, and launched the fractured-mirror Superman tales of the Bizarro World. For almost twenty years, Binder contributed more new elements to the Superman legend than anyone since the original creative team of Jerry Siegel and Joe Shuster.

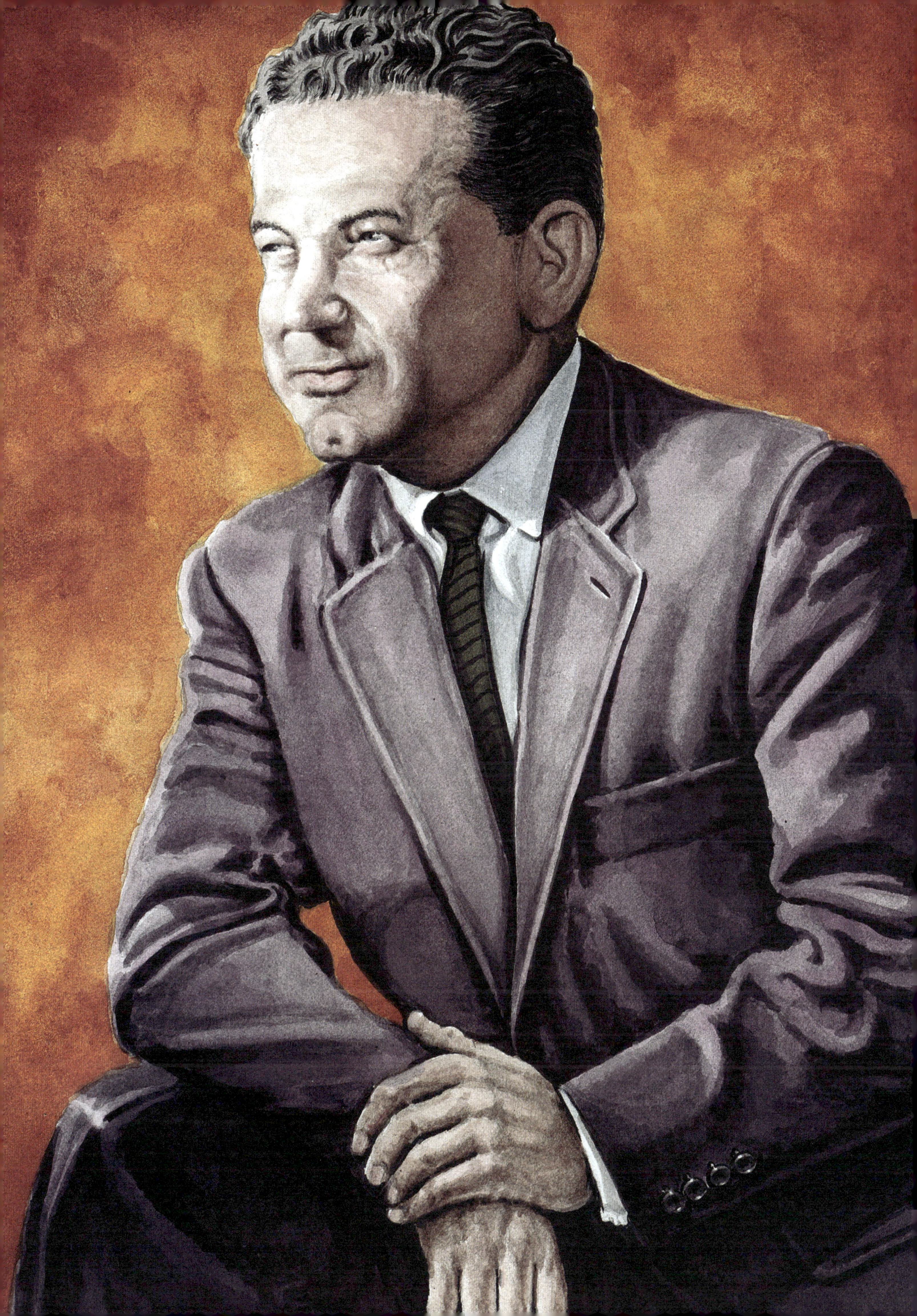

AUDREY BLUM

1918–1973

plate 12

Audrey Anthony "Toni" Blum was born in Philadelphia, and moved with her family to New York during the Depression. At the age of eighteen, Blum became the only woman staff member at Will Eisner and Jerry Iger's comic book production shop. Her father Alex Blum, an illustrator and portrait artist, joined the shop the following year. Audrey Blum, an aspiring playwright, was the only staff writer employed at Eisner & Iger. She worked under a variety of different pen names throughout her career, making an accurate chronology of her work difficult, but her earliest comic book contribution was most likely "Vladim the Voodoo Master" in Fox Comics' *Blue Beetle* #1, published in 1939. She was credited with co-creating Prop Powers, Sally O'Neil, Policewoman, and Wonder Boy, all in a single issue of Quality Comics' *National Comics* #1.

When Eisner and Iger parted ways in 1939, Blum remained with Iger for three more years before deciding to join Eisner on his new project *The Spirit*. When Eisner entered military service in 1942, she took over scripting duties. Blum and Eisner's (alleged) brief romantic entanglement was fictionalized in Eisner's graphic novel about the early comic book industry, *The Dreamer*. After the war, she married Eisner & Iger artist Bill Bossert. The couple soon left the comic book business and moved to Pleasantville, New York, where she settled into life as a housewife.

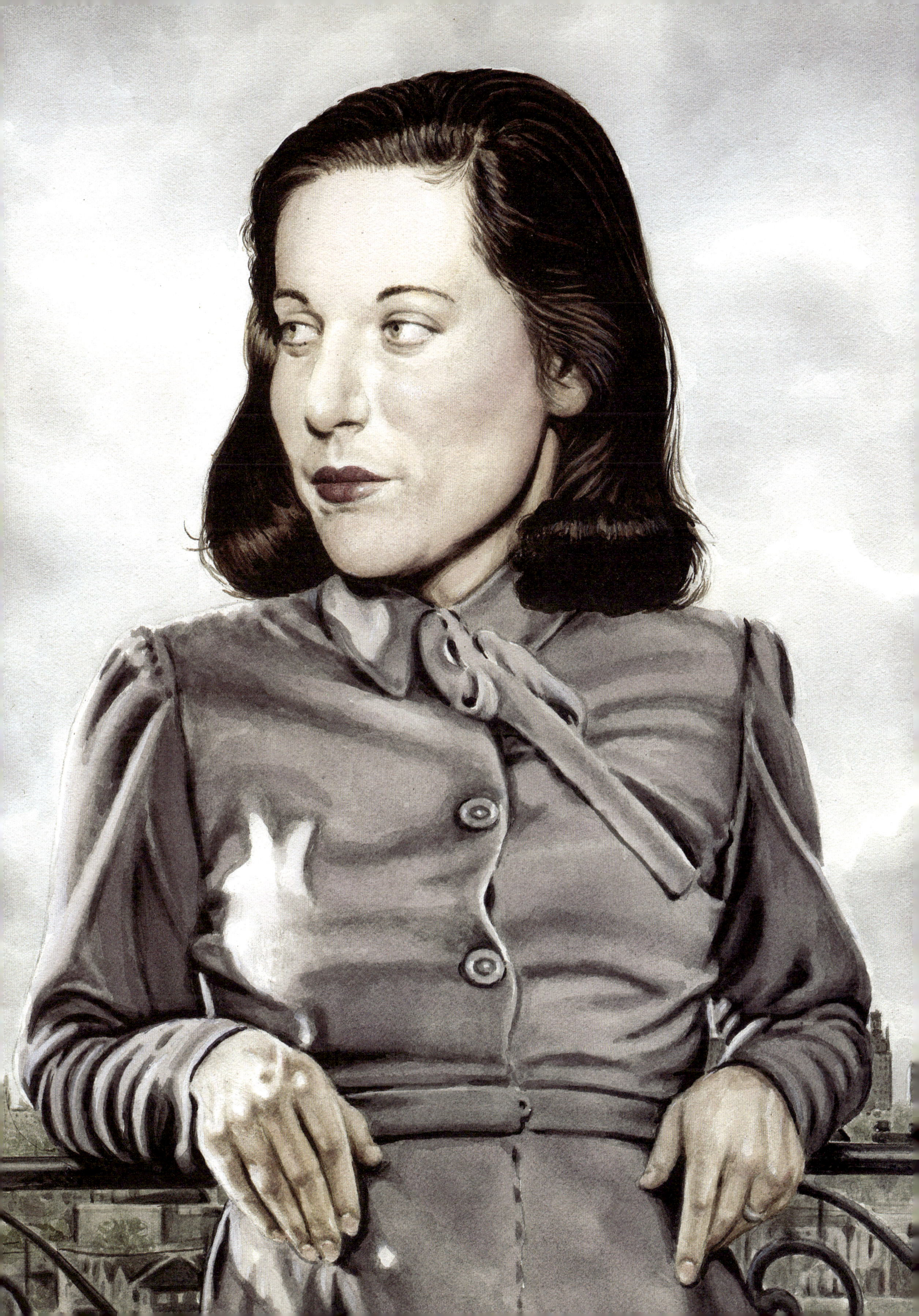

BOB BOLLING

b. 1928

plate 13

Born in Brockton, Massachusetts, Bob Bolling served two years in the US Navy after graduating high school in 1946. After the navy, Bolling spent three years studying at Boston's Vesper George Art School. Bolling worked in the art department at the *Boston Record American* before landing a job assisting cartoonist George Shedd on his adventure comic strip, *Marlin Keel*. When the strip was canceled a year later, a friend steered him towards a freelance position drawing joke pages for Archie Comics. He soon progressed to drawing a *Dennis the Menace* knockoff, *Pat the Brat*.

In 1956, Archie Comics publisher John Goldwater tasked Bolling with creating Little Archie, a younger, more whimsical version of Archie Andrews and his pals. He rose to the occasion, creating a world far richer than the one inhabited by teenaged Archie. *Little Archie* featured longer stories (eighty-page issues were common), and incorporated elements of fantasy and adventure.

Bolling wrote, penciled, inked, and lettered most of his own *Little Archie* stories. He left the title in 1965, but continued drawing for Archie Comics into his eighties.

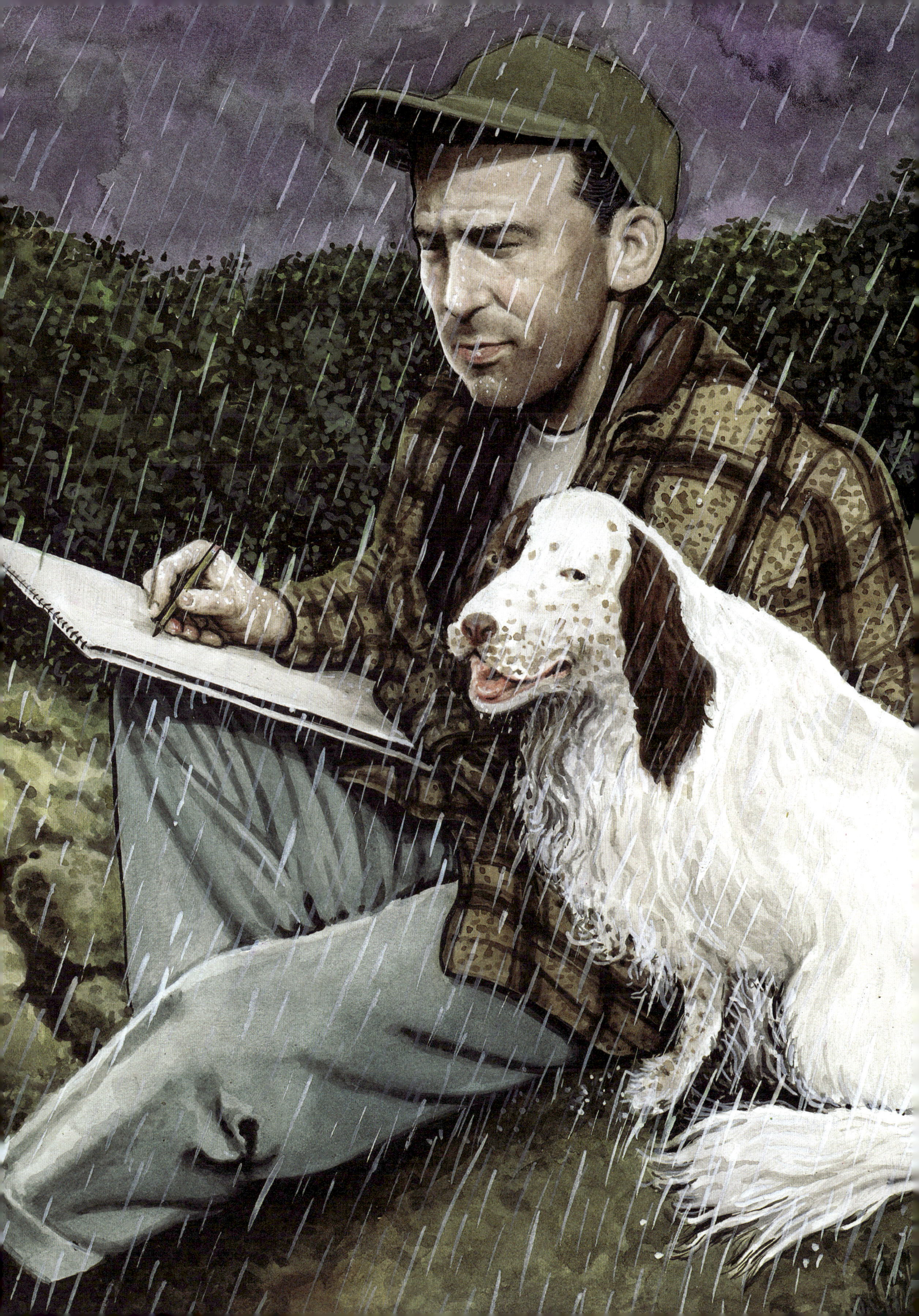

RAY BRADBURY

1920-2012

plate 14

The famed science fiction author Raymond Douglas Bradbury was born in Waukegan, Illinois, and moved to Los Angeles with his family when he was fourteen. A chance meeting with radio comedian George Burns led to Bradbury's first paid writing assignment on the *Burns and Allen Show*.

"Hollerbochen's Dilemma," in Forrest J. Ackerman's fanzine, *Imagination*, in 1938, was his first published story; he sold his first professional story when he was twenty-two, and his first book, a collection of short stories, *Dark Carnival*, was published in 1947.

By 1951, Bradbury was riding high on the success of his first published novel, *The Martian Chronicles*. That same year, EC Comics published Al Feldstein's "A Strange Undertaking!" in the *Haunt of Fear* #6. Feldstein's script was an uncredited swipe of Bradbury's "The Handler," originally published in the pulp magazine *Weird Tales* in 1947.

Several other EC stories followed that were remarkably similar to Bradbury stories. Bradbury finally contacted EC publisher William M. Gaines with a very polite letter, asking for a modest $50 payment for the rights. Gaines gladly agreed to the terms.

Soon after, Bradbury's work became a regular (credited) presence in EC titles like *The Vault of Horror*, *Weird Fantasy*, and *Weird Science,* with his name often appearing on the covers. Bradbury was delighted with the comic book adaptions of his stories. EC adapted a total of twenty-seven Bradbury stories until they closed shop in 1955. In 1965, Ballantine Books compiled sixteen of the Bradbury EC stories stories in two paperbacks, *The Autumn People* and *Tomorrow Midnight*.

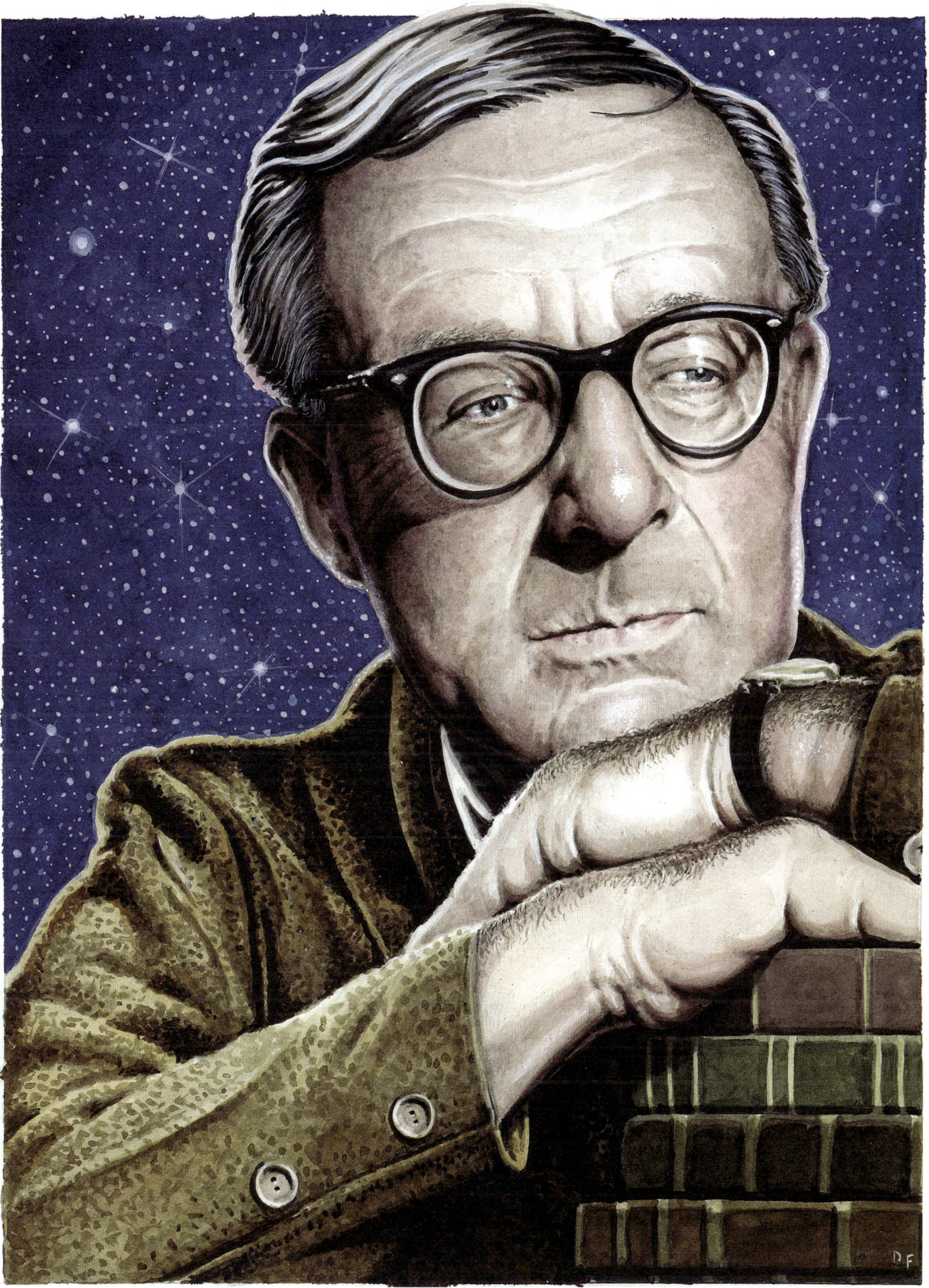

SOL BRODSKY

1923–1984

plate
15

Born in Brooklyn, Brodsky's earliest comic book work was sweeping the floors at MLJ Comics as a teenager. Brodsky soon moved onward and upward to Timely Comics, writing and drawing a single-page filler "The Portrait Artist" in *Mystic Comics* #10 in 1940. Brodsky's six-page "The Enemy Falcon" for Holyoke Publishing's *Cat-Man Comics* #14 was his earliest published story.

World War II interrupted his comics career. After the war, he returned to freelancing for Holyoke's *Captain Aero Comics*, Catholic Publications' *Catholic Comics*, and others, before reuniting with Stan Lee in 1954 at Atlas Comics to handle production chores across the line.

By 1957, Atlas publisher Martin Goodman laid off most of the staff except for his wife's cousin, Stan Lee. Brodsky was freelancing again, creating promotional comics for clients like Big Boy restaurants and Bird's Eye frozen foods.

In 1958, Brodsky became the founding editor of *Mad* imitator *Cracked* magazine and remained there until rejoining Stan Lee once more, at Timely/Atlas successor Marvel Comics, as production manager. There he worked closely with editor Lee, handling a multitude of tasks from inking and corrections to supervising engravers and printers. In 1970, Brodsky left Marvel for a few months to help launch Skywald Publication's black-and-white horror magazines *Psycho* and *Nightmare*. When Brodsky rejoined Marvel, he had a new title: "Vice President of Operations."

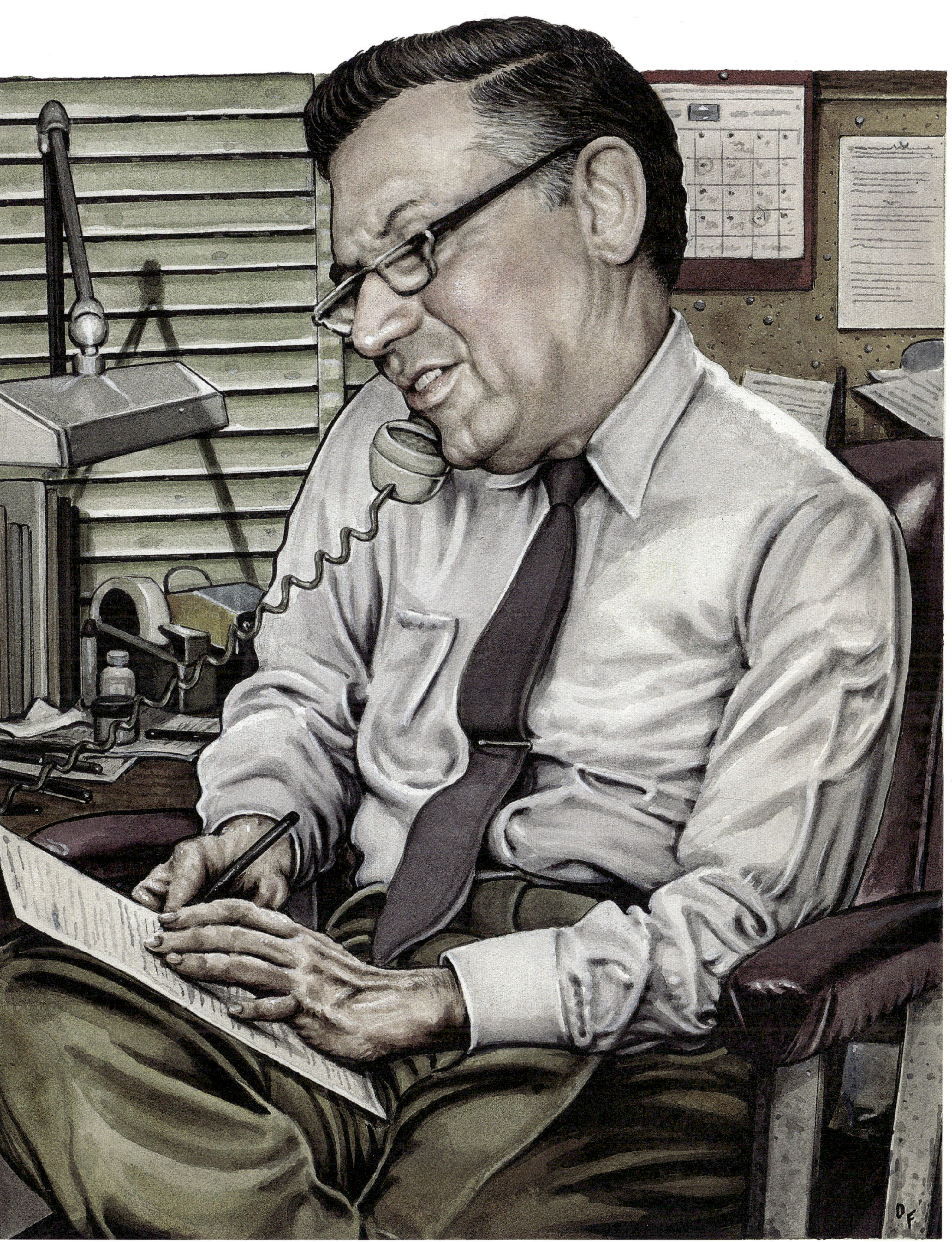

JOHN BROOME

1913–1999

plate **16**

Born in New York, John Broome's first comic book work was in 1936, writing a two-page humor story for Centaur Publication's *Funny Pages* #7. Broome also wrote text pieces for Fawcett titles like *Captain Marvel Adventure*, using one of his many pseudonyms, "Ron Broome."

Broome's former agent at Solar Sales Service, Julius Schwartz, had become an editor at DC Comics, and recruited him to work on superhero tales. His first confirmed script was a thirteen-page Flash story, "The City of Shifting Sand," published in *All-Flash* #22 in 1946. For the rest of the decade, he specialized in scripting Green Lantern tales for *All-American Comics*, as well as the bimonthly *Green Lantern* series. He also made ongoing contributions to Justice Society of America stories in *All-American Comics.*

He continued at DC through the '50s, helping to revive the Flash in 1956, and Green Lantern three years later. With Gil Kane, he created the modern version of the character. He also worked with Schwartz and Carmine Infantino to excise some of the campy aspects that had crept into *Detective Comics* after the success of the 1966 Batman television series.

Broome last worked for DC in 1970 and spent the rest of his life traveling and teaching English abroad.

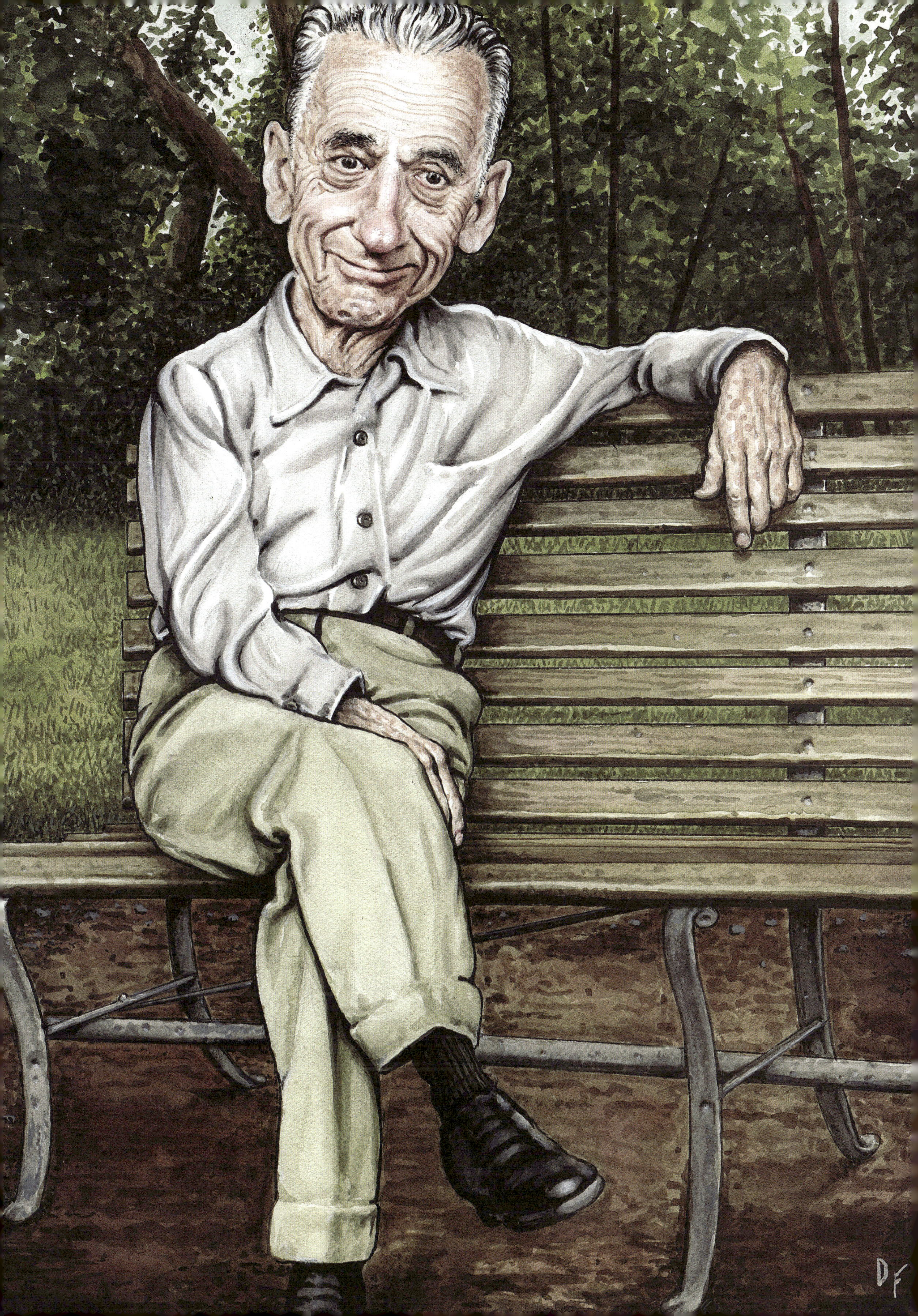
DF

JACK BURNLEY

1911-2006

plate **17**

Hardin Jack Burnley began his career in 1929 as an art assistant at King Features Syndicate. By 1938, he was drawing his own sports cartoon feature for the company. When the feature was canceled, he contacted DC/National Comics editor Whitney Ellsworth, a former King Features employee.

Burnley's first work for DC/National was the cover of *New York World's Fair Comics* in 1940. It was the first time Superman, Batman, and Robin were shown together. In 1941, he became the second artist, after co-creator Joe Shuster, to draw Superman, uncredited, for *Action Comics*, and remained an uncredited contributor for the next six years. He joined the daily *Superman* comic strip in 1941, also uncredited. By 1944, he was anonymously penciling both Bob Kane's *Batman* and Siegel & Shuster's *Superman* Sunday pages. Burnley had the distinction of being DC's top "ghost artist." (Basically, his entire career drawing Superman and Batman went uncredited.)

Burnley left comic books in 1947 to once again work as a newspaper sports cartoonist (finally credited). He retired from his staff position at the *San Francisco News* in 1976.

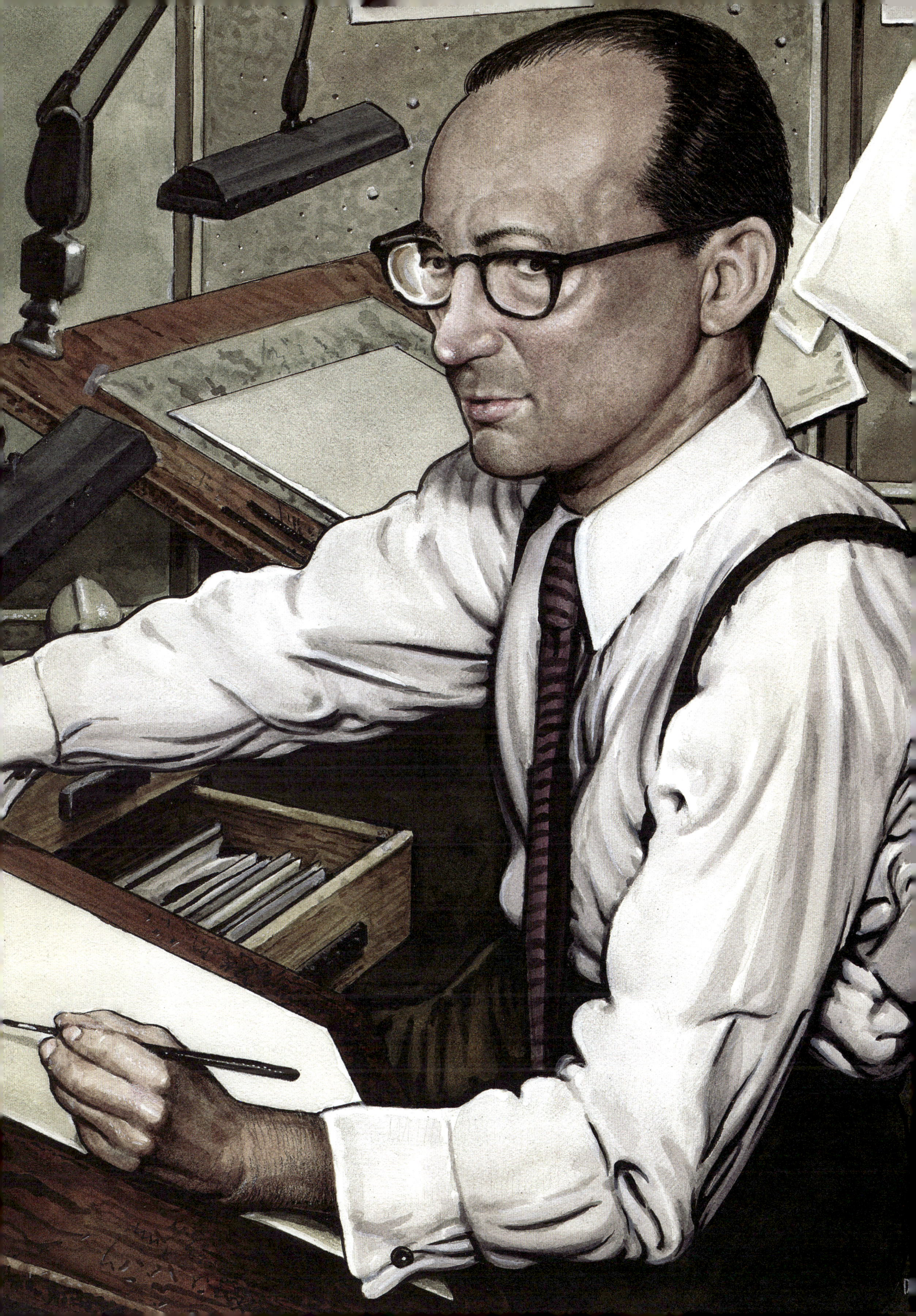

JOHN BUSCEMA

1927-2002

plate **18**

Giovanni Natale Buscema was born in Brooklyn and attended the High School of Music and Art in Manhattan. Buscema's formal art training consisted of night classes at Pratt Institute and life-drawing sessions at the Brooklyn Museum. At the time, the physically large Buscema envisioned a career as a boxer and earned extra money painting portraits of his fellow fighters. Buscema also contributed to the *Hobo News.*

In 1948, Buscema saw a help wanted ad in the *New York Times* placed by Timely Comics. There he met editor Stan Lee, who invited the nineteen-year-old to join Timely's in-house bullpen. Buscema's first published story was the four page "Till Crime Do You Part" in *Lawbreakers Always Lose.* Buscema spent several years on staff at Timely making contributions to western titles like *Cowboy Romances* and *The Two-Gun Kid,* as well as "real life" books *True Adventures* and *Man Comics.*

By 1957, Buscema was freelancing for Timely's successor, Atlas, as well as Dell and AGC, but the future looked bleak for comic book artists. He left the business and joined the staff of the Alexander E. Chaite Studio, the prestigious New York advertising firm. Buscema spent the next few years creating layouts, illustrations, and storyboards for Madison Avenue.

Buscema returned to Marvel in 1966 at the behest of Stan Lee, who offered to let him work from home. For his return, Buscema penciled a Nick Fury story (over Jack Kirby layouts) for *Strange Tales.* The new-style Marvel look was substantially different from his earlier work, and he leaned heavily on Kirby's distinctive style at first.

Buscema soon became the quintessential Marvel artist, with long runs on flagship titles *The Avengers, The Fantastic Four,* and *The Silver Surfer*—and later, *Conan the Barbarian.*

In 1978 he and Stan Lee collaborated on the best-selling *How to Draw Comics the Marvel Way,* a distillation of the cartooning class he had taught for years.

"Big" John Buscema was buried with a pen in his drawing hand.

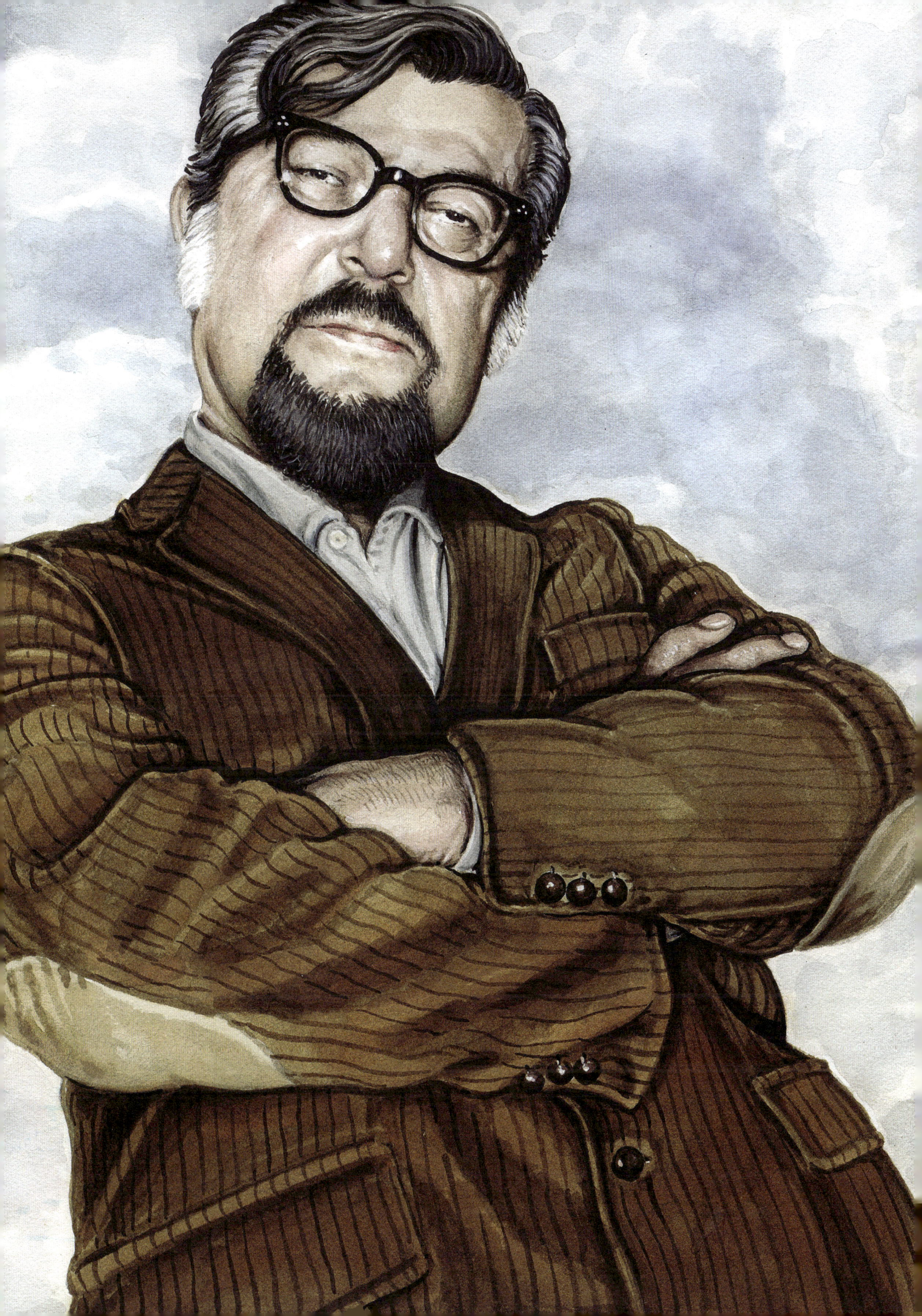

NICK CARDY

1920–2013

plate **19**

Nicholas Viscardi was born the son of Italian immigrants on New York's Lower East Side. Viscardi attended the School of Industrial Arts, and studied life drawing at the Art Students League of New York. After a brief stint in advertising, Viscardi joined the comic book business in 1939, at the Eisner & Iger shop. Viscardi's earliest work included drawing the jungle explorer Roy Lance in Fiction House's *Jungle Comics* #7 (1940). For ten months, Viscardi drew *Lady Luck*, a four-page backup feature in Will Eisner's *Spirit* section. When Viscardi was eventually allowed to sign his work, he adapted the pseudonym "Cardy."

In 1943, Cardy was drafted into the US Army and saw combat in Europe as an assistant tank driver. He returned to civilian life having earned two Purple Hearts for battlefield injuries. Cardy did advertising art and spent six months in 1950 drawing the *Tarzan* daily comic strip for United Feature Syndicate. But National Comics (soon to become DC Comics) was where he would make his biggest impact. His first published story for DC was in 1948, a six-page "Customs Cop" for *Gang Busters* #6. During the '50s, he worked across a host of genres, handling westerns like *Tomahawk* and mystery titles *House of Secrets* and *Tales of the Unexpected.* During the superhero revival of the early '60s, he flourished, drawing the first thirty-nine issues of *Aquaman* and launching the *Teen Titans* into their own book in 1965. He was among DC's most prolific cover artists until he left the company in 1974 to concentrate on the lucrative field of movie posters. Using the name "Nick Cardi" he created posters—some used, some not—for *The Street Fighter, Movie Movie, Meatballs Part II* and others. When producers were unhappy with artist Tom Jung's poster for 1977's *Star Wars,* Cardy was called in to add images of C-3PO and R2-D2 to Jung's original painting.

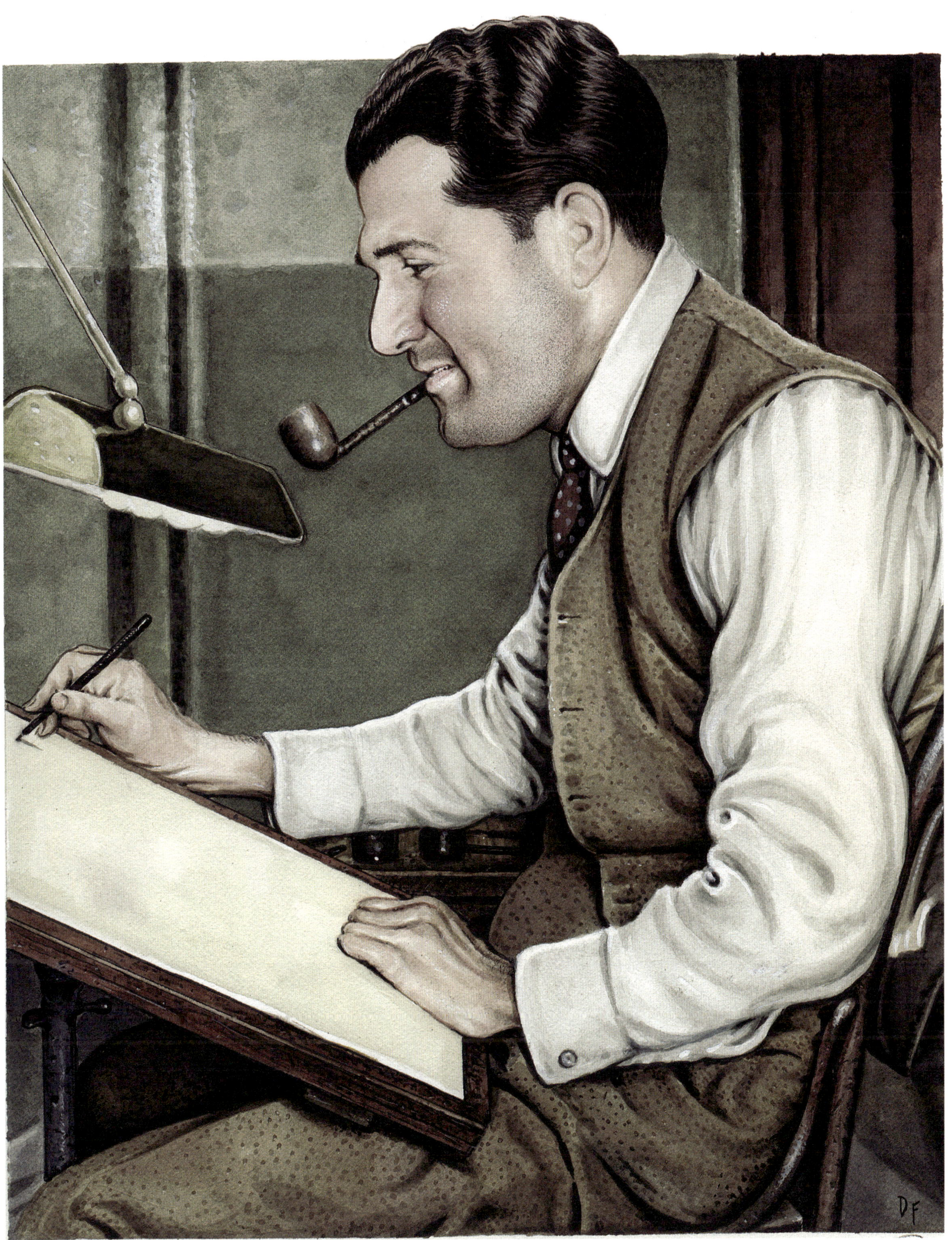

GENE COLAN

1926-2011

plate 20

Bronx-born Eugene Jules Colan attended the Art Students League in Manhattan, and published his first comics work in 1944: a single-page, nonfiction filler in Fiction House's *Wings Comics*. His first full-length story appeared in the next issue. The following year, Colan enlisted in the Army Air Corps, eventually finding himself in the Philippines and contributing illustrations to the *Manilla Times*. When the war ended, Colan was back in his parent's home, writing and drawing a story to use as a calling card for publishers. Colan's spec story led to a job at Timely as an uncredited staff artist; he was making $60 a week.

Although Colan published at least one Captain America story during his Timely years, the Golden Age of superhero comics was winding down postwar. By 1948, Timely had pruned most of its staff and he began freelancing at National Comics and Martin Goodman's post–Timely endeavor, Atlas Comics.

The 1950s found him honing his craft on a variety of books, from licensed titles—such as National's *Hopalong Cassidy* and Dell's *Ben Casey*—to grittier, military fare, like *Our Army at War*, *All-American Men at War*, and *Navy Combat*. He was illustrating romance titles for DC when the early 1960s superhero boom was blasting off at Marvel, and occasionally contributed to the rival company using the pseudonym Adam Austin. Stan Lee convinced him to make the jump to Marvel, where became one of the prime movers of the company's new style of superhero books. Colan had long runs on the influential titles *Iron Man*, *Doctor Strange*, *The Avengers*, *Tomb of Dracula*, and especially, the noir-ish and moody *Daredevil*.

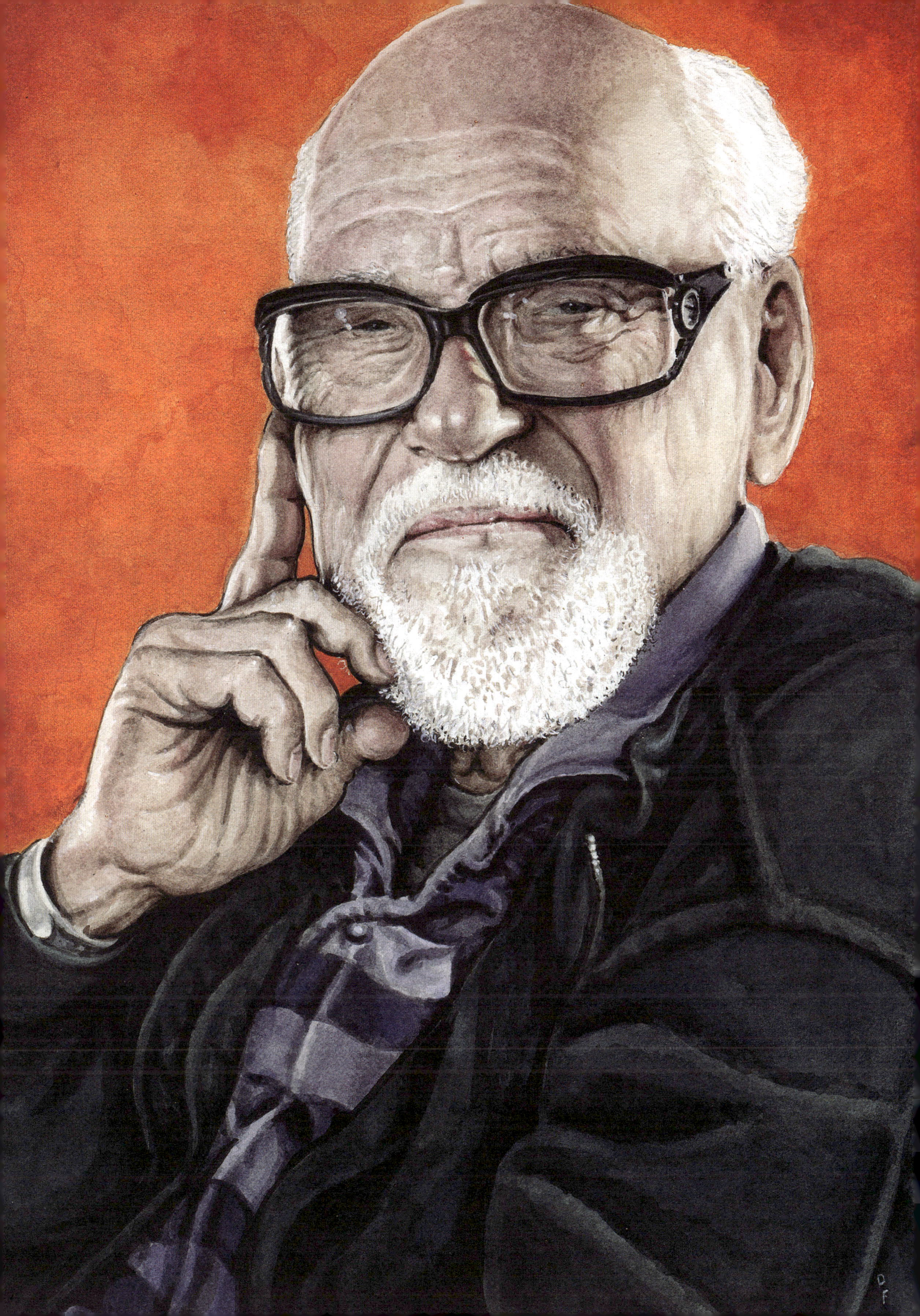

VINCE COLLETTA

1923–1991

plate 21

Born in Casteldaccia, Italy, Vincente Joseph Colletta emigrated to the United States in 1943. After a brief period in Brooklyn, his family moved to New Jersey, where Coletta studied at the New Jersey Academy of Fine Arts. His earliest known comic book work was penciling and inking a 1952 six-page romance story, "Please Don't Love Me," in *Daring Love* #15, published by Pix-Parade. Over the next few years, he penciled and inked romance stories for various publishers, like Atlas, Standard, and Youthful. *Daring Confessions*, *Popular Romances*, and *Thrilling Romances* were typical titles during the heyday of the romance comic books. In 1957, with Atlas Comics seemingly on life-support, he worked on romance titles for other companies before returning to work for Stan Lee at the latest incarnation of Martin Goodman's company, now called Marvel Comics.

Colletta's first task at Marvel was inking Jack Kirby's pencils for the cover of the one-hundredth issue of *Kid Colt: Outlaw* in 1961. Although in later years, his inking style would lead to accusations that he simplified Kirby's detailed line work for the sake of speed, Lee appreciated Colletta for his ability to deliver under pressure and on time. He spent the better part of the decade as one of the most prolific inkers in Marvel's bullpen. He worked on almost every Marvel comic book; he spent six years on Kirby's *The Mighty Thor.* At the start of the '70s, he followed Kirby to DC Comics where he inked his work on *Superman's Pal, Jimmy Olsen*, *The Forever People*, and *Mister Miracle.* Colletta was named art director at DC in 1976.

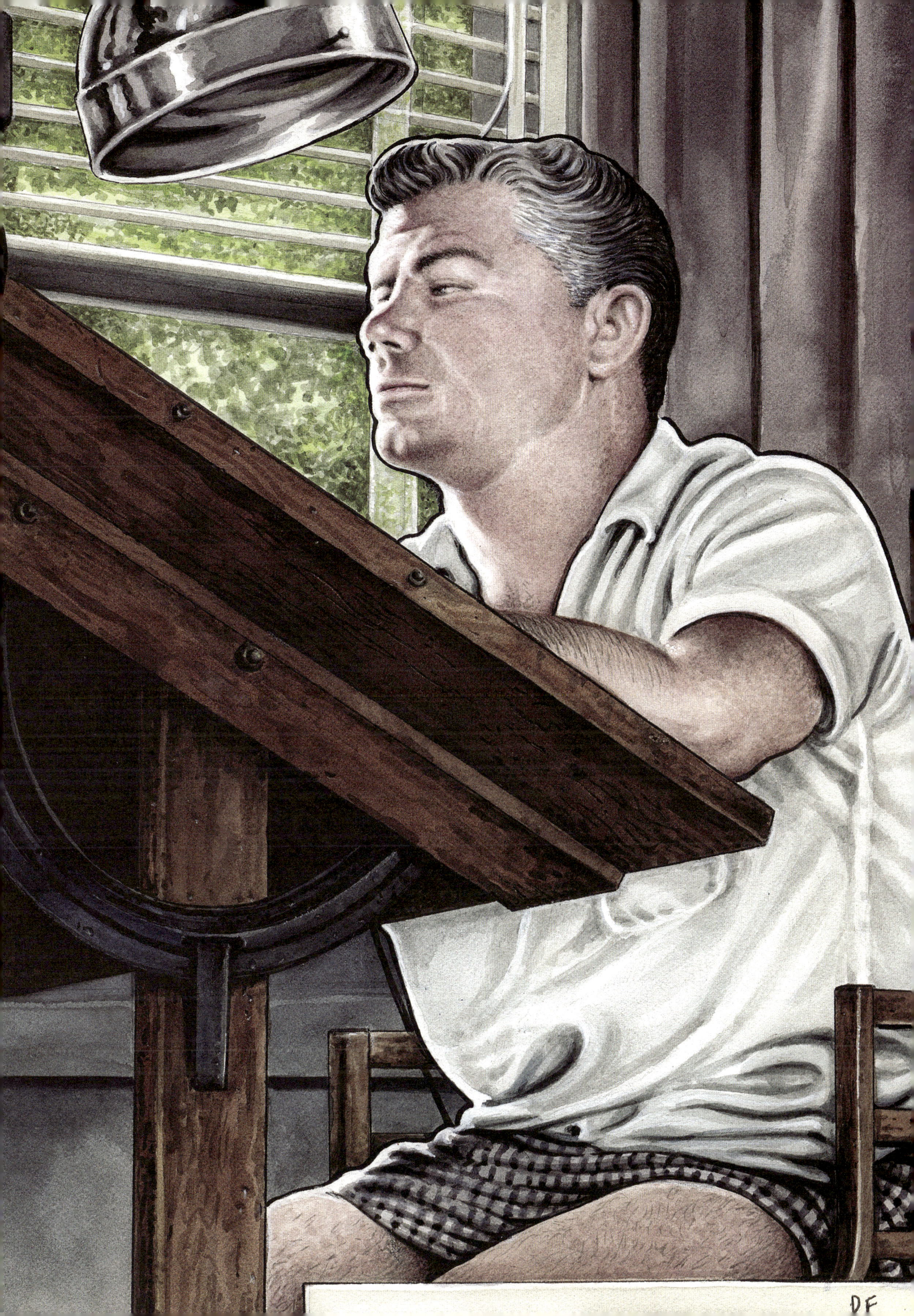
DF

CHASE CRAIG

1910-2001

plate 22

Born in Ennis, Texas, Chase Craig studied at the Chicago Academy of Fine Arts. After graduating, he drew a gag panel, *Little Chauncey*, for *The Christian Science Monitor.* He headed for Hollywood in 1935 and spent the next four years in Leon Schlesinger's animation unit at Warner Bros. He started freelancing for newspaper comic strips at the end of the '30s, drawing *Hollywood Hams*, *Mortimer & Charlie*, and six weeks of *Bugs Bunny* Sunday comic pages.

Craig worked for Dell Comics in the early '40s, drawing some of the first *Bugs Bunny* and *Porky Pig* comic books for Western Publishing before enlisting in the navy on the eve of World War II. He remained in Hollywood during the war, illustrating training manuals like the whimsically titled safety guide "Don't Kill Your Friends."

After the war, Craig continued what would be a career-long association with Western Publishing and its partners, Dell Comics and Gold Key. He served as editor of Dell's *Four Color* anthology, the longest-running comic book ever published. Each issue featured a single, licensed property. Anything from *This is Your Life Donald Duck* (*Four Color* #1109) to *The Danny Thomas Show* (*Four Color* #1180.) He also created original characters for Gold Key, including the popular Magnus, Robot Fighter. Craig also served as Carl Bark's last editor at Dell. He retired from Western in 1975.

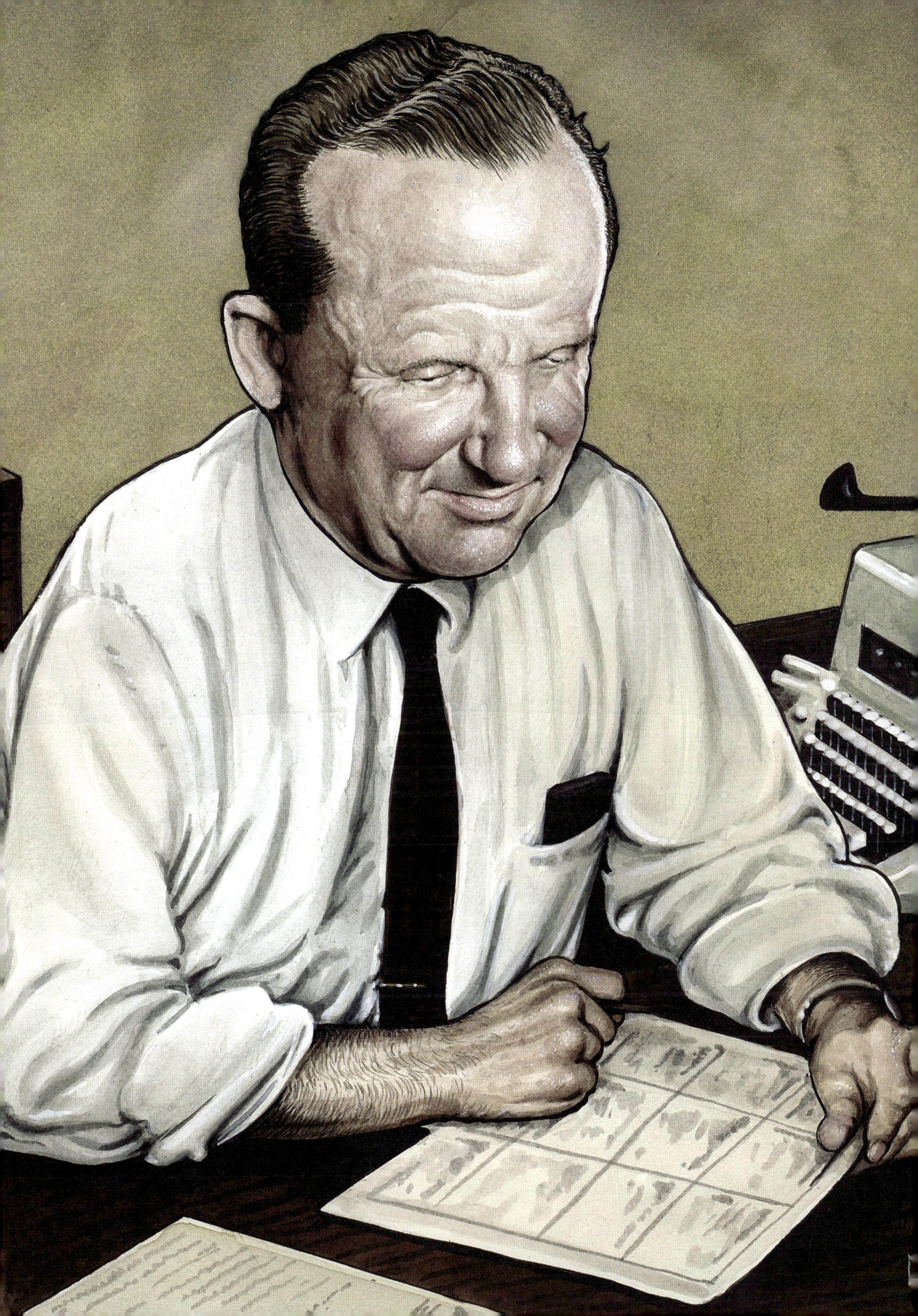

DAN DECARLO

1919-2001

plate
23

Daniel S. DeCarlo, famed for his "DeCarlo Girls," was born in New Rochelle, New York. After graduating from New Rochelle High School, he attended the Art Students League. In 1941, he was drafted into the US Army. He spent the war years in Great Britain, working as a draftsman and drawing a weekly comic strip the *418th Scandal Sheet*.

After the war, DeCarlo was working for his father when a help wanted ad led him to Stan Lee at Timely Comics. His first confirmed work for Timely was penciling and inking a five-page untitled story, featuring "Jeanie," in *Patsy Walker* #24 for editor Al Jaffee in 1949. He spent less than a year on *Patsy Walker* before Lee put him to work on another teen-oriented title, *Millie the Model*. He would spend ten years on *Millie the Model*, sometimes drawing several stories in each issue. He also worked on Atlas titles *My Friend Irma* and *Sherry the Showgirl*, and contributed racy gag cartoons and pinup art to Martin Goodman's *Humorama* digest.

DeCarlo drew for Archie comics for the next forty-three years, updating their look and style and bringing the characters into the (more or less) modern world. He contributed many original characters to the world of Archie, including the popular *Josie and the Pussycats*.

A contentious lawsuit over the rights to *Josie and the Pussycats* led to Archie Comics terminating him in 2001. DeCarlo's final comic book work was published in Bongo Comics' *Bart Simpson* #8 in 2001.

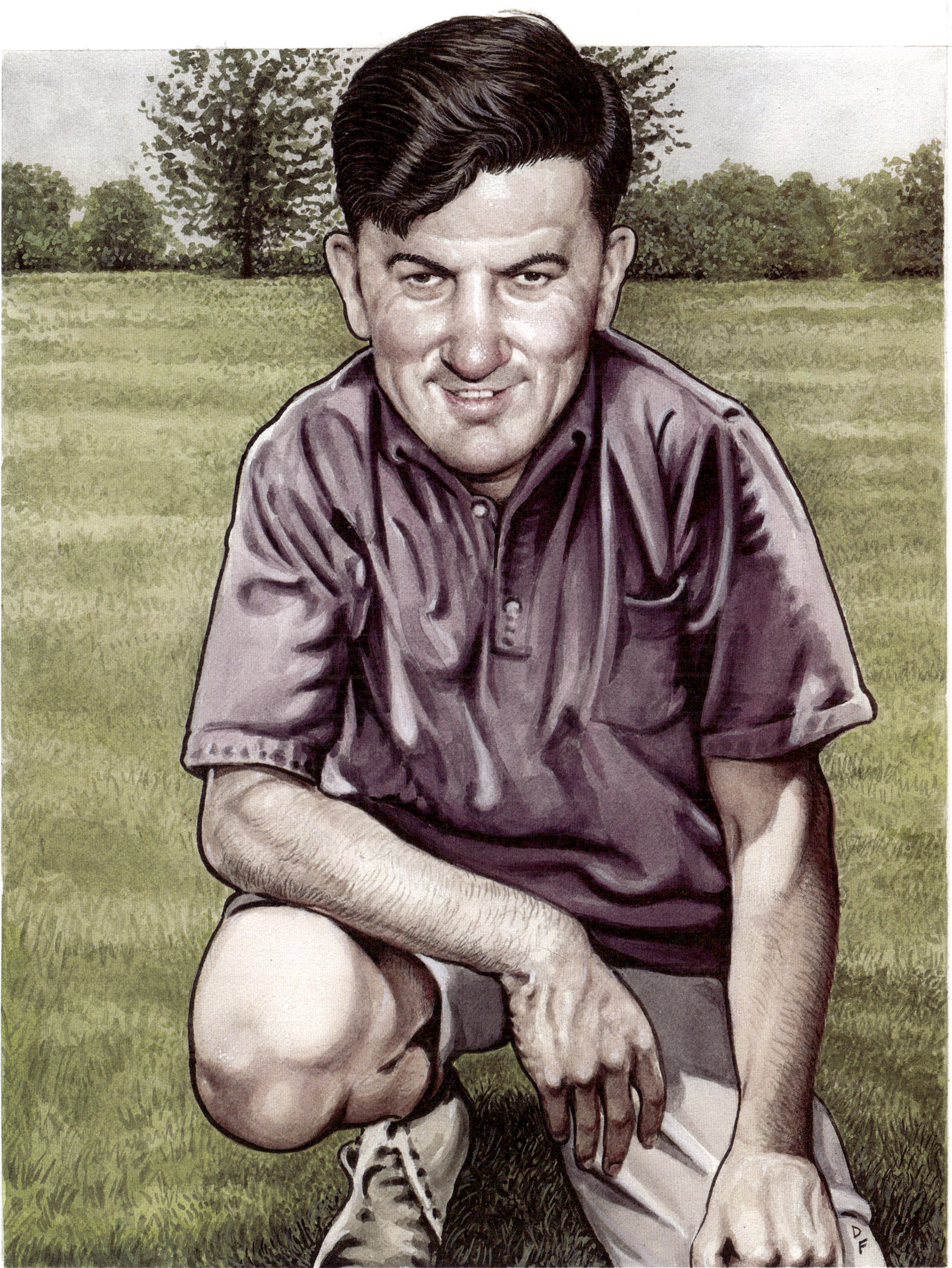
DF

HARRY DONENFELD

1893–1965

plate 24

Harry Donenfeld was born in Romania, and emigrated to the United States with his family in 1900. He grew up on the Lower East Side of New York, sporadically attending school and drifting in and out of street gangs. Meanwhile, his brothers Charlie and Mike were hard at work, establishing a printing business in New York.

In 1919, Donenfeld married and opened a clothing store in Newark, New Jersey. The store went out of business in 1921, and he turned to his brothers for help. Donenfeld became a salesman for Martin Press, and the business thrived. In 1925, he began producing pulp magazines, with titles like *Spicy Adventure Stories* and *Spicy Detective Stories.* A few years later, he hired accountant Jack Liebowitz, and they created their own distribution arm, Independent News Company.

Major Malcolm Wheeler-Nicholson's company National Allied Publications had launched one of the earliest comics books in 1935, but financial and distribution problems led him to Donenfeld and Independent News. Donenfeld, Liebowitz, and Wheeler-Nicholson joined forces as Detective Comics, and published *New Comics* and *Detective Comics.* Less than a year later, Wheeler-Nicholson was bankrupt, and Liebowitz and Donenfeld controlled National Allied Publications.

In 1938, National published *Action Comics* #1, featuring the first appearance of Siegel and Shuster's Superman, and the rest is history. Donenfeld would remain active in the company until the early '60s. His son Irwin worked as editorial director, and finally executive vice president of DC.

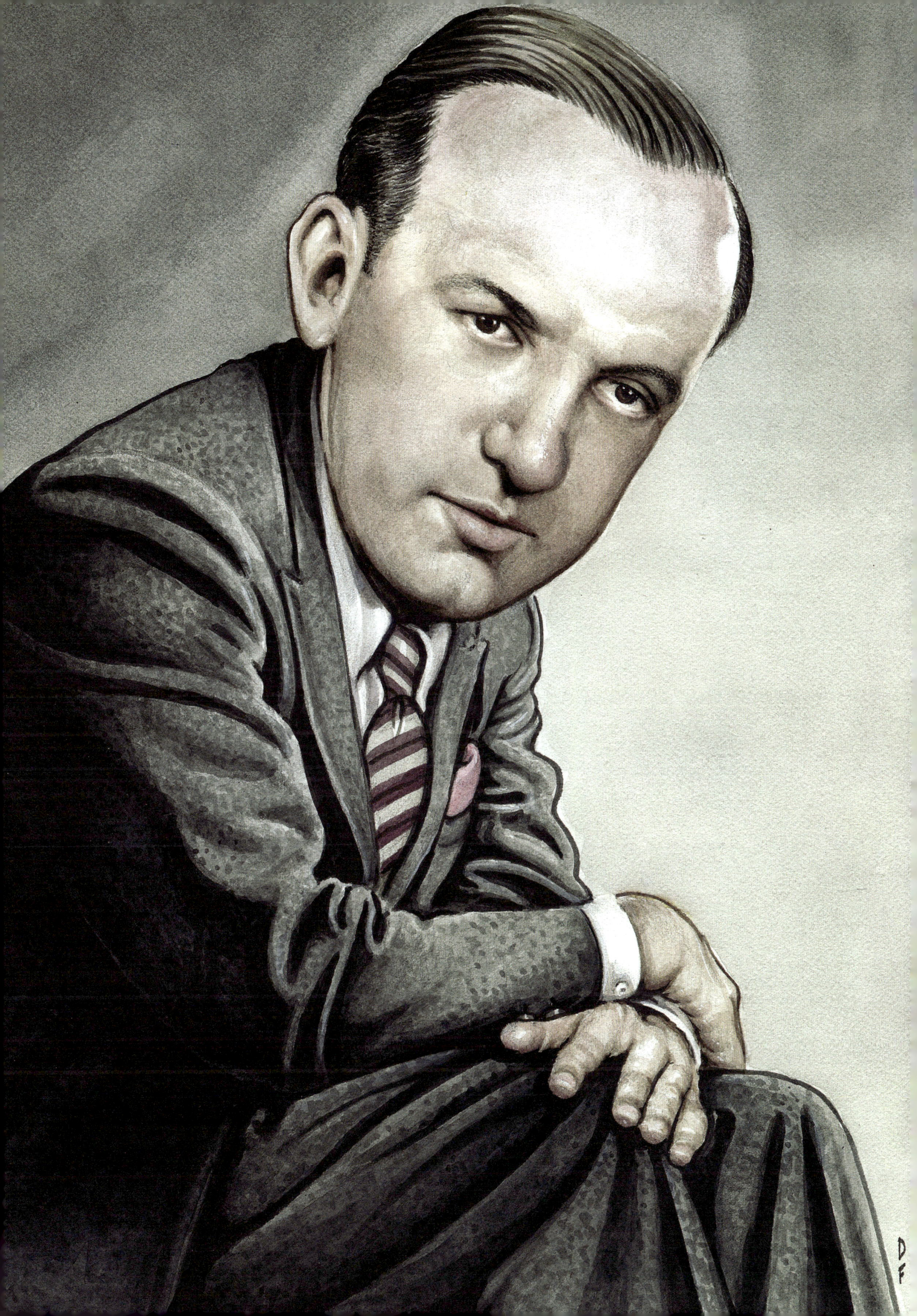

ARNOLD DRAKE

1924-2007

plate
25

Born in Queens, Arnold Drake spent a year in bed after contracting scarlet fever. He spent his convalescence writing and drawing his own comic strips. He later studied journalism at the University of Missouri and New York University.

In 1950, Drake collaborated with another writer, Leslie Walker, and artist Matt Baker on *It Rhymes with Lust,* an early "graphic novel."

Batman artist Bob Kane was Drake's brother's neighbor; he introduced Drake to editors at DC Comics. His first work for DC was in 1956, on an eight-page story, "The Return of Mister Future," in *Batman* #98. He supplied a number of Batman stories over the next few years, but also scripted ghost stories for *House of Mystery* and humor tales for *The Adventures of Jerry Lewis* and *The Adventures of Bob Hope.*

Drake and artist Bruno Premiani created the *Doom Patrol* for DC in 1963 and would script almost every single issue for the next five years. In 1966, Drake and Win Mortimer created *Stanley and His Monster* as a backup feature in *The Fox and the Crow* #95. The story of a six-year-old boy and his pet monster soon earned its own solo title. He also helped DC revive the Golden Age favorite Plastic Man in 1966.

Drake was also the screenwriter of the 1964 cult horror film *The Flesh Eaters*, and 1965's *Who Killed Teddy Bear?,* starring Sal Mineo, Juliet Prowse, and Jan Murray.

Carmine Infantino and Drake created the supernaturally tinged Deadman in 1967. Working for Marvel in 1968, he wrote several issues of the *X-Men* and *Captain Marvel*, as well as *Not Brand Ecch.* For Gold Key Comics, he scripted licensed TV adaptations, like *Dark Shadows* and *Star Trek.* His last published comic work was "Tripping Out," published in *Heavy Metal* in 2003.

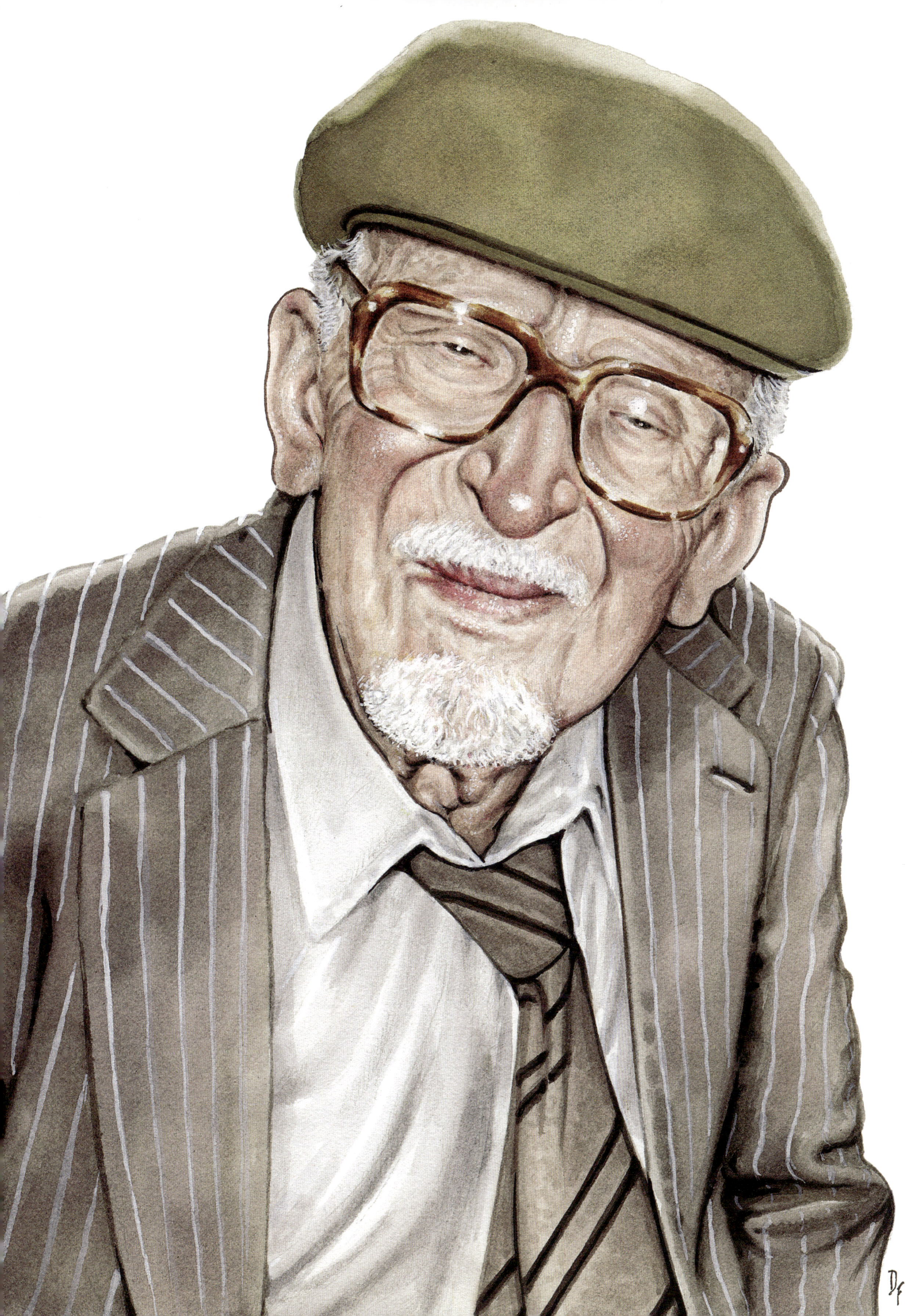

GAYLORD DU BOIS

1899–1993

plate 26

Gaylord McIlvaine Du Bois was born in Winthrop, Massachusetts, and attended Boston University and Trinity College. Before embarking on a thirty-year career as a writer, Du Bois drifted from job to job, spending time as a deputy sheriff in Wyoming and a retail clerk in New York. In 1935, bedridden in his parent's home with chronic brucellosis, he wrote an old college friend at Whitman Publishing looking for ways he could earn some money. The friend sent him a *Lone Ranger* radio script and challenged him to turn it into a 60,000-word novel. The book was published the next year and Du Bois launched a new career writing for licensed characters in novels, Big Little Books, and comic books.

Du Bois's earliest comic book work is likely a two-page Tom Mix story, "The Fighting Cowboy," published by Dell in 1936 in *Popular Comics* #4. Other early work includes *Raggedy Ann* and *Andy Panda* stories for Dell's *New Funnies*. He wrote for Dell and Gold Key for the next twenty-five years, publishing more than 3,000 stories in almost every genre.

Du Bois excelled at westerns, penning tales about Tom Mix, Gene Autry, and Red Ryder. He also specialized in animal stories featuring four-legged stars for *The Lone Ranger's Famous Horse Hi-Yo Silver, Roy Rogers' Trigger*, and *Lassie*. He was the main writer on Dell and Gold Key's *Tarzan* comics from 1947 to 1972, when the rights were sold to DC.

Du Bois's last published work was the six-page story "Fight with Philistines" in the 1993 Christian comic book *Aida-Zee*.

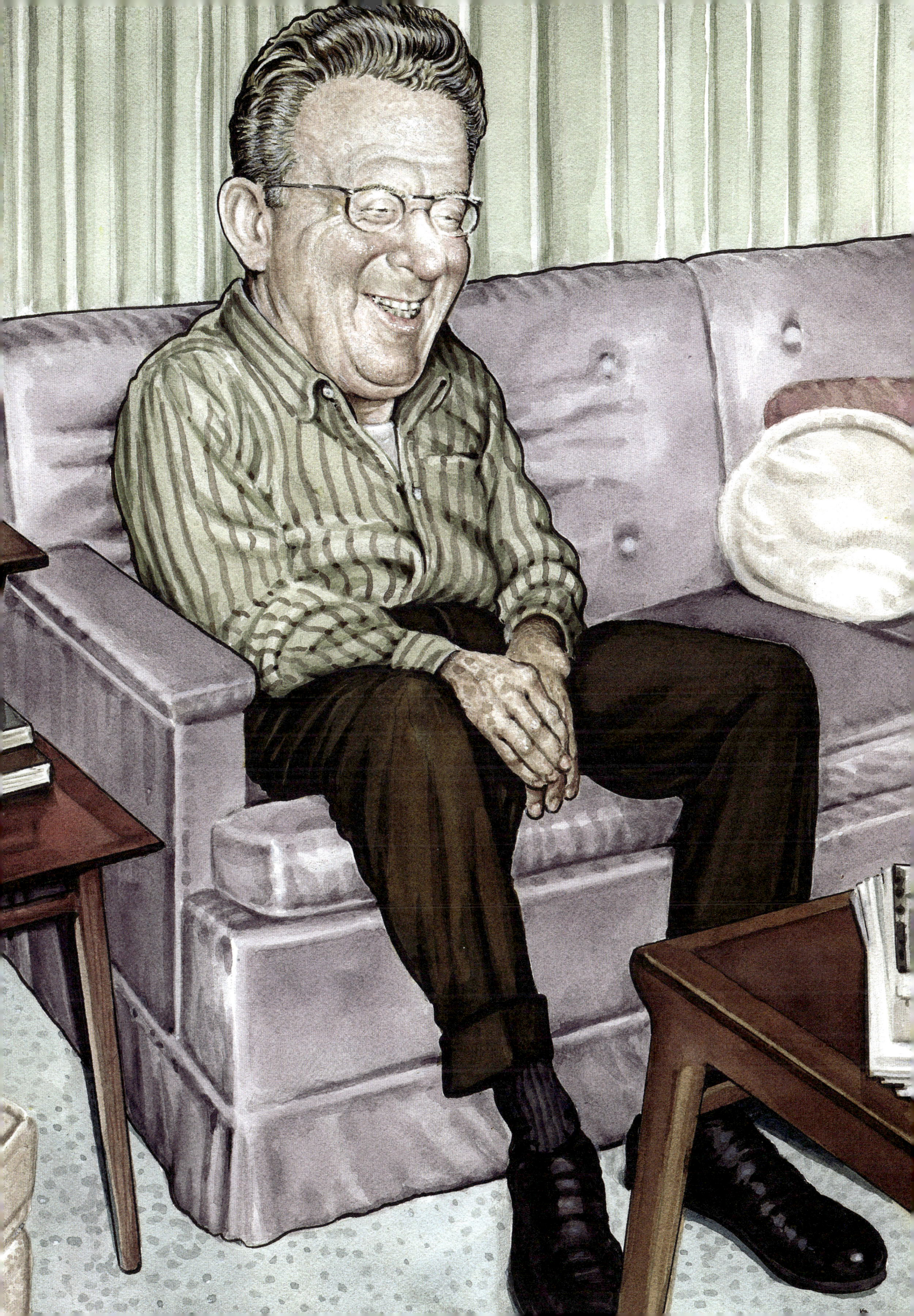

WHITNEY ELLSWORTH

1908–1980

plate 27

Frederic Whitney Ellsworth was born in Brooklyn. His education as a future comic book writer and editor consisted of a cartooning course at the Brooklyn YMCA, taught by cartoonist Ad Carter (creator of newspaper strip *Just Kids*), who would later introduce Ellsworth to his editors at King Features Syndicate.

During the Depression, he worked for King Features, performing various production chores on *Dumb Dora* and *Tillie the Toiler.* He was a jack-of-all-trades, penciling, inking, and coming up with gags. He also contributed illustrations to the *Newark Star Ledger.*

In 1934, Ellsworth became an assistant editor for Major Malcolm Wheeler-Nicholson's National Allied Publications, home of pioneering comic books like *New Fun, Adventure Comics*, and *Detective Comics.* Ellsworth not only edited the titles, but made suggestions for covers, and sketched out rough drafts for artists to follow. He eventually became an editorial director, taking charge of every facet of DC Comics for the next few years.

Starting with the 1948 movie serial *Superman*, he became DC Comics' Hollywood liaison, responsible for shepherding the company's properties through film and television adaptations. He had a hands-on role in script and production matters for such projects as the 1951 feature, *Superman and the Mole Men*, which led directly to 1952's *The Adventures of Superman*, starring George Reeves. He later wrote and produced a bizarre television pilot, *Super Pup*, that replaced the Superman cast with little people wearing fiberglass dog masks. Ellsworth also oversaw an unsuccessful attempt to bring *Superboy* to television in 1961.

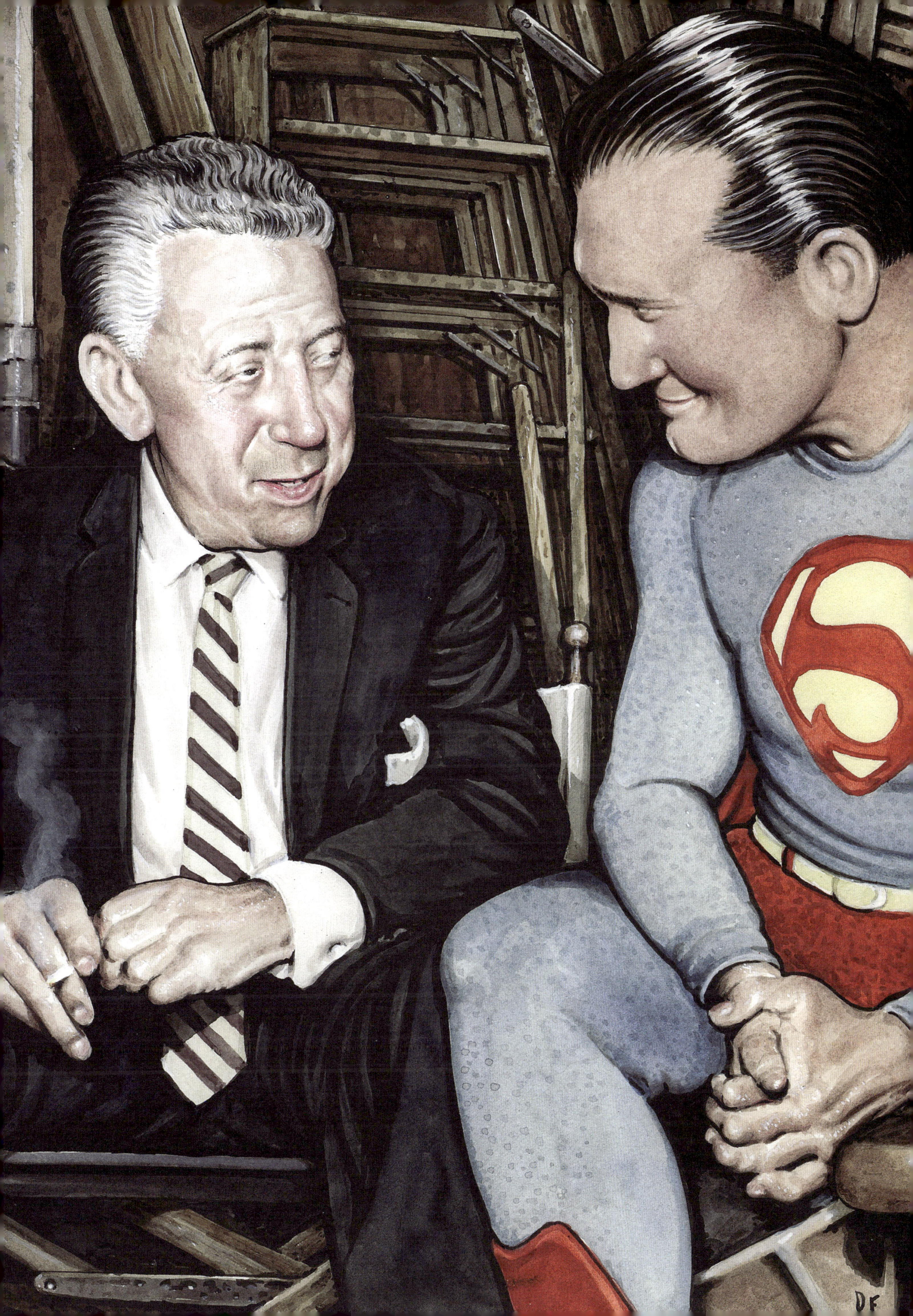
DF

MIKE ESPOSITO

1927-2010

plate 28

Mike Esposito was born in New York and attended the High School of Music & Art, where he met his future collaborator, artist Ross Andru. Esposito was drafted into the US Army in 1945. Esposito was stationed in Germany, and illustrated venereal disease prevention posters.

Esposito left the service in 1947, and joined his friend Andru at the Cartoonists and Illustrators School in New York. Esposito entered the comic book business in 1948 with his first published work: a ten-page western story, “Trouble Huntin’ in Dark Canyon,” in Fiction House’s *Western Thrillers* #4. Esposito and Andru’s first team effort came two years later, in Hillman Periodicals *Western Fighters* Vol. 2 #12.

Esposito went to work as a staff penciler for Stan Lee at Atlas Comics in 1951. His first published work was penciling and inking a six-page story, “Heat of Battle!,” in *Men’s Adventure* #6.

It wasn’t long before Esposito left Atlas to rejoin Andru and co-own the publishing company Mikeross Publications. They produced *3-D Romance*, *3-D Love*, and two other titles before the company dissolved. In 1962, Esposito and Andru began their long association with DC Comics, with extended runs on *Wonder Woman* and co-creating *Metal Men*.

Esposito began accepting assignments from Marvel Comics while still working with Andru at rival DC. Esposito inked without credit or under a pseudonym on *Amazing Spider-Man* with John Romita until he finally began using his real name in 1968.

Andru joined Esposito at Marvel in 1972, and they enjoyed a long run on the *Amazing Spider-Man*. Esposito left Marvel in 1988, and by the late ’90s, he had also completed hundreds of pages of inking for Archie Comics.

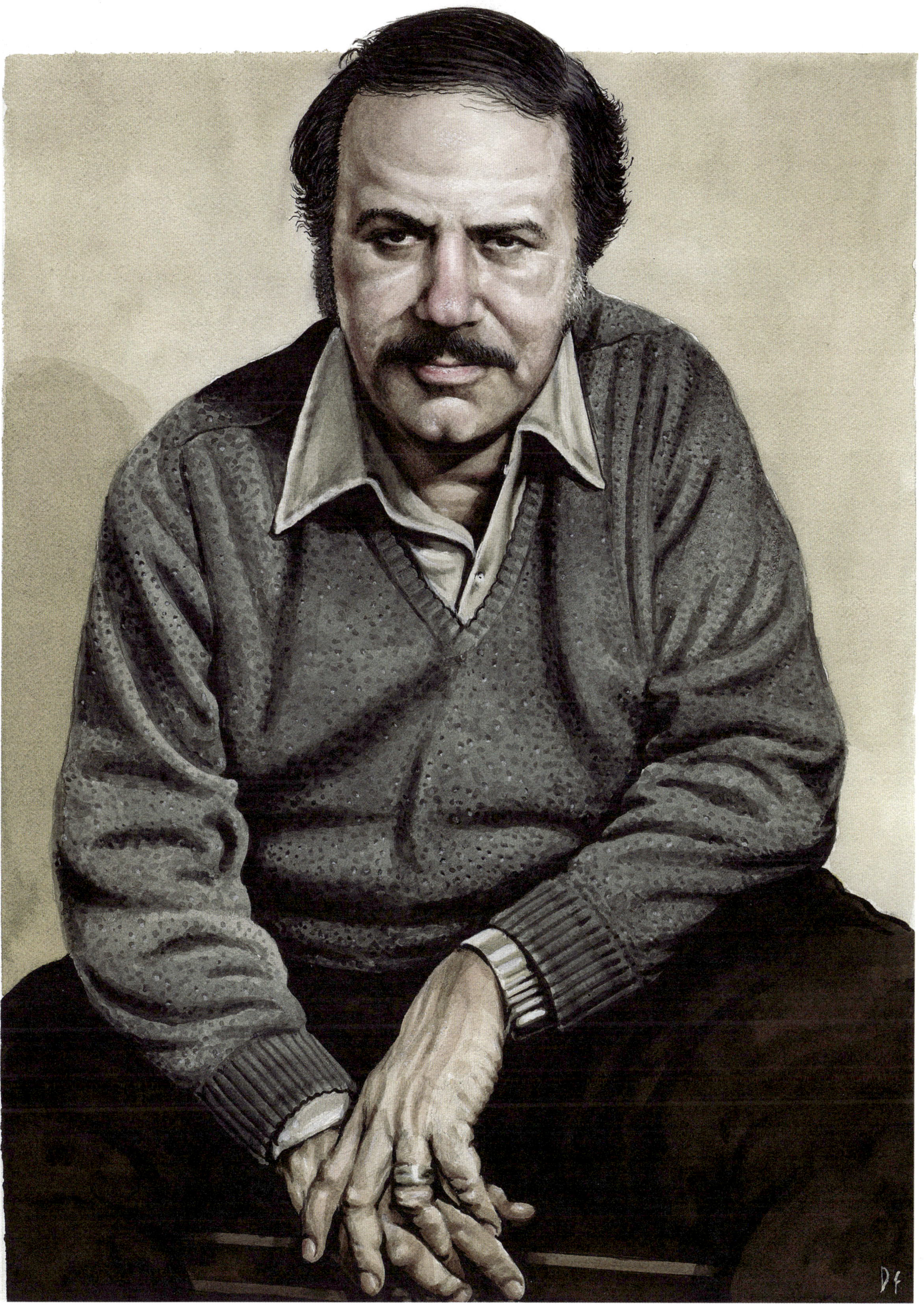

RIC ESTRADA

1928-2009

plate 29

Ric Estrada was born in Havana, Cuba, and attended the University of Havana. In 1946, Estrada met Ernest Hemingway, who assisted him in leaving Cuba for New York. In New York, he studied at the Art Students League, the Cartoonists and Illustrators School, and New York University.

Estrada's earliest comic book work was penciling and inking the eight-page story "No Scruples" for St. John's *Wartime Romances* #9, in 1951, and he regularly contributed to their romance titles, like *Teen-Age Temptations*, *Pictorial Romances*, and *True-Love Pictorial.*

His collaboration with editor/writer Harvey Kurtzman, "Bunker," for EC Comic's *Two-Fisted Tales* in 1952, was the first comic book story to feature an African American hero.

Estrada's work on superhero titles was rare. A notable exception was his work for the revival of DC Comic's *All-Star Comics* in 1976. He also drew a comic book adaptation of the New Testament for the Church of Jesus Christ of Latter-Day Saints.

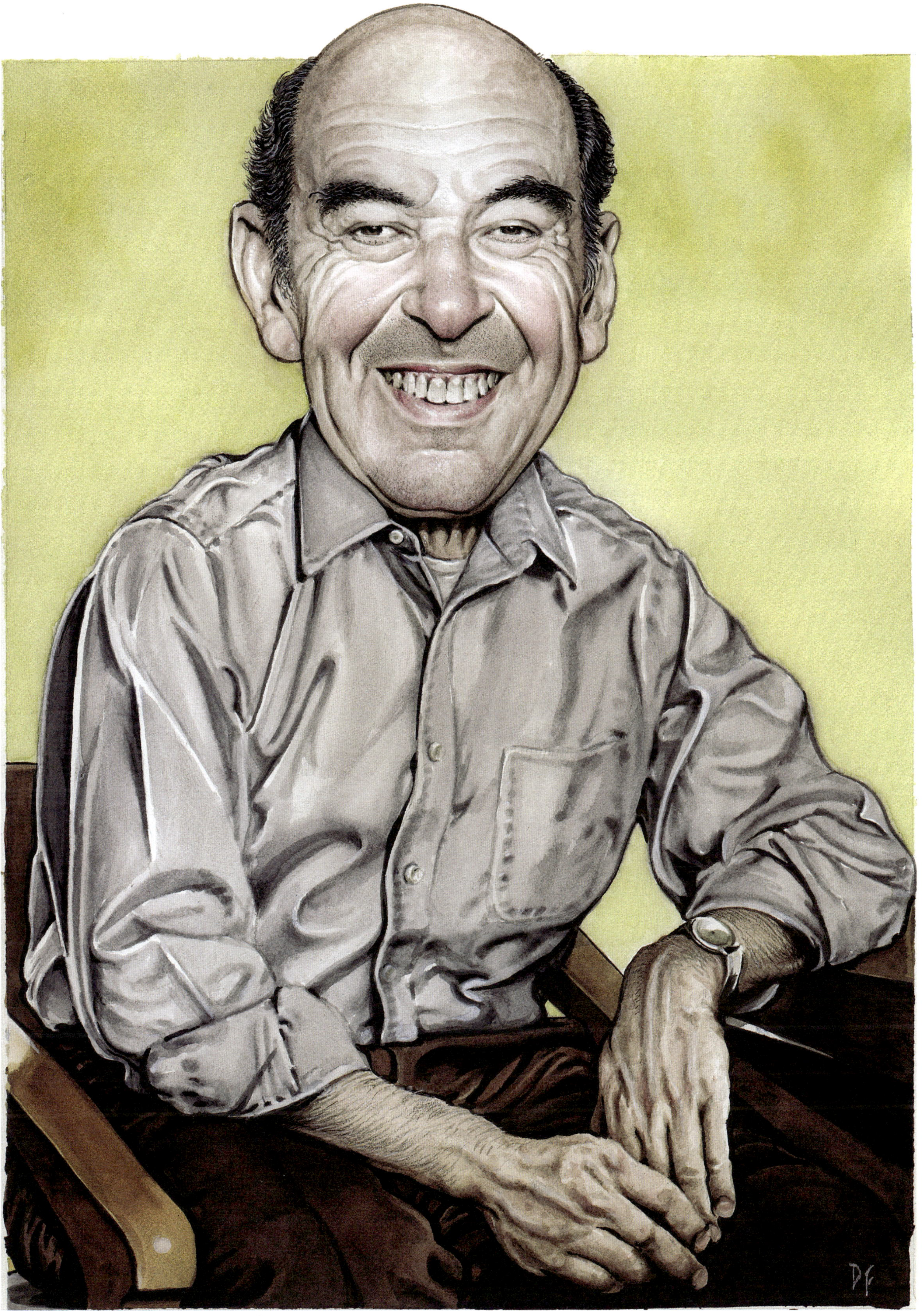

ORRIN C. EVANS

1902-1971

plate 30

Orrin Cromwell Evans was born in Steelton, Pennsylvania. Evans's mother, Maude, was the first African American to graduate from Williamsport Teacher's College.

Evans dropped out of school at seventeen, and worked for *Sportsman's Magazine* and the black-owned *Philadelphia Tribune*. In the early '30s, he landed a job as a general assignment reporter, for the 100-percent-white-staffed *Philadelphia Record*. Evans was not always readily accepted as a journalist. Meeting with reporters after his son was kidnapped in 1932, Charles Lindbergh refused to start the press conference until Evans was removed from the room. Evans' wartime exposé of racial segregation in the Armed Forces resulted in death threats.

After the war, the owners of the *Record* responded to a prolonged labor action by shutting the paper down for good. In 1947, Orrin C. Evans would become the first African American publisher of comic books, joining forces with his former editor, Harry T. Saylor, to launch *All-Negro Comics*. The first issue featured art by Evans's brother, George J. Evans Jr. and black artists from Philadelphia and Baltimore. The book's content was a grab-bag of detective, humor, and adventure stories, featuring characters like Lion Man, Li'l Eggie, and Ace Harlem. *Time* magazine said *All-Negro Comics* was "the first to be drawn by negro artists and peopled entirely by negro characters." Although a second issue was prepared, it never saw print. Newsprint vendors refused to sell to Evans, and the series was abandoned. Soon after, mainstream publishers began publishing comic books (like Fawcett's *Negro Romance*), targeted at a black readership.

Evans returned to newspapers, working at the *Chester Times* and the *Philadelphia Bulletin*.

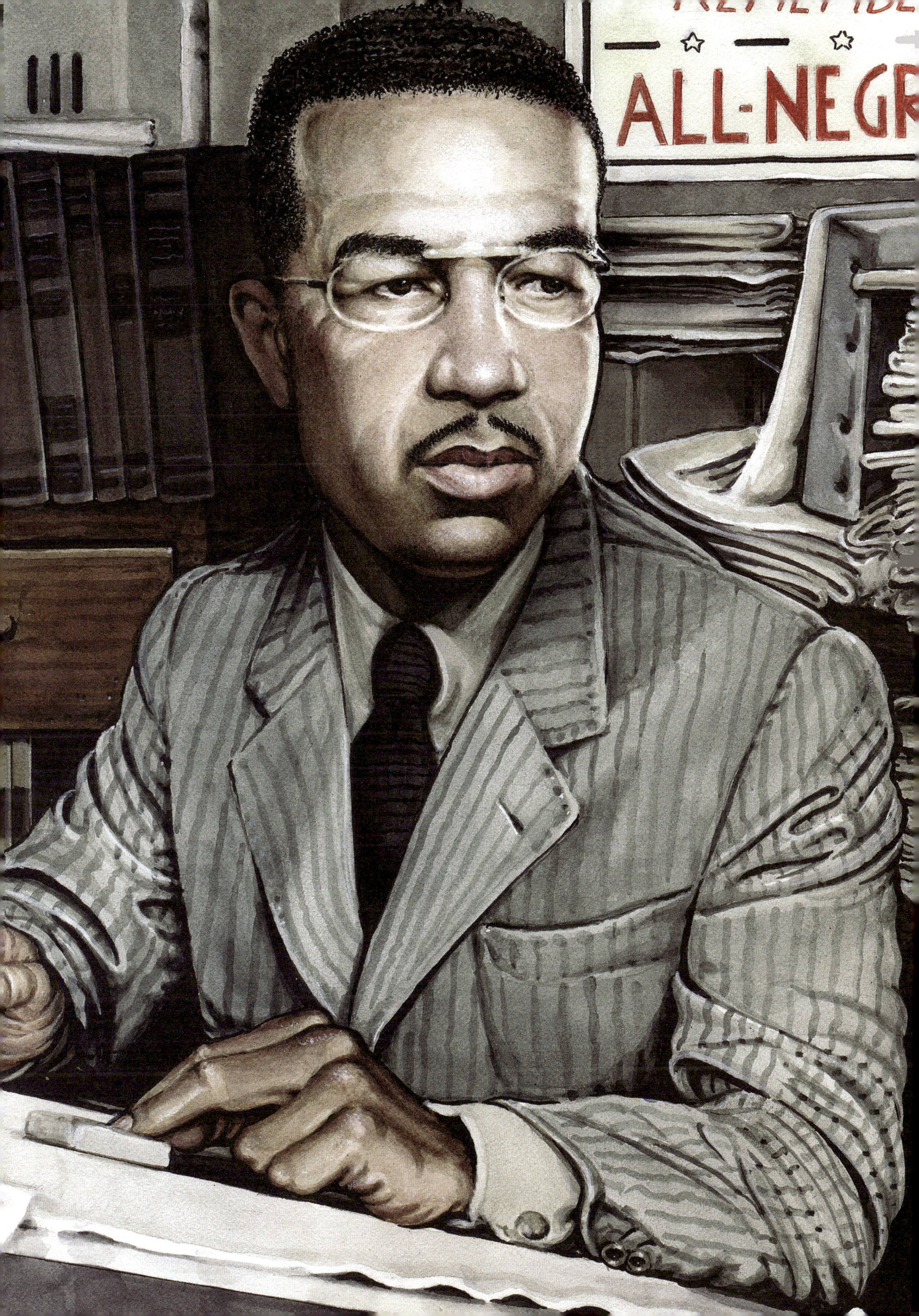
ALL-NEGR

AL FAGO

1904–1978

plate 31

Born in Yonkers, New York, Alfred V. Fago attended trade school and got a job in the design department of the Alexander Smith Rug Company in 1922. Fago's younger brother, Vince, was also a comic book artist and animator. The Fago brothers occasionally worked together on funny animal titles like Al's *Frisky Fables,* which made its debut in 1945 and went through three different publishers during its five-year run. In the early '50s, Fago became a managing editor at Charlton Comics, where he published his own creations: funny animal superheroes Atomic Mouse and Atomic Rabbit. In 1956, he created *Timmy the Timid Ghost* for Charlton, a brazen attempt to capitalize on the success of Harvey's *Casper the Friendly Ghost. Timmy the Timid Ghost* lasted for almost fifteen years.

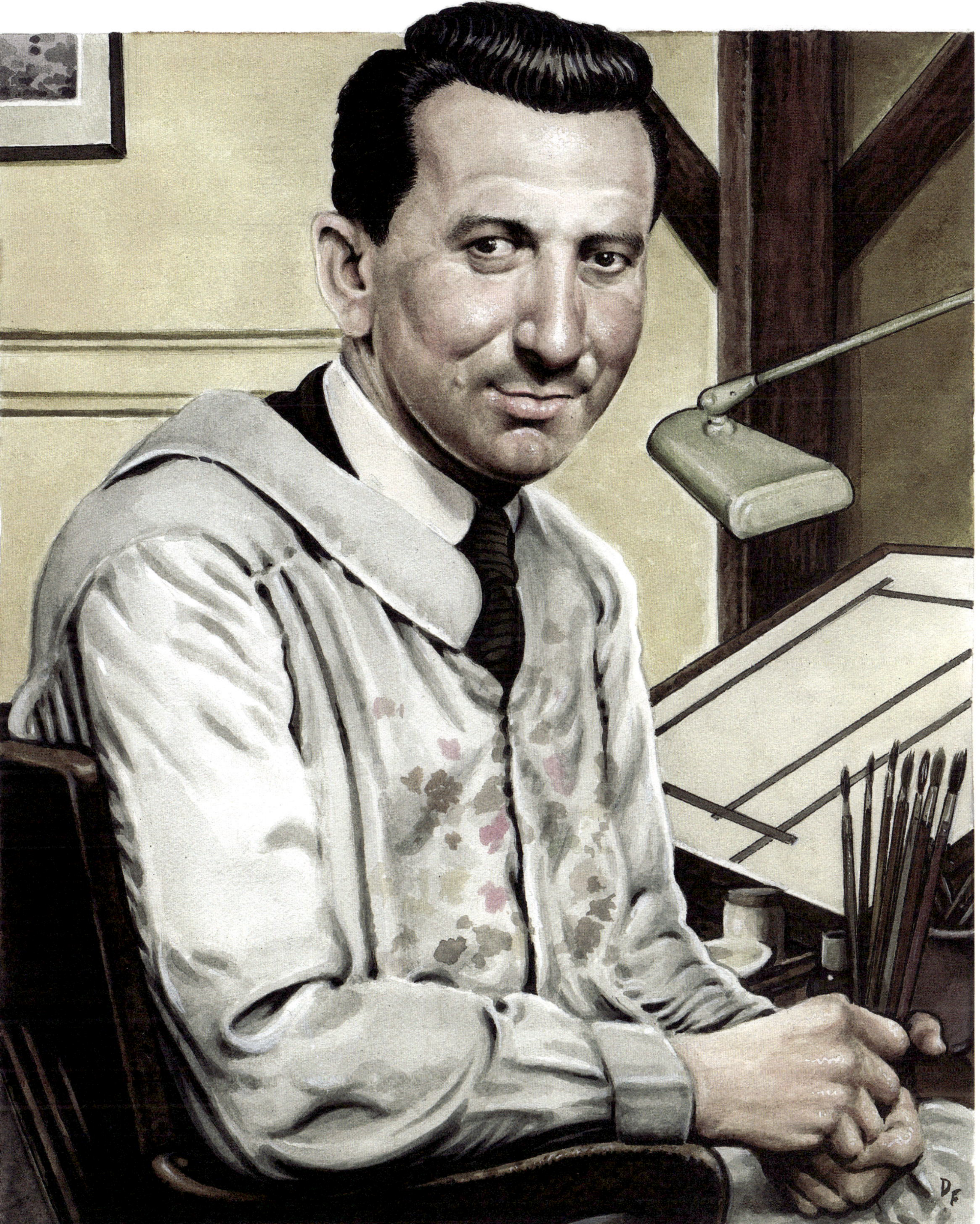

VINCE FAGO

1914-2002

plate 32

Born in Yonkers, New York, Vincenzo Francisco Gennaro Di Fago attended DeWitt Clinton High School in the Bronx. After graduating (at the age of twenty), he worked in industrial animation production for the Jam Handy Studio in Detroit. Fago returned to New York for a job as an assistant animator for the Fleischer Brothers' studio, where he worked on *Popeye* shorts and the influential *Superman* serial.

Fago followed the studio's move to Florida when Paramount Pictures gained control of the Fleischer's operation. After the bombing of Pearl Harbor in 1941, Fago returned to New York where he met Timely Comics editor Stan Lee. Lee gave him freelance penciling work on books like *Terrytoons Comics*, which feature funny animal characters Dinky and Frenchy Rabbit.

Fago had vision in only one eye, making him ineligible for military service. When Fago's close friend Lee left to join the service, he became interim editor and art director at Timely. Upon Lee's return, he worked in independent comics production, and illustrated *Golden Books*. Fago did extensive work in the '70s for Now Age Books, producing *Classics Illustrated*-style adaptations of literature for the educational market.

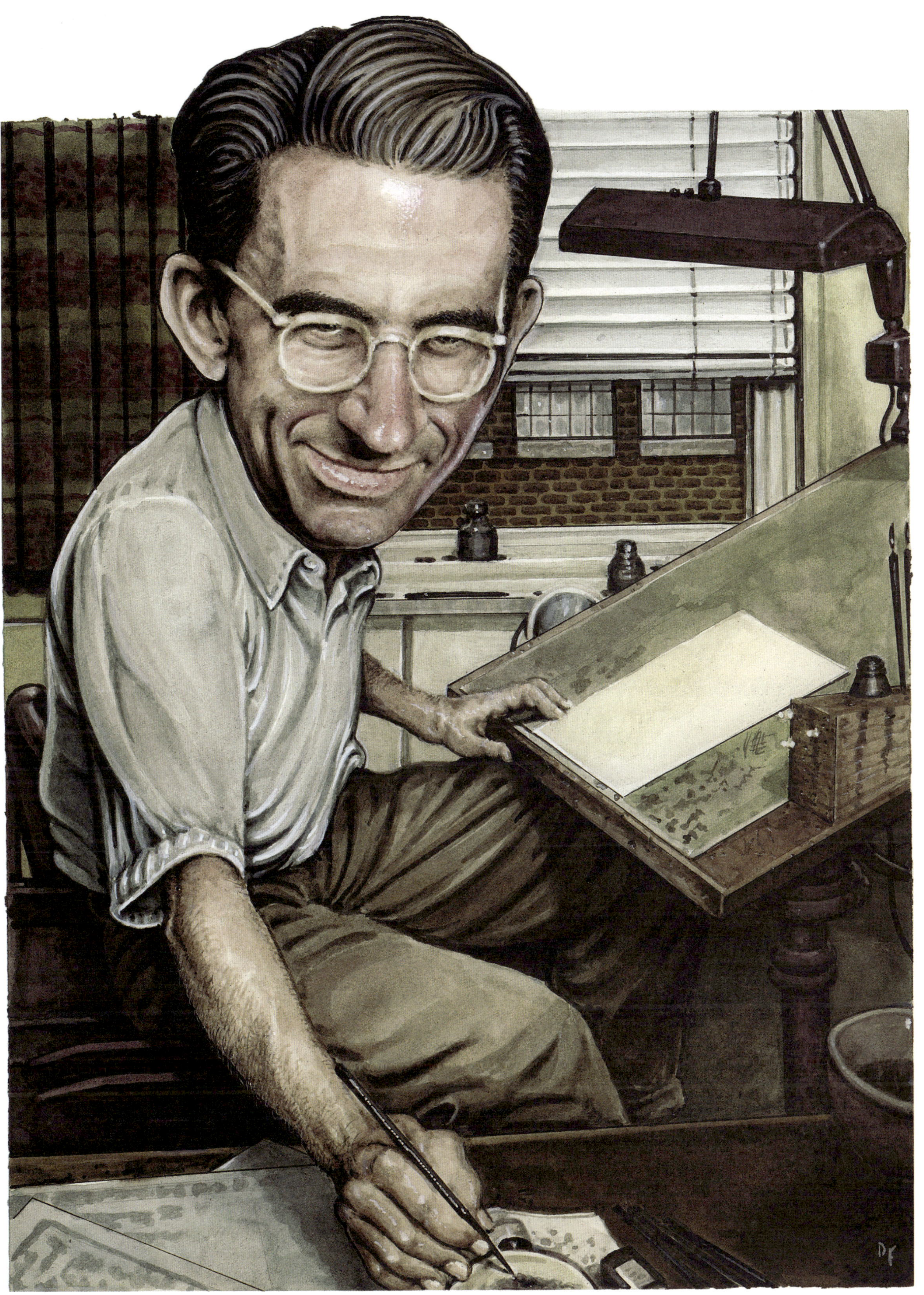

ROBERT W. FARRELL

1908-1986

plate 33

Isidore Katz was born in New York, and graduated from Far Rockaway High School in 1926. After spending ten years as a lawyer, Katz changed his name to Robert W. Farrell and began a freelance writing career working for the Eisner & Iger shop. Farrell also worked with artist Frank Robbins on the syndicated comic strip *Scorchy Smith*. In 1939, Farrell and Victor S. Fox patented the *Comicscope*, a cheaply made slide projector that they hawked through Victor S. Fox's comic book ads.

By 1940, Farrell had left Fox to start his own company, Farrell Publications, which published titles like *Captain Flight Comics* and *U.S. Jones*. In 1943, he was drafted into the US Army and stationed in Alabama for the next three years. By 1951, Farrell Publications had become Farrell Comics Group, with a bewildering array of imprints: *America's Best*, *Ajax Publications*, *Red Top Comics*, *Steinway Comics*, and several others. Farrell hired the S. M. Iger Studio to produce a line of horror titles: *Fantastic Fears*, *Haunted Thrills*, *Strange Fantasy*, and *Voodoo*. After the Comics Code Authority put an end to most horror comics, he edited a humor magazine called *Panic* (no relation to the earlier EC comic with the same name). In 1966, he (briefly) partnered with Myron Fass to publish a line of black-and-white horror comics magazines under the Eerie Publications banner, beginning with *Weird*. They were mainly reprints of his pre-Code horror stories, with some added-on blood. Farrell also briefly revived the newspapers the *Brooklyn Eagle*, and later the *New York Daily Mirror*.

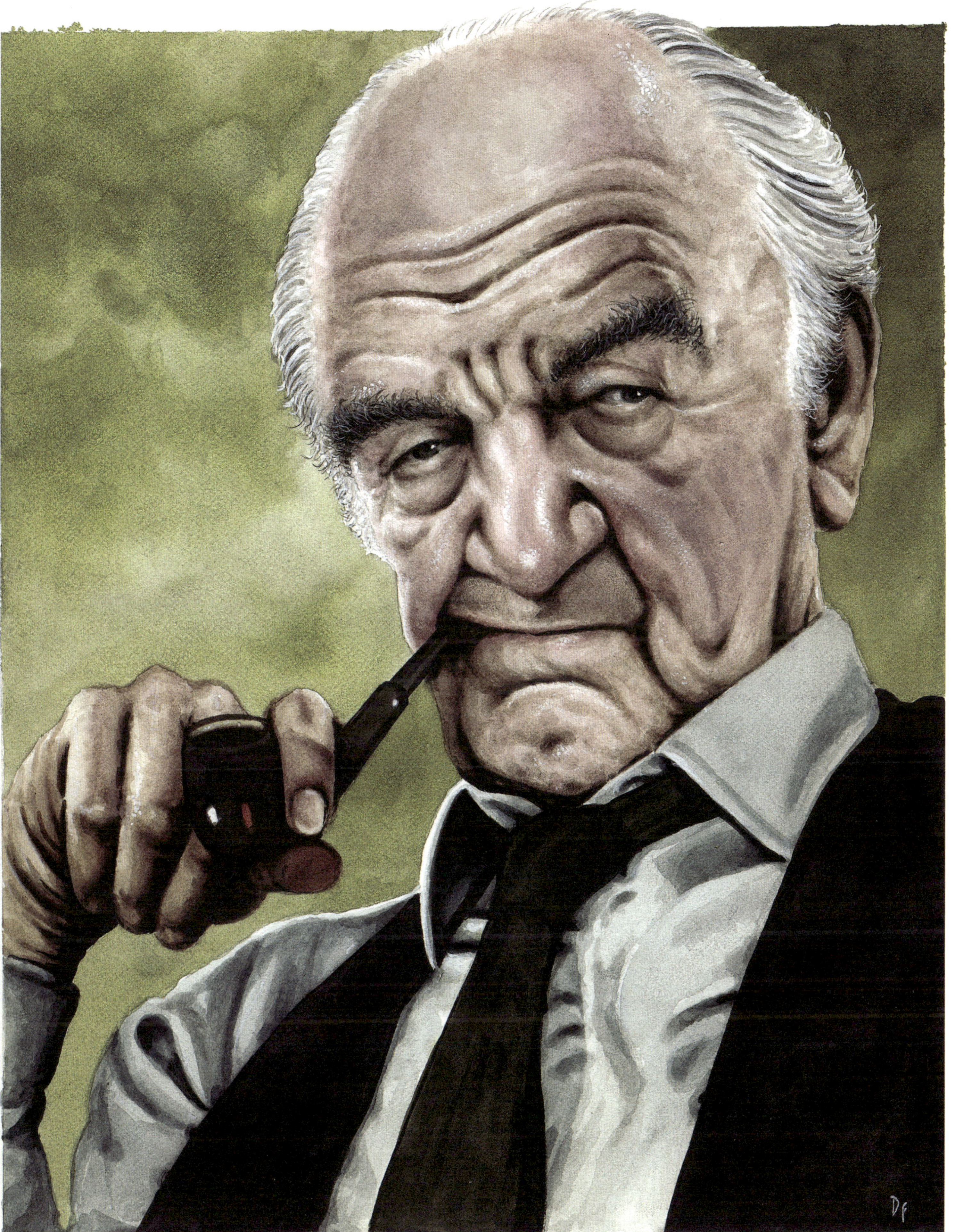

MYRON FASS

1926-2006

plate 34

While few comic book artists have ever reinvented themselves as publishing moguls, Brooklyn-born Myron Fass did so with a gold-plated revolver strapped to his waist while seated beneath a large portrait of himself as Jesus Christ.

A few years after World War II, in the midst of a declining, postwar comic book market, Fass was making a living drawing western, romance, and horror titles, spending time at Marvel, Street & Smith, Lev Gleason Enterprises, and other publishers. Fass worked on titles like *John Wayne Adventures*, *Hollywood Love Doctor*, and *Great Lover Romances*.

By 1956, shrinking sales, senate investigations, and Dr. Fredric Wertham's *Seduction of the Innocent* had gutted the industry. EC publisher William M. Gaines retooled his *Mad* comic book into a magazine format, avoiding the oppressive oversight of the newly formed Comics Code Authority. Fass packaged one of the very first *Mad* imitators, *Lunatickle*, for a subsidiary of Fawcett Publications. Fass later bragged that the first issue of *Lunatickle* sold a million copies—and was canceled before the third issue made it to press.

But Fass was off and running with a template for creating quick-to-market publications designed to fill practically any uncharted niche on the newsstand. Fass began publishing girlie magazines and gossip rags in the early '60s. By the middle of the decade, he had appropriated the name of the now-defunct *Captain Marvel* comic book, with art by the Human Torch creator Carl Burgos, to cash in on the latest comic book boom. When Warren Publishing made a splash with horror magazine titles *Creepy* and *Eerie* in the mid-'60s, Fass launched his own delightfully depraved black-and-white horror comics magazine line with titles like *Weird, Horror Tales*, and *Tales of Voodoo*, and even borrowed Gaines's old EC title (for one issue): *Tales from The Crypt*. Fass shamelessly named his operation Eerie Publications.

In his last decades, he ran his own Countrywide Publications—whose titles included the *Heavy Metal* clone, *Gasm*—then focused on producing weapon and hunting magazines and operating his Florida gun shop.

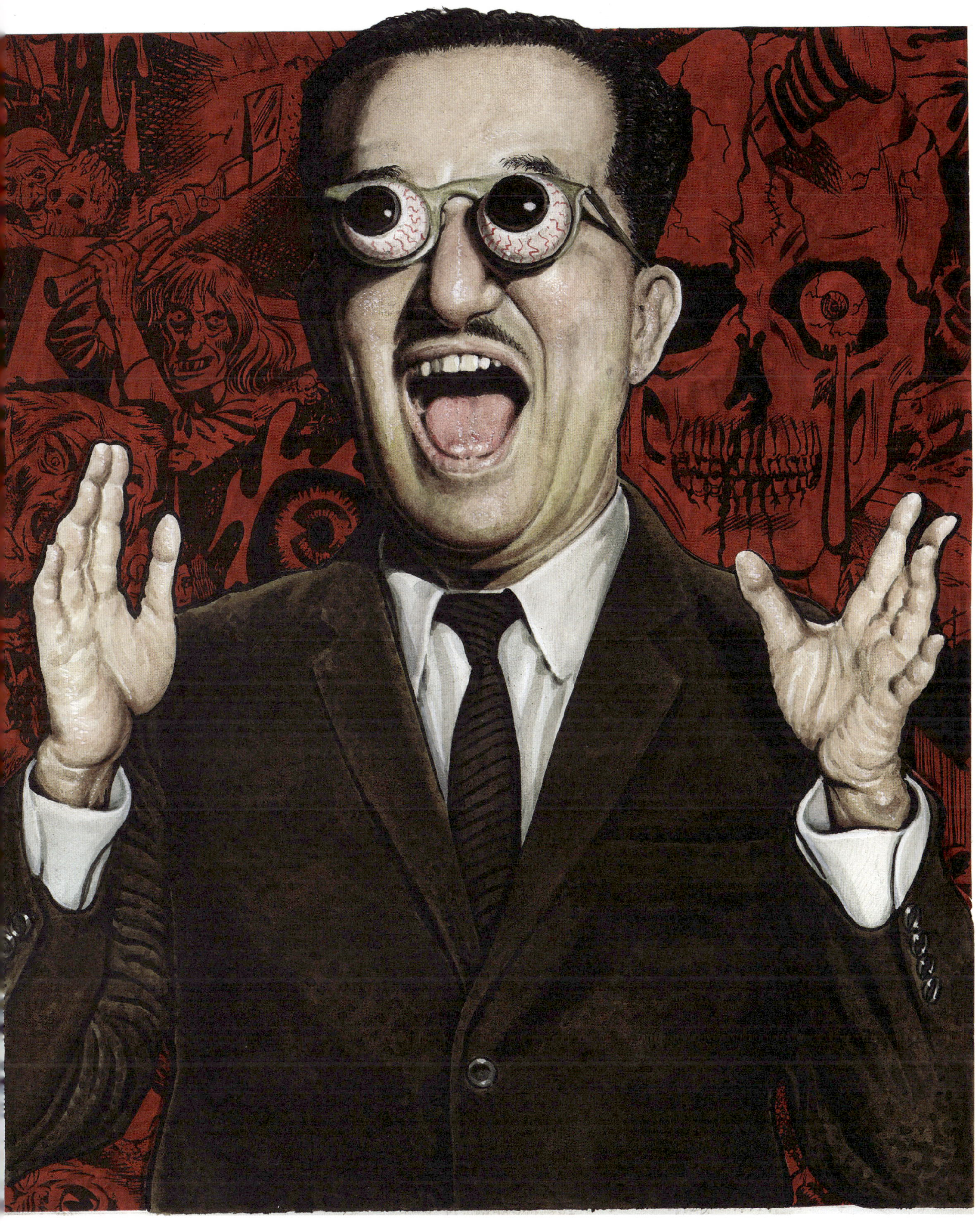

JULES FEIFFER

b. 1929

plate 35

Jules Ralph Feiffer was born in the Bronx. His mother was a fashion designer who encouraged his drawing abilities by enrolling him in the Art Students League when he was thirteen. Feiffer took comics seriously even as a youngster, deconstructing layouts and composition. He graduated from James Monroe High School in 1947 and soon made his way to Will Eisner's studio to ask *The Spirit* artist for a job. Eisner was delighted to hire an assistant who required so little financial compensation. Feiffer began doing odd jobs like filling in backgrounds and drawing word balloons until he eventually worked his way up, scripting Spirit stories from Eisner's prompts. When he asked for a raise, Eisner countered with an offer to feature his humor strip *Clifford* on the back page of the widely distributed *Spirit* newspaper sections. Feiffer also made known to his boss his objection to the stereotyping of the black character, Ebony.

By 1956, Feiffer had a weekly comic strip in the *Village Voice*, originally titled *Sick, Sick, Sick*. The strip was rechristened *Feiffer* by the time it was nationally syndicated in 1959. A kinetic, loosely drawn combination of Jewish angst and New York politics, it ran for 42 years, and has been anthologized in a number of books. His 1961 film *Munro* won the Academy Award for best animated short.

Feiffer paid tribute to Eisner and the comic book heroes of his youth with 1965's landmark book on comics history, *The Great Comic Book Heroes*, published by Bonanza. Part memoir, part anthology, the book was one of the first to document the Golden Age of comics.

Feiffer wrote the screenplay for Robert Altman's live action 1980 film *Popeye*, starring Robin Williams.

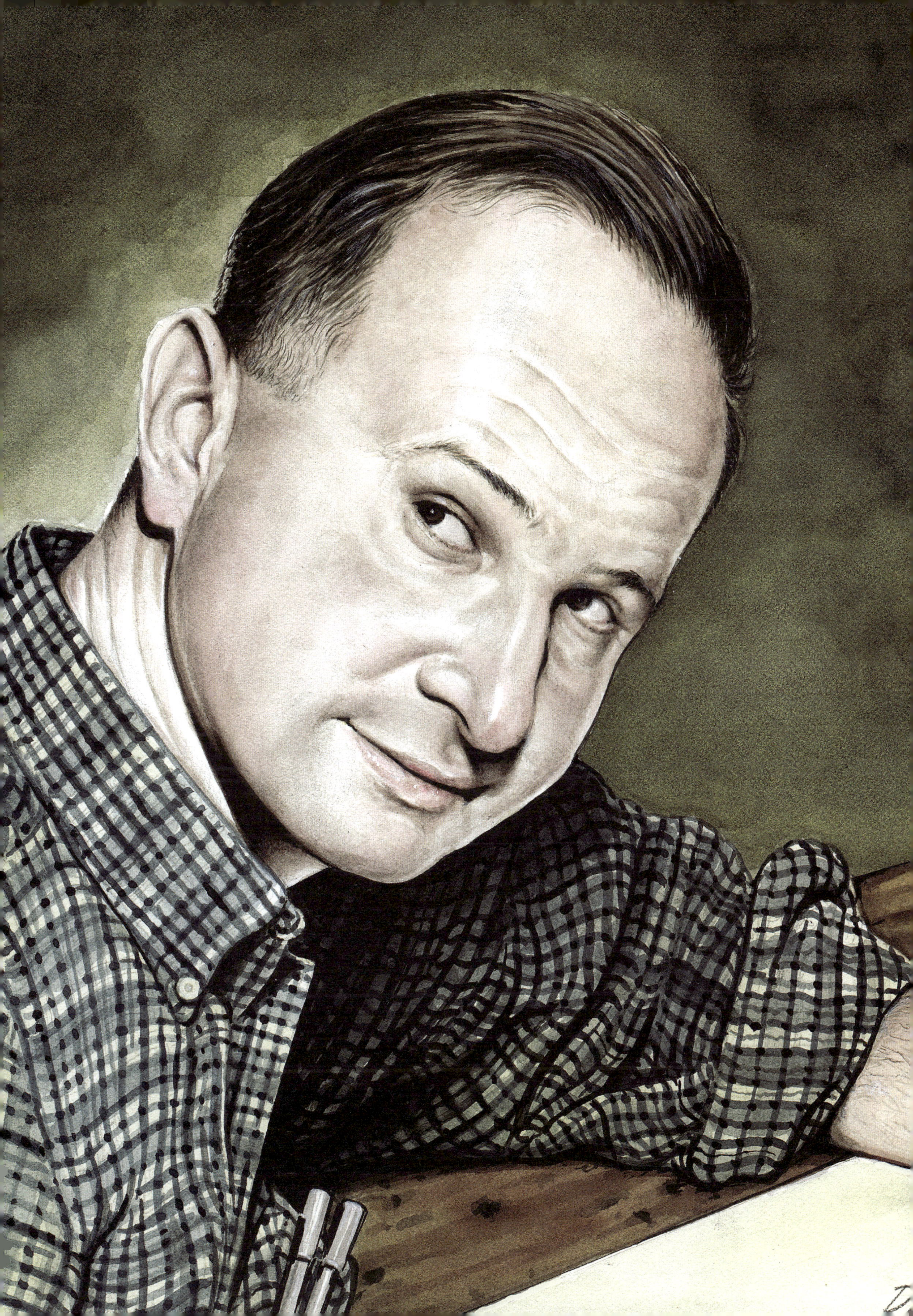

LOUIS FERSTADT

1900-1954

plate 36

In 1910, Louis Goodman Ferstadt emigrated to Chicago from Ukraine. Ferstadt spent four years studying at the Art Institute of Chicago before winning a scholarship to attend the Art Students League of New York. Ferstadt worked in advertising before publishing his first comic strip in 1926, *The Kids in Our Block*, for the *New York Evening Graphic Standard*. In the '30s, he did freelance work for the Demby Studio and Eisner & Iger. Working for the WPA, he created murals for the 1939 World's Fair and New York's RCA building.

Ferstadt launched his own studio in 1942, employing a young Harvey Kurtzman, among others. His studio produced work for Ace Comics, Harvey Comics, etc. Before closing his studio in 1945 and taking an art director job at Fox, he drew Flash and Green Lantern for National Publications' *Comics Cavalcade*. An avowed Communist, he contributed a strip to *The Daily Worker*.

Ferstadt died of a heart attack while camping in 1954.

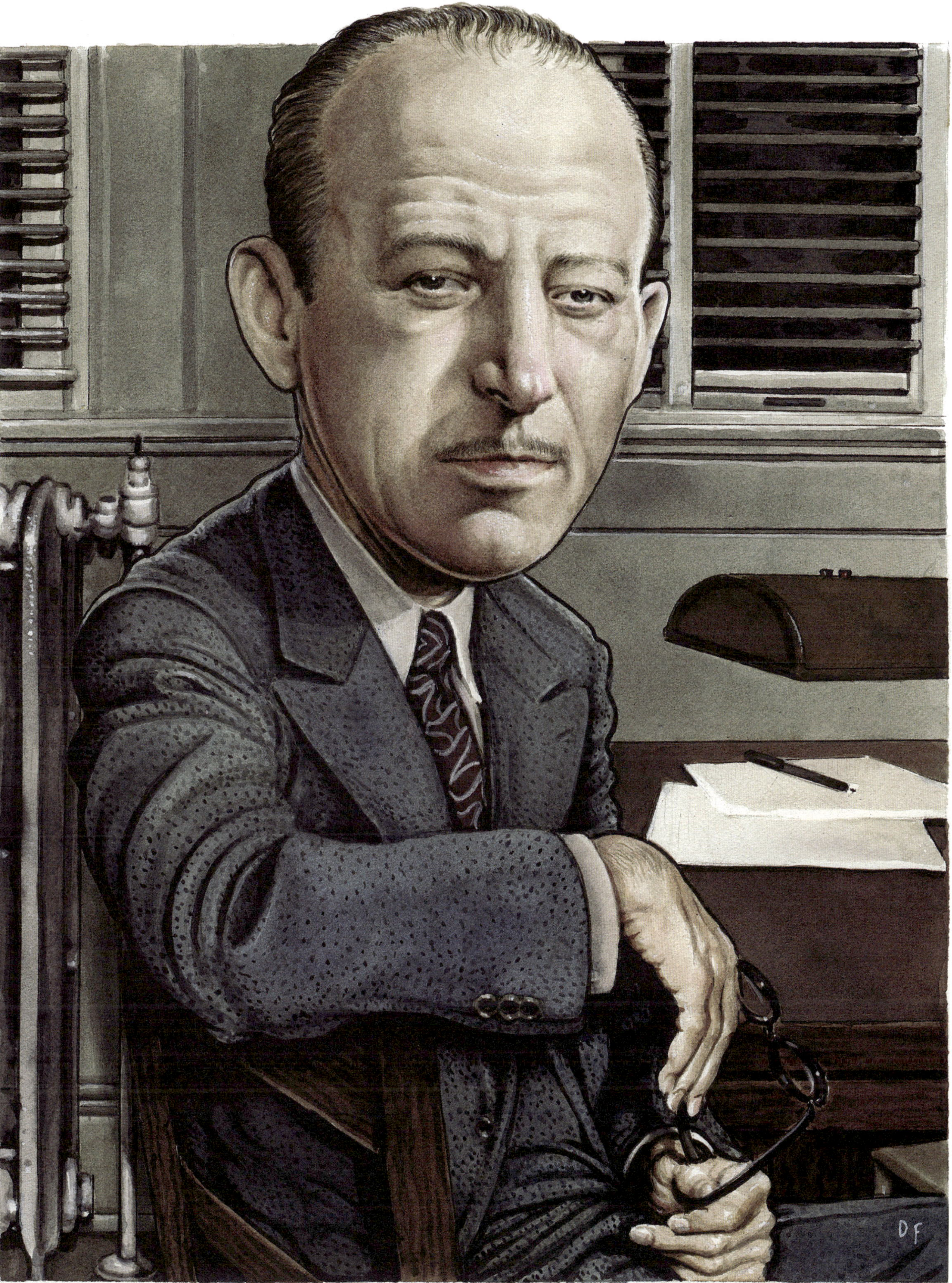
DF

VICTOR FOX

1893–1957

plate 37

Samuel Victor Joseph Fox was born in Nottinghamshire, England. Fox and his family emigrated to New York when Fox was six. Fox's early career on Wall Street was overshadowed by indictments for mail fraud. Several years later, Fox found himself working as an accountant for DC Comics precursor, National Comics Publications. Legend has it that, one morning, Fox saw the booming sales figures for comic books and, by that afternoon, had set up shop on another floor. He commissioned his first title, *Wonder Comics*, from Eisner & Iger's comic book shop. The rotund, fedora-wearing Fox would soon anoint himself, to all who would listen, "the King of Comics!"

Wonder Comics hit the stands in 1939; National Comics quickly sued, claiming it hewed a bit too closely to their *Action Comics* and its star, Superman. Fox pressured Eisner to take the fall and claim that Wonder Man was entirely his idea. Fox lost the suit, and, afterward, would routinely stop the elevator at National's offices to spit on the floor before continuing on to his own offices.

Fox originated the long-running *Blue Beetle* and also published girlie magazines but went out of business in the mid-1950s, another victim of declining sales and the Comics Code Authority. The *Blue Beetle* continued on at Charlton Comics.

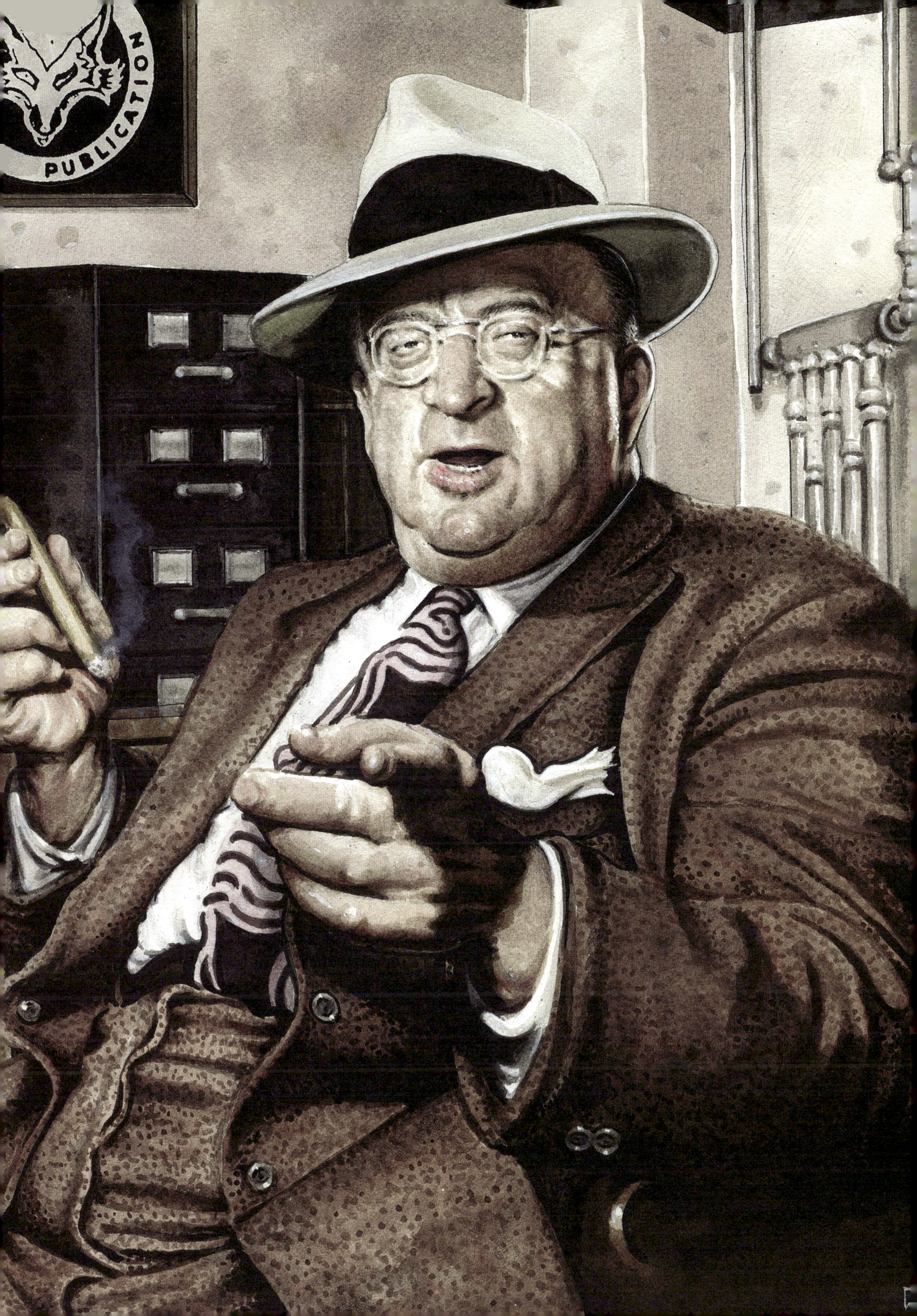
PUBLICATION

FRANK GIACOIA

1924–1988

plate 38

Born in New York, Frank Giacoia attended the School of Industrial Art in Manhattan, and continued his education at the Art Students League of New York.

Giacoia joined Eisner & Iger's comic book production shop in 1941. His very first documented work was inking Allen Simon's pencils for the cover of *Sub-Mariner Comics* #7. His earliest published interior work was penciling and inking the eight-page story "The Millen-Faber Case" in Lev Gleason's *Crime Does Not Pay* #24 (1942).

Giacoia worked as a penciler and inker for different publishers for the next two decades, but probably made his biggest impact as a Marvel Comics inker. Starting in the mid-'60s, while still working for DC, he collaborated with the company's most prolific artists, inking Jack Kirby, John Romita, Gil Kane, and others on virtually every important Marvel title. Frank Giacoia used a number of pseudonyms while freelancing for rival companies, such as Frankie Ray, Phil Zupa, and Espoia.

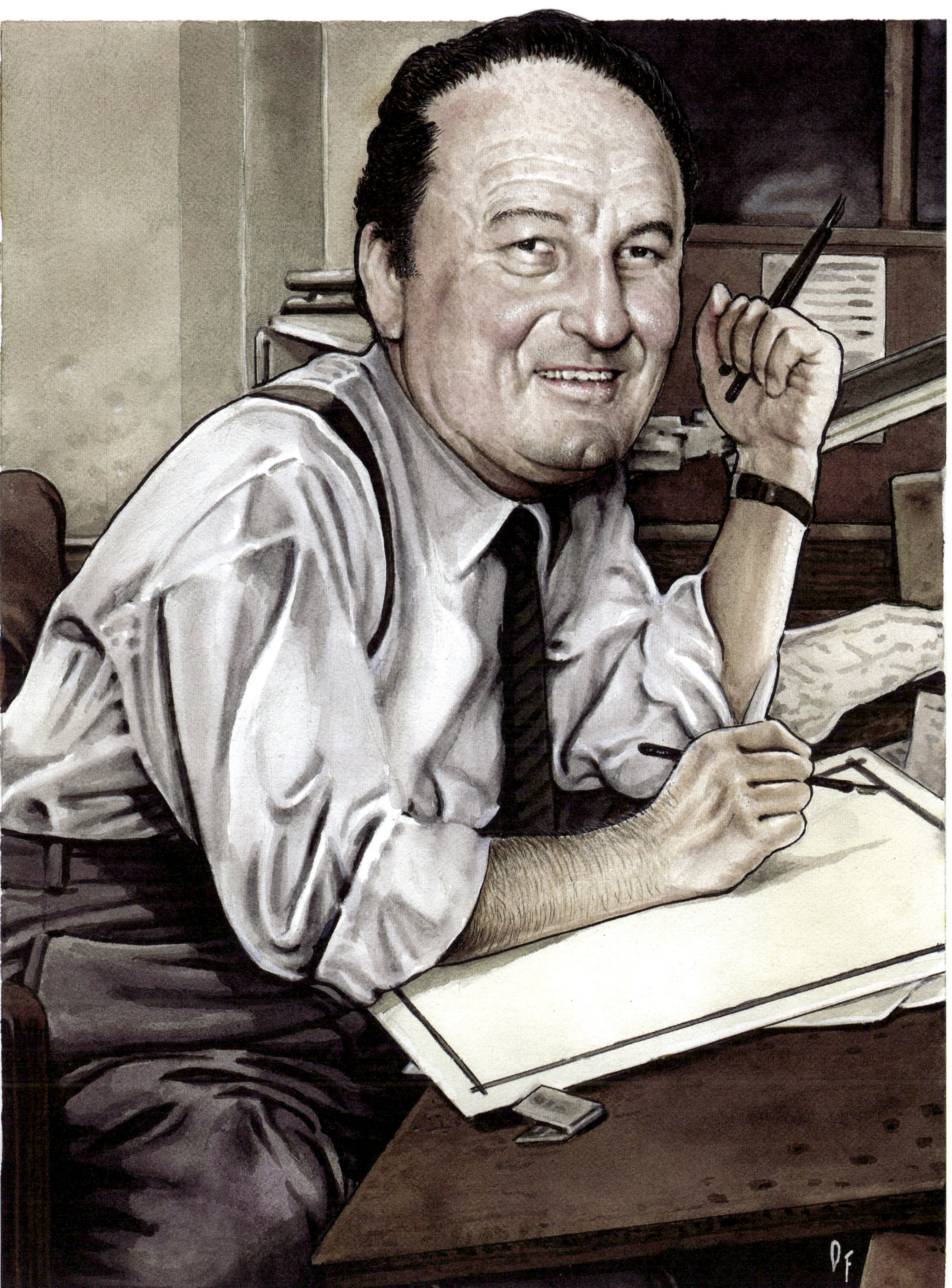

STAN GOLDBERG

1932-2014

plate 39

Born in the Bronx, Stan Goldberg graduated from the School of Industrial Art. He joined Timely Comics as a colorist right out of high school. Within two years, he would be promoted to head of the coloring department. He also drew the occasional horror tale, the earliest example being a three-page story appearing in 1952, "The Cave of Death," in *Marvel Tales* #109. He remained on staff at Timely as the company evolved into Atlas.

He returned to art school in 1958, studying under Batman artist Jerry Robinson at the School of Visual Arts, and worked as a freelancer for Atlas's new incarnation Marvel Comics. He was involved in color design for many of Marvel's earliest, groundbreaking titles, like *Spider-Man*, *The Fantastic Four*, and the *Hulk*.

Goldberg continued to ink and draw, mainly for Marvel's romance comics. He employed his teen-art style on *Millie the Model* and *Patsy Walker,* and later for DC on titles like *Binky*.

In 1975, he began an association with Archie Comics that would continue for nearly forty years.

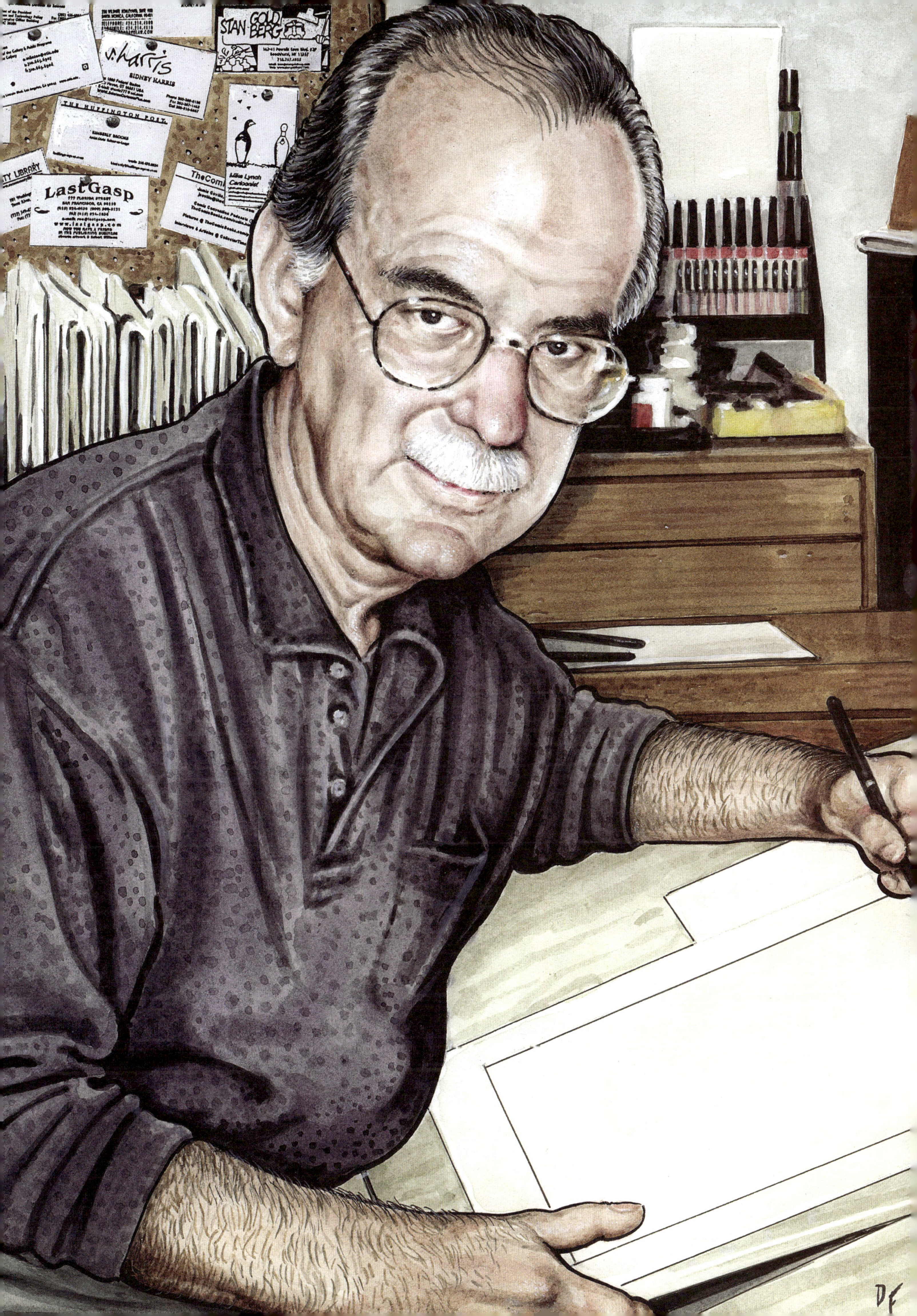

s.harris
SIDNEY HARRIS
STAN GOLDBERG
THE HUFFINGTON POST
LastGasp
Mike Lynch Cartoonist
DF

FRED GUARDINEER

1913-2002

plate **40**

Fredrick B. Guardineer was born in Albany, New York, and studied art at Syracuse University. After graduating and spending time abroad in Europe, he moved to New York in search of a job. He worked on illustrations for pulp publisher Street & Smith, before going to work for the comic book production shop of Harry "A" Chesler in 1937. His first substantial published work was "The Cowgirl," a single-page humor piece in *Star Ranger* #6 in 1937 by Chesler Publications, Inc.

Guardineer left Chesler to freelance for DC and Centaur Publications, drawing covers and spot illustrations. In 1938, his twelve-page story, "The Mystery of the Freight Train Robberies," appeared alongside the first appearance of Superman in *Action Comics* #1. After a brief stint in the military, he returned to the comic book business, working for DC, Hillman Publications, Lev Gleason, and others. In 1943, Guardineer replaced artist Bob Powell, drawing *Mr. Mystic* for Will Eisner's weekly *The Spirit* newspaper insert, until the strip was dropped the following year.

In 1955, Guardineer left the comic book business for a job with the US Postal Service. He retired in 1975.

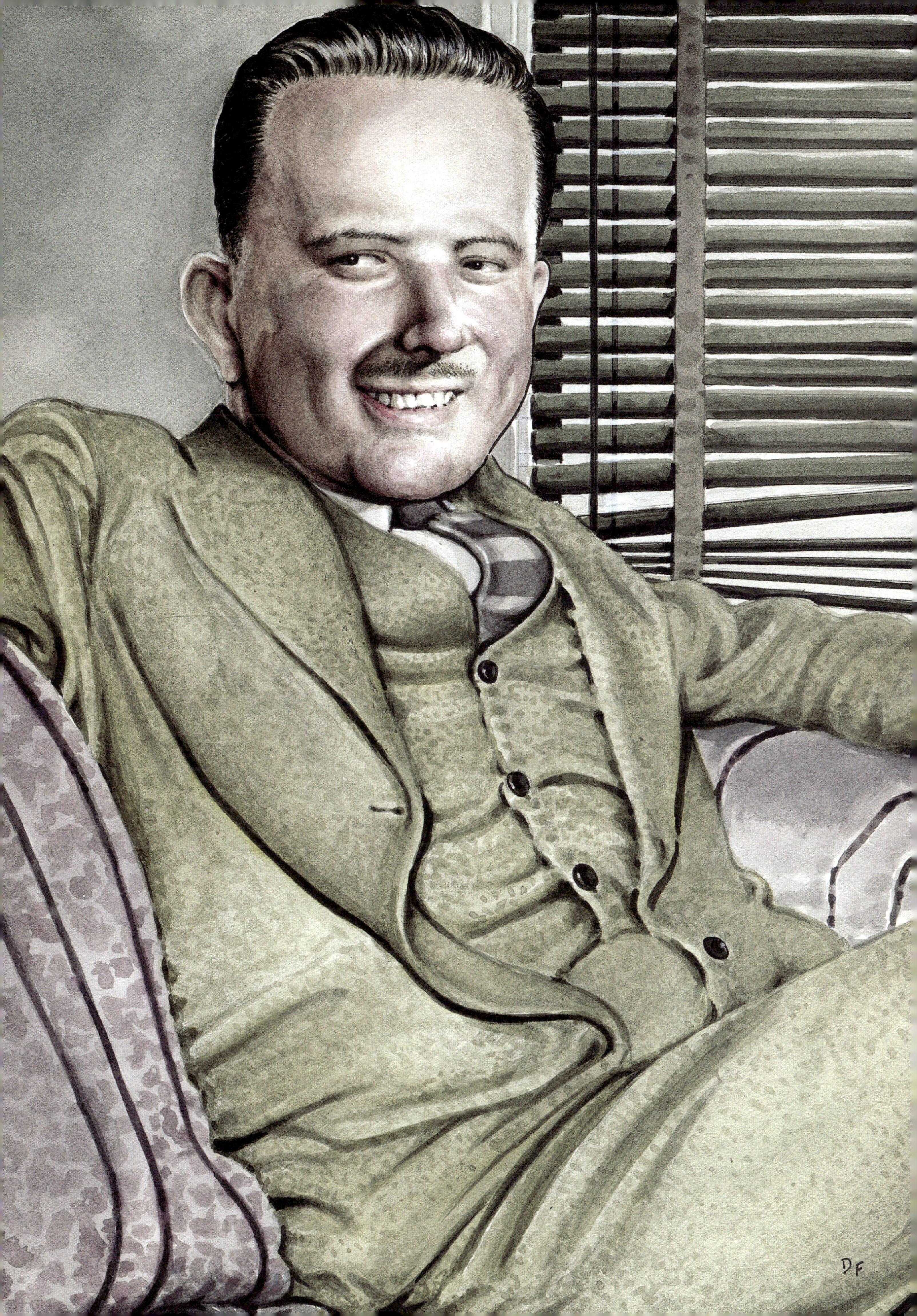
DF

BOB HANEY

1926-2004

plate 41

Robert G. Haney grew up in Philadelphia, and attended Swarthmore College before enlisting in the US Navy at the start of World War II. After the war, Haney earned a master's degree in French history from Columbia University, and entered the comic book business in 1948. His earliest credit was a ten-page story, "College for Murder," in Harvey's *Black Cat* #9. He spent the next several years writing for *Black Cat* and was a prolific contributor to DC war titles like *All-American Men of War*, *G.I. Combat*, and *Our Fighting Forces*.

In 1964, Haney created the Teen Titans, penning their debut story for *The Brave and the Bold* #54. The Teen Titans were spun off into their own title two years later, scripted by Haney. Two months after creating the Teen Titans, Haney and artist Ramona Fradon's Metamorpho character made his debut in *The Brave and the Bold* #57. Metamorpho would also merit his own title before the year was over. His work on *The Brave and the Bold* extended from the title's earliest days in the '50s, as a vehicle for Robin Hood and Viking Prince stories, to its later incarnation as a showcase for Batman team-ups. His efforts to produce work that was in line with contemporary youth culture often put him at odds with DC editors.

After leaving DC in the early '80s, Haney scripted animated cartoons like *ThunderCats* and *Silverhawks*.

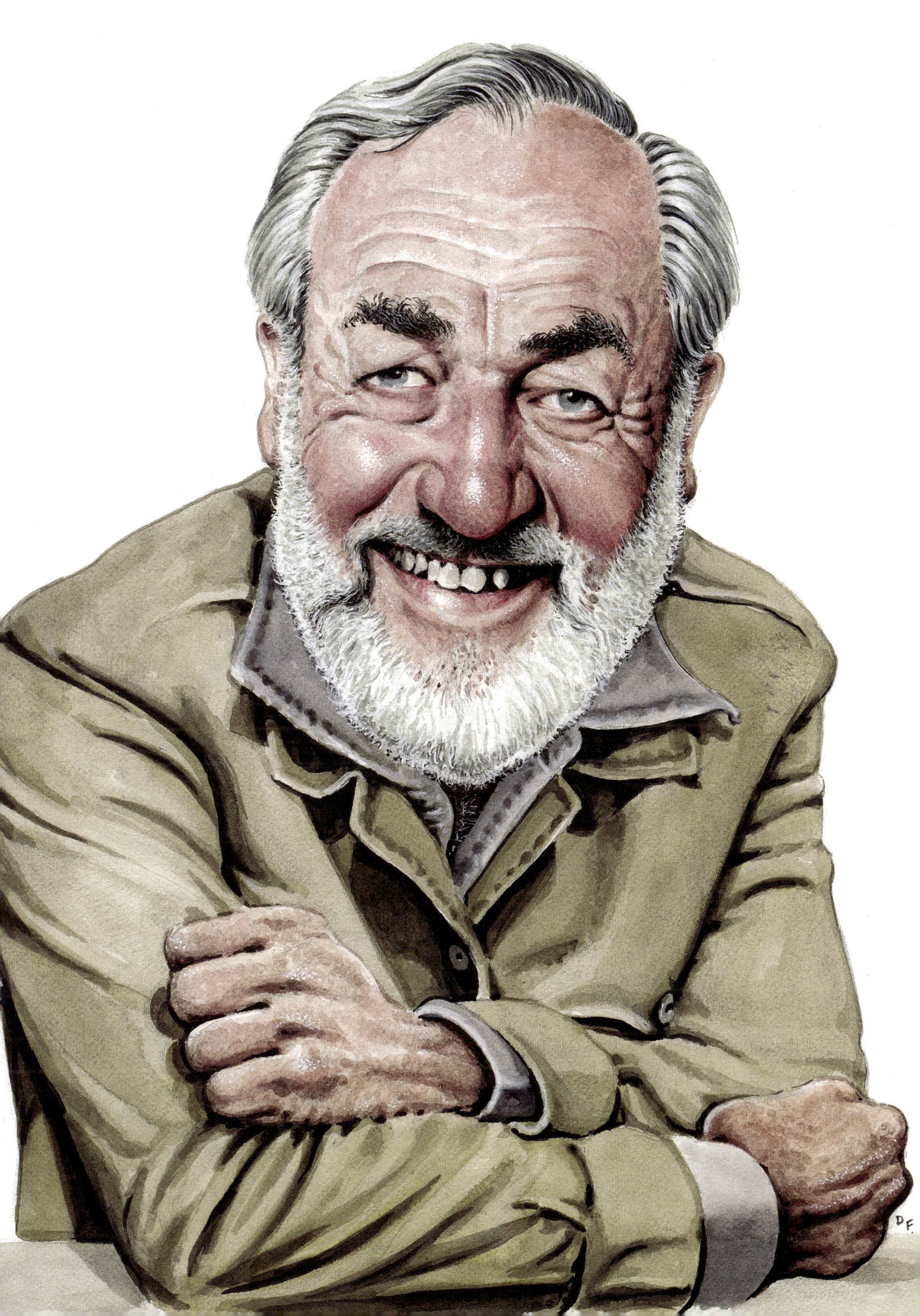
DF.

HARRY HARRISON

1925-2012

plate 42

Henry Maxwell Dempsey was born in Stamford, Connecticut, and raised in Brooklyn and Queens. Harrison graduated Forest Hills High School in 1943 with few prospects as a draft-eligible eighteen-year-old during World War II. Harrison enlisted in the Army Air Corps and spent three years stateside in Colorado, Texas, and Florida as a military policeman and weapons instructor.

Harrison was discharged in 1946 and studied art at New York's Hunter College and the Cartoonists and Illustrators School, where he met artist Wallace Wood. Wood and Harrison teamed up to produce romance comic books for Fox Comics, with titles like *My Confession, My Secret Life*, and *My True Love*. The duo's work at Fox led to their first job for EC Comics in 1949, a seven-page story, "Too Busy for Love," in *Modern Love* #5. Later that year, they delivered "I Was a Wild Girl" for *A Moon, A Girl . . . Romance* #10. Three issues later, *A Moon, A Girl . . . Romance* was retitled *Weird Fantasy,* which featured a seven-page story, "The Black Arts," that was written and inked by Harrison over Wood's pencils. Years later, Harrison said he and Wood had strongly encouraged EC publisher William Gaines to enter the science fiction and fantasy markets. Harrison left EC soon after, and, while he dabbled in comics over the next few years, in 1951 he published his first science fiction short story, "Rock Diver," in the February 1951 *Worlds Beyond.* Harrison became a globetrotting itinerant writer moving from Mexico to England to Italy while freelancing for men's adventure magazines and science fiction monthlies. His first novel, *Deathworld,* was published in 1962. His 1966 novel *Make Room! Make Room!* was the basis for the 1972 film *Soylent Green.*

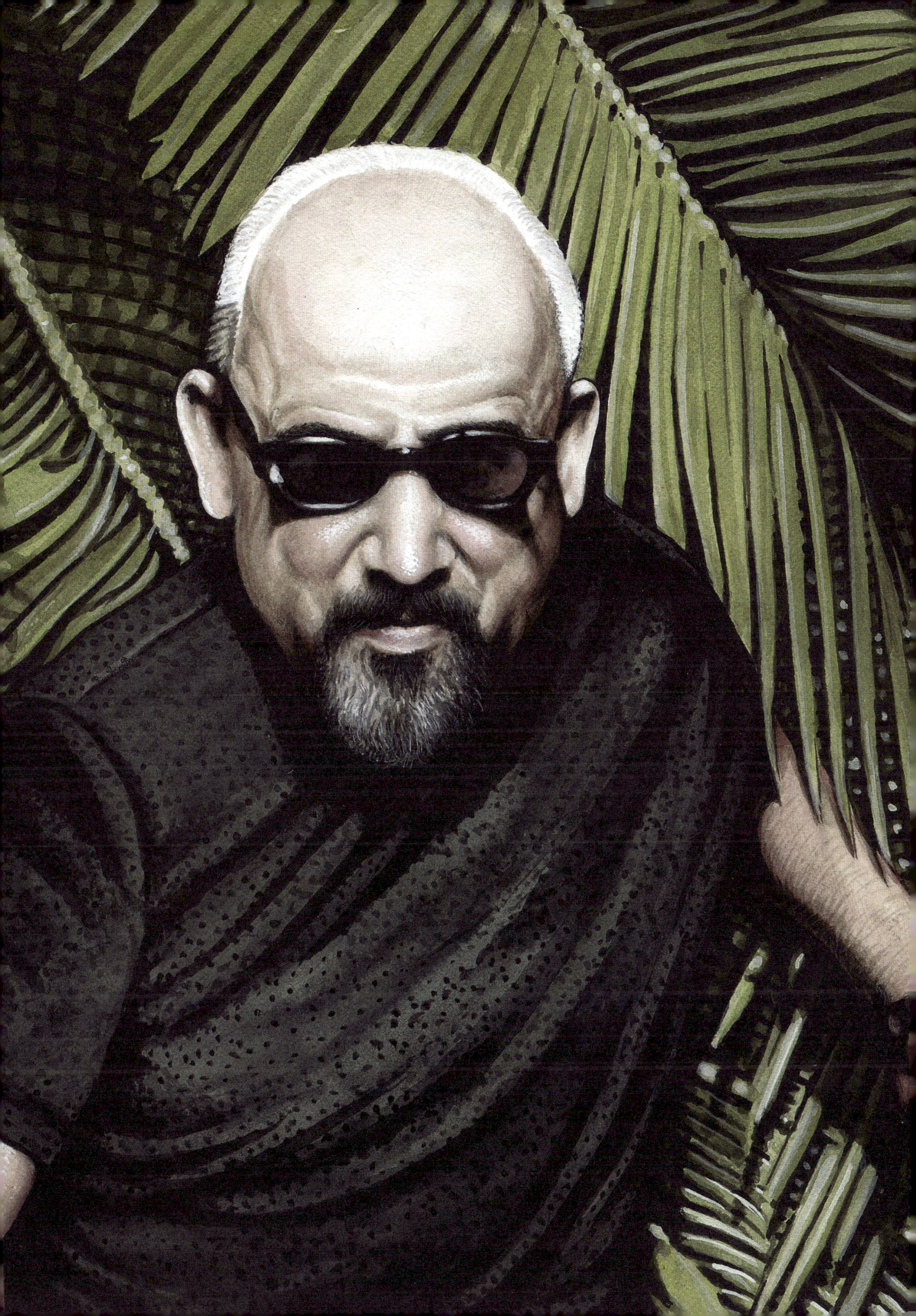

SOL HARRISON

1917-1989

plate 43

Sol Harrison started his career in 1933 at the very beginning of the comic book business. While on staff at Rex Engraving, Harrison created color separations for Eastern Color Printing salesman Max Gaines's pet project, *Famous Funnies. Famous Funnies* is generally recognized as the first modern comic book. In the early years of comic book production, coloring was an arcane, complicated process. Color decisions were an afterthought. Frequently left to the printer's discretion, the results were dubious. Harrison's experience producing newpaper strip sections gave him a useful skillset for the comic book business.

In 1943, Harrison landed a job as art director for DC predecessor All-American Publications. Harrison brought coloring and production chores in house, rising quickly to production manager. He would stay on through various mergers and ownership changes at the company, eventually becoming president of DC Comics in 1977.

In 1972, he developed the *Limited Collectors' Edition,* an anthology series of mostly reprinted material in an oversized format, designed to maximize newsstand impact. He retired in 1981.

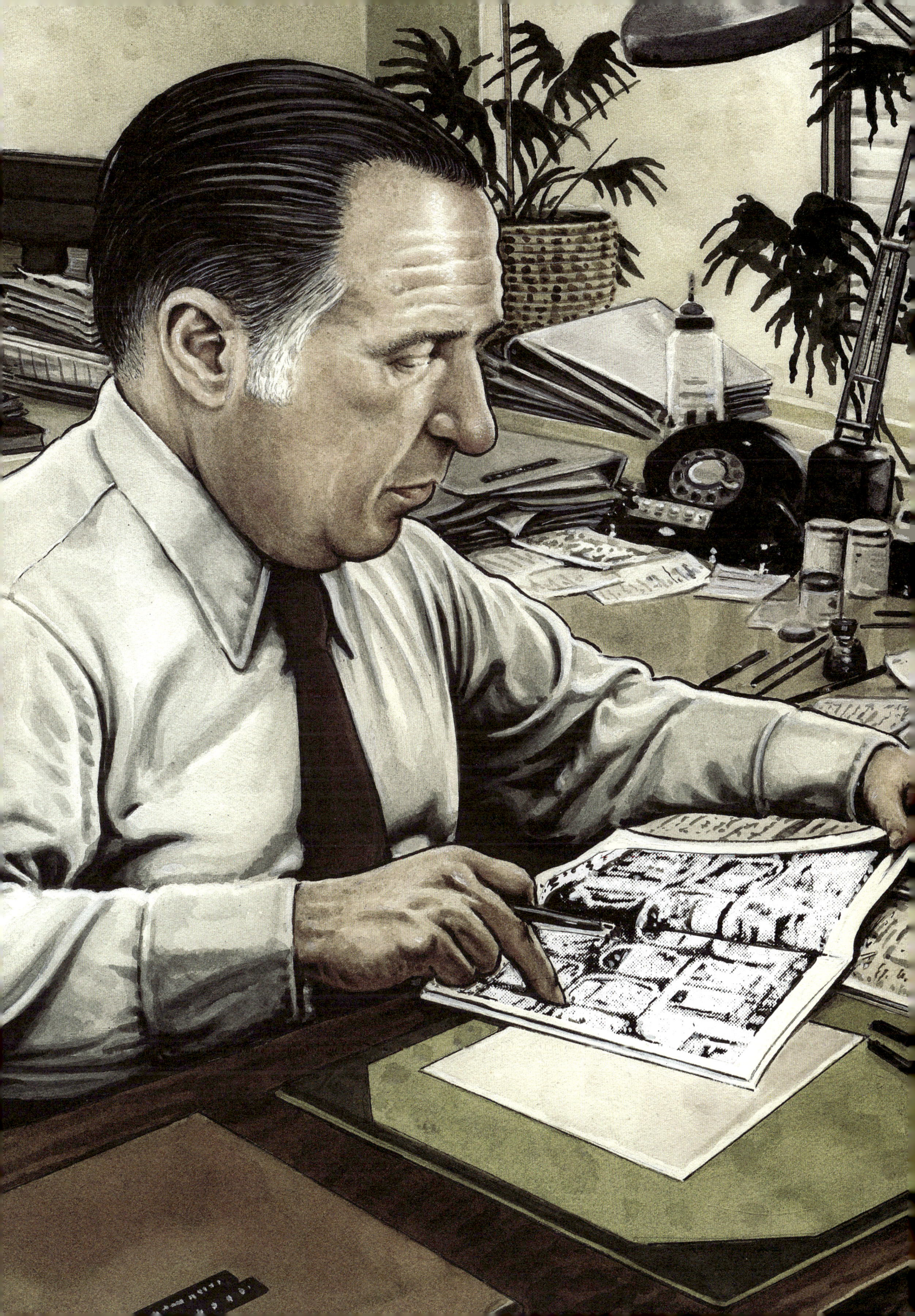

DON HECK

1929–1995

plate 44

Queens-born Donald L. Heck's post-high school art training consisted of community college in Brooklyn, supplemented by a correspondence course. His education continued when he was hired to do paste-ups for Harvey Comics in 1949. At Harvey, Heck was tasked with reconfiguring Milton Caniff's *Terry and the Pirates* dailies into comic book form.

After more than two years at Harvey, Heck jumped ship to join former Harvey employee Allen Hardy's newly launched company, Comic Media. His first published work was "The Unconquered" in the September 1952 debut issue of *War Fury*. Comic Media folded two years later. He spent the next few years freelancing for publishers such as Toby Press, US Pictorial, and Hillman Comics, contributing to western and romance titles like *Captain Gallant of the Foreign Legion* and *Billy the Kid Adventure Magazine*.

Heck's first work for Stan Lee at Atlas was "Werewolf Beware" in *Mystery Tales* #25. Heck drew for a steady stream of horror, war, and western comics for the company, but near the end of the decade Atlas was in turmoil as a result of declining sales and distribution problems.

By the early '60s, Atlas had transitioned into Marvel Comics, initially relying a steady stream of monster stories from the prolific Jack Kirby. Heck returned to the company shortly before the superhero revival put Marvel at the center of a pop culture phenomenon. By 1963, Heck had introduced Iron Man in *Tales of Suspense* #39, and a year later he took over for Kirby on *The Avengers*. Heck's pencils showed up in flagship Marvel titles *The Amazing Spider-Man* and *The X-Men*, as well as horror books like *Chamber of Darkness*.

Heck was unhappy with some of his Marvel inkers, and started freelancing for DC in 1970 on books like *House of Secrets* #85 and *Flash* #198. Heck occasionally did work for Marvel, handling art on various issues of *Daredevil, Sub-Mariner*, and *Ghost Rider*, but, by 1977, his output would be mostly for DC.

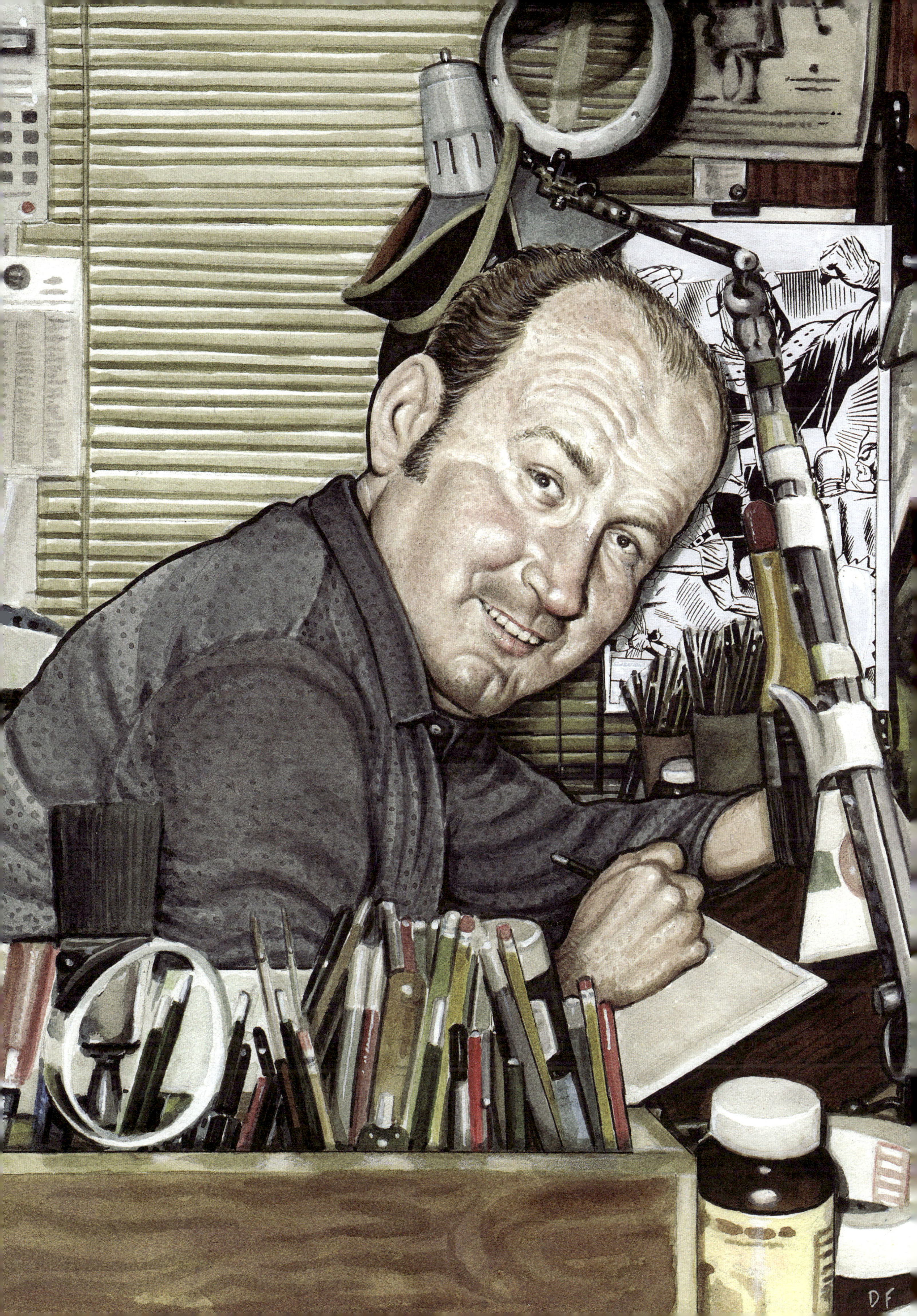

PATRICIA HIGHSMITH

1921-1995

plate 45

Born Mary Patricia Plangman in Fort Worth, Texas; her parents divorced shortly after her birth. Her mother married Stanley Highsmith, and the new family moved to New York when she was six. Highsmith graduated from Barnard College in 1942 with an English degree, but had little success securing work in New York's bustling magazine business.

Highsmith answered a help wanted ad for a writer which led to a $55 a week job at the Pines-Sangor shop. Ned L. Pines and Benjamin W. Sangor produced comic books for National Publications as well as Pines imprints Standard Comics and Better Comics. Her first published work was scripting a seven-page story about boxer and war hero Barney Ross in *Real Life Comics* #13.

Highsmith scripted *Jap-Buster Johnson* and *The Destroyer* for U.S.A. Comics. She penned stories for Charlton characters Crisco and Jasper. She also wrote text-only pieces—a regular feature of Golden Age comics—about historical figures like Catherine the Great and Eddie Rickenbacker.

By the time her first novel, *Strangers on a Train*, was published in 1950, she had left comics. Alfred Hitchcock's now-classic film adaptation appeared a year later.

Highsmith's second novel, *The Price of Salt*, was published under the nom de-plume Claire Morgan. It was viewed as a groundbreaking work of lesbian fiction in which the protagonists emerge relatively unscathed at the novel's end. She would not acknowledge authorship until 1990, when the book was republished as *Carol*.

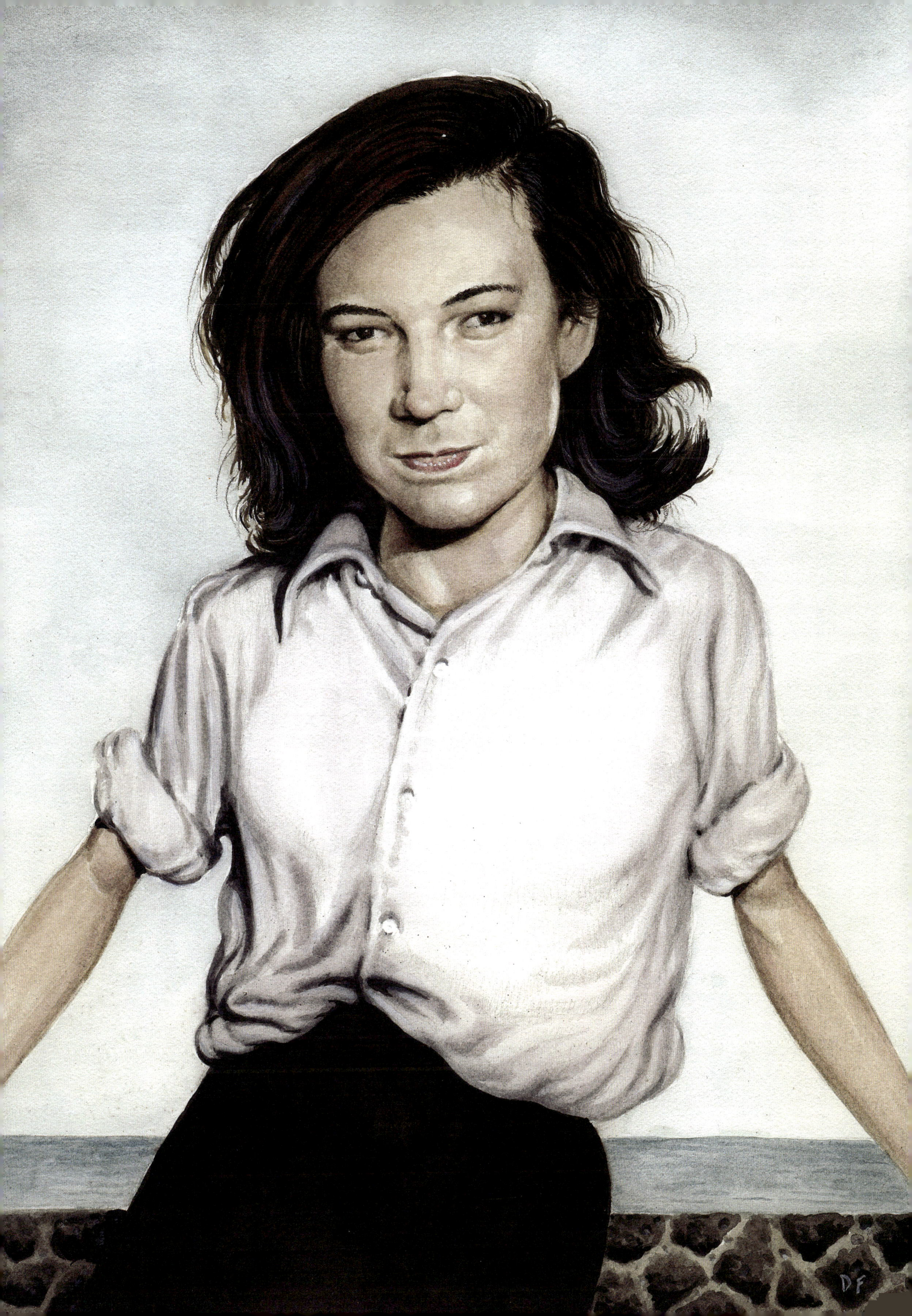
DF

LLOYD JACQUET

1899–1970

plate 46

Lloyd Victor Francis Jacquet was born in Brooklyn and educated at the Manual Training High School of Brooklyn. He was drafted into the US Navy in 1918, and spent a year aboard a supply ship as a radio operator. He left the navy a year later, and briefly returned to college before taking a job at the *Brooklyn Daily Eagle*. His experience with radio eventually led to editorial positions at *Amateur Radio Magazine* and *Radio Digest*.

Major Malcolm Wheeler-Nicholson, president of National Allied Publications, hired Jacquet in 1935 to edit *New Fun* #1. *New Fun* was the first comic book to feature all-new, original content, in lieu of reprinted newspaper comics strips. The interior pages of *New Fun* were printed at the *Brooklyn Daily Eagle*, while the covers were printed by Eastern Color Printing in Waterbury, Connecticut.

Jacquet left after four issues and spent time as an art director at Centaur Publications, before establishing First Funnies Inc. in 1939. Jacquet's first project was creating *Motion Picture Funnies Weekly*. The comic book was intended as a promotional giveaway in theaters, but the project was abandoned. *Motion Picture Funnies Weekly* contained the first appearance of Sub-Mariner, in an eight-page origin story that Bill Everett would expand later that year when it was reprinted in Timely's *Marvel Comics* #1.

First Funnies Inc. would become known as Funnies Inc., one of the earliest comic book production shops. It supplied creative services to publishers such as Gilbertson (*Classics Illustrated*), Hillman Periodicals, and Timely. Timely publisher Martin Goodman would eventually recruit his own bullpen of in-house artists and writers to lessen his dependency on outside contractors. Funnies Inc. would be gone by the end of the decade.

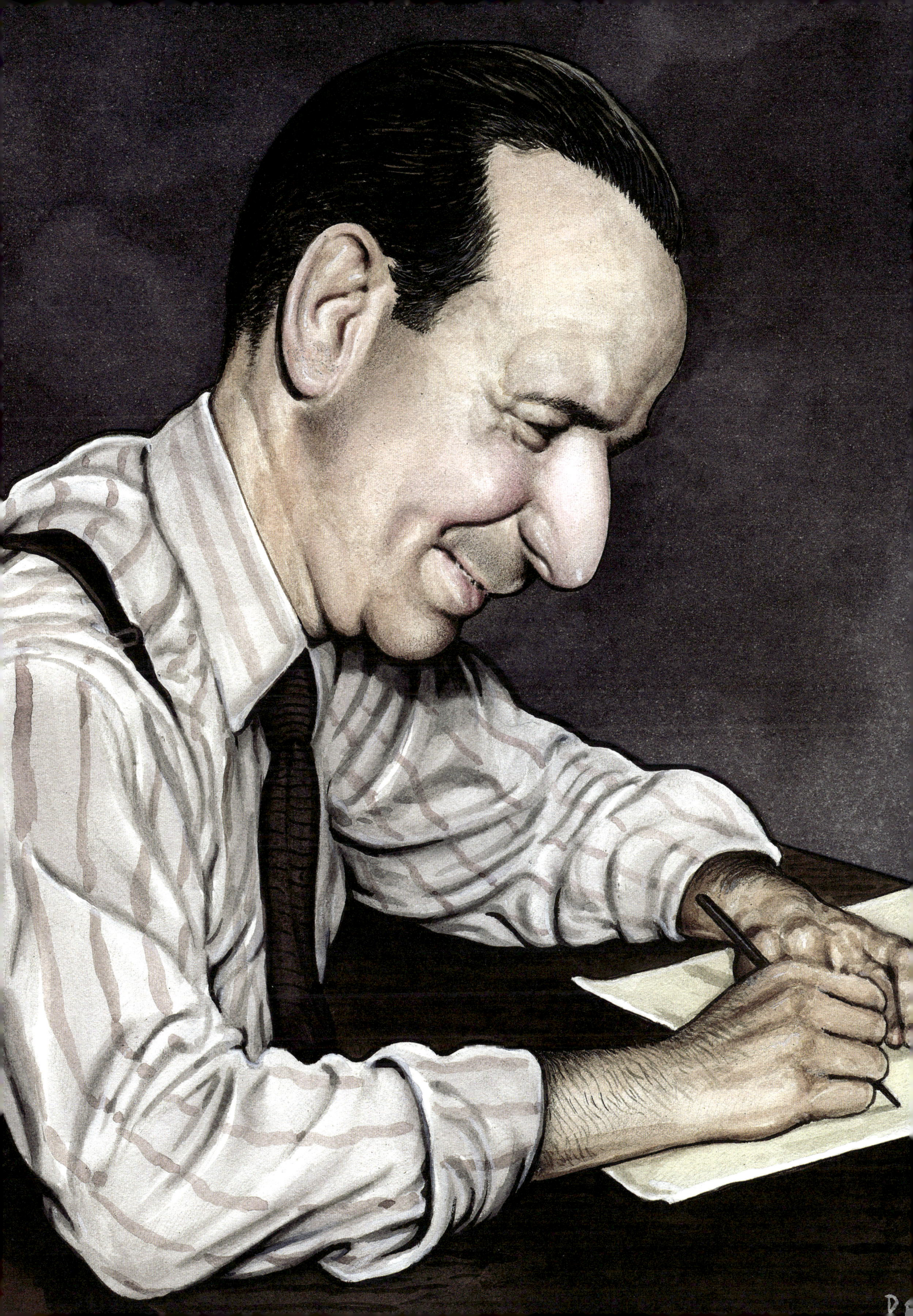

ABE KANEGSON

1921–1965

plate
47

Born in Eastern Europe, Abe Kanegson moved to New York as a child and attended James Monroe High School in the Bronx, and later City College. Remembered primarily for his exemplary lettering on Will Eisner's *The Spirit*, he has virtually no other comic credits, other than lettering *The Secret Files of Dr. Drew*, a backup feature for Fiction House's *Rangers Comics* that was conceived by Eisner and executed by *The Spirit* associates Marilyn Mercer and Jerry Grandenetti.

Kanegson lettered for Eisner's *The Spirit* from 1947 to 1951. His work was uniquely alive and evocative, adding tone and inflection to speeches, as well as feeling and mood to captions. Similar to the technique Walt Kelly used later in *Pogo*, he varied his style, using different "fonts" to suit what was being said. His sound effects become part of the art, integrated into the scene rather than looking like an afterthought.

Kanegson disappeared from comics lettering after a "pay dispute" with Eisner. Although he had a prominent stutter, he was an accomplished square-dance caller, operating the Village Folk Dance Studio and performing at the Indian Neck Folk Festival in 1961, sharing the bill with a young Bob Dylan. Published examples of his compositions include "Abe's Skirt Swisher." Kanegson died of leukemia in 1965. Kanegson's self-titled square dance album was released posthumously on Homesteadfast Records in 1969.

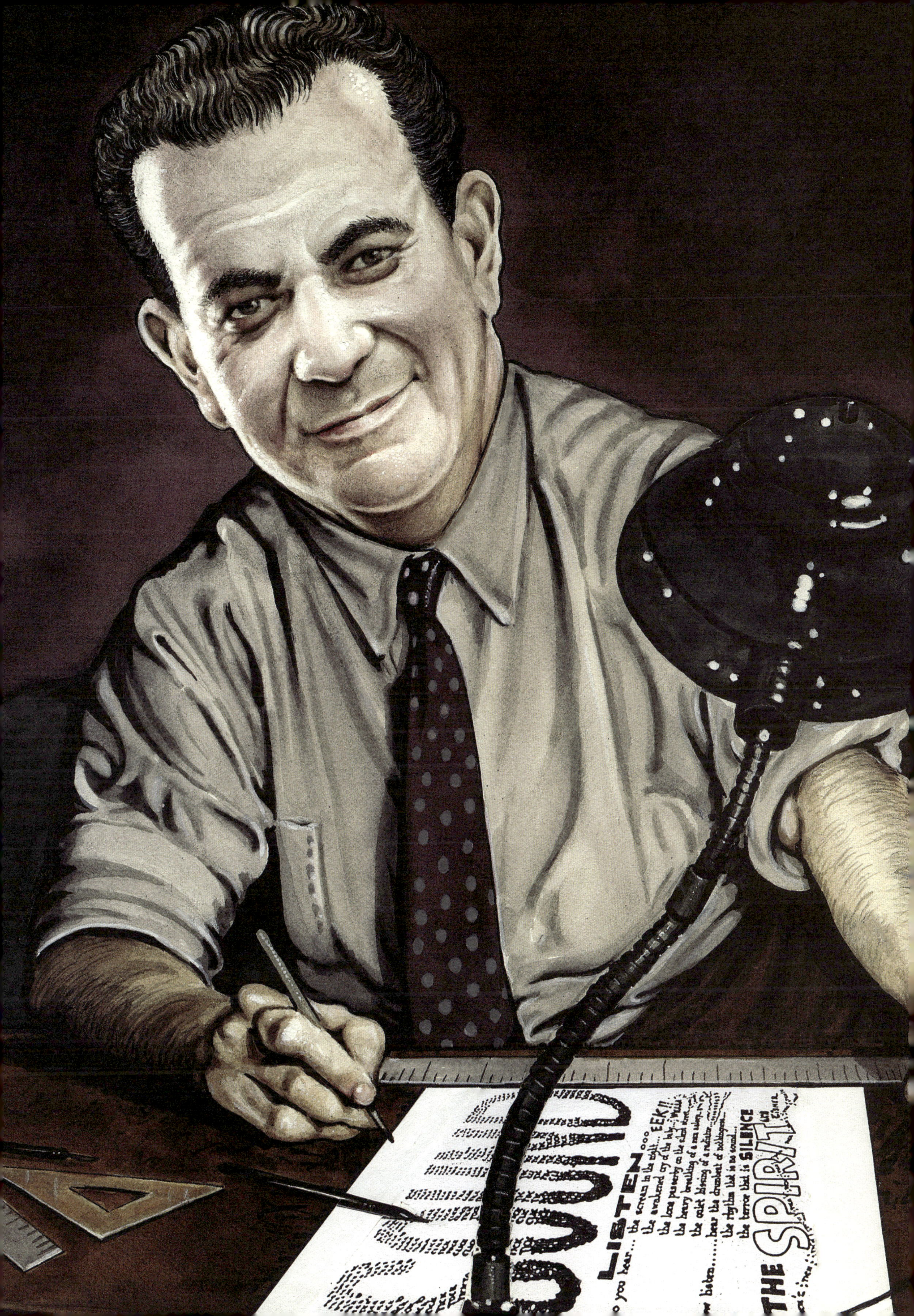
LISTEN
EEK!!
SILENCE
THE SPIRIT

ROBERT KANIGHER

1915-2002

plate 48

New York-born Robert Kanigher started selling short stories while still an adolescent. At age seventeen, he won a *New York Times* collegiate short story competition. Young Kanigher also contributed scripts to the radio drama *House of Mystery*.

Kanigher claimed to have never read a comic book when his comics career started in 1940. He wrote scripts for Fox Comic's *Blue Beetle*, Fawcett's *Captain Marvel Adventures*, and MLJ's *Steel Sterling*. Less than three years after his comic book debut, he wrote one of the first books on the subject: *How to Make Money Writing for Comics Magazines*.

In 1946, shortly before All-American Comics and DC comics merged into National Periodical Publications, Sheldon Mayer hired Kanigher to script *Flash, Green Lantern, Hawkman*, and the *Justice Society of America*. When *Wonder Woman* scribe William Moulton Marston died the following year, Kanigher took over the writing duties on the book. He stayed with the title for more than two decades.

By 1956, while superhero comic books were taking a backseat to horror, mystery, and romance titles, Kanigher and Carmine Infantino revived the Golden Age Flash and helped usher in a new era of costumed heroes. In the midst of the Korean War, Kanigher was the main creative force behind a line of war comic books that included *Our Army at War, Star Spangled War Stories, All-American Men Of War*, and *Our Fighting Forces*. With artist Joe Kubert, Kanigher popularized *Sgt. Rock*, DC's most enduring military character.

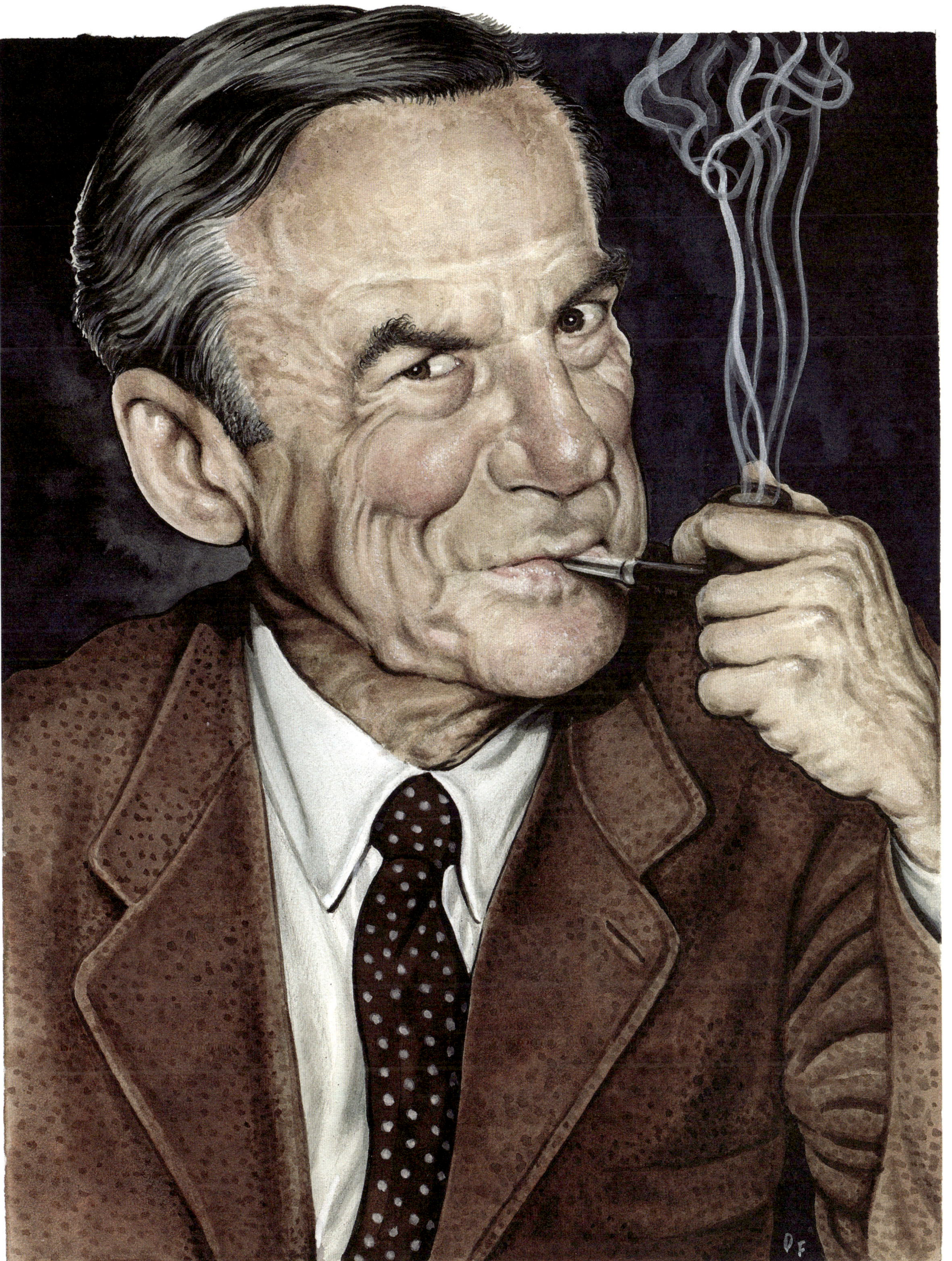
DF

FRED KIDA

1920-2014

plate 49

Japanese American Fred Kida was raised in Manhattan and attended the American School of Design. He launched his comic book career in 1941, at the Jerry Iger Studio, as an inker and background artist. That same year, he also worked briefly as an assistant to Will Eisner on *The Spirit*. The following year, he took a staff position at Quality Comics, where he penciled and inked his first credited story: the eight-page "Introducing the Phantom Clipper" in *Military Comics* #9.

In 1942, Kida started at Hillman Periodicals and commenced his long association with Airboy in *Air Fighter Comics* and *Airboy*. Kida also worked on other Hillman titles, featuring characters like Gunmaster, The Heap, and The Challenger. During this period, he also drew two monthly features—*Science Silhouettes* and *The Eagle Traveller*—for *Boy's Life*, as well as several issues of a promotional Buster Brown comic for the children's shoe company.

Near the end of the decade, with superhero sales declining, he worked at Lev Gleason Publications on *Crime Does Not Pay*, as well as western and romance titles. In 1952, he started associating with Stan Lee and Atlas Comics. For Atlas, he worked on a range of titles, including westerns such as the *Ringo Kid* and the *Two-Gun Kid*, and collaborated with Lee on the short-lived humor comic, *Willie the Wiseguy*.

Kida returned to Marvel in the '70s, primarily as an inker, and in 1981, he took over drawing duties on the syndicated *Amazing Spider-Man* newspaper comic strip. He remained there until his retirement in 1991.

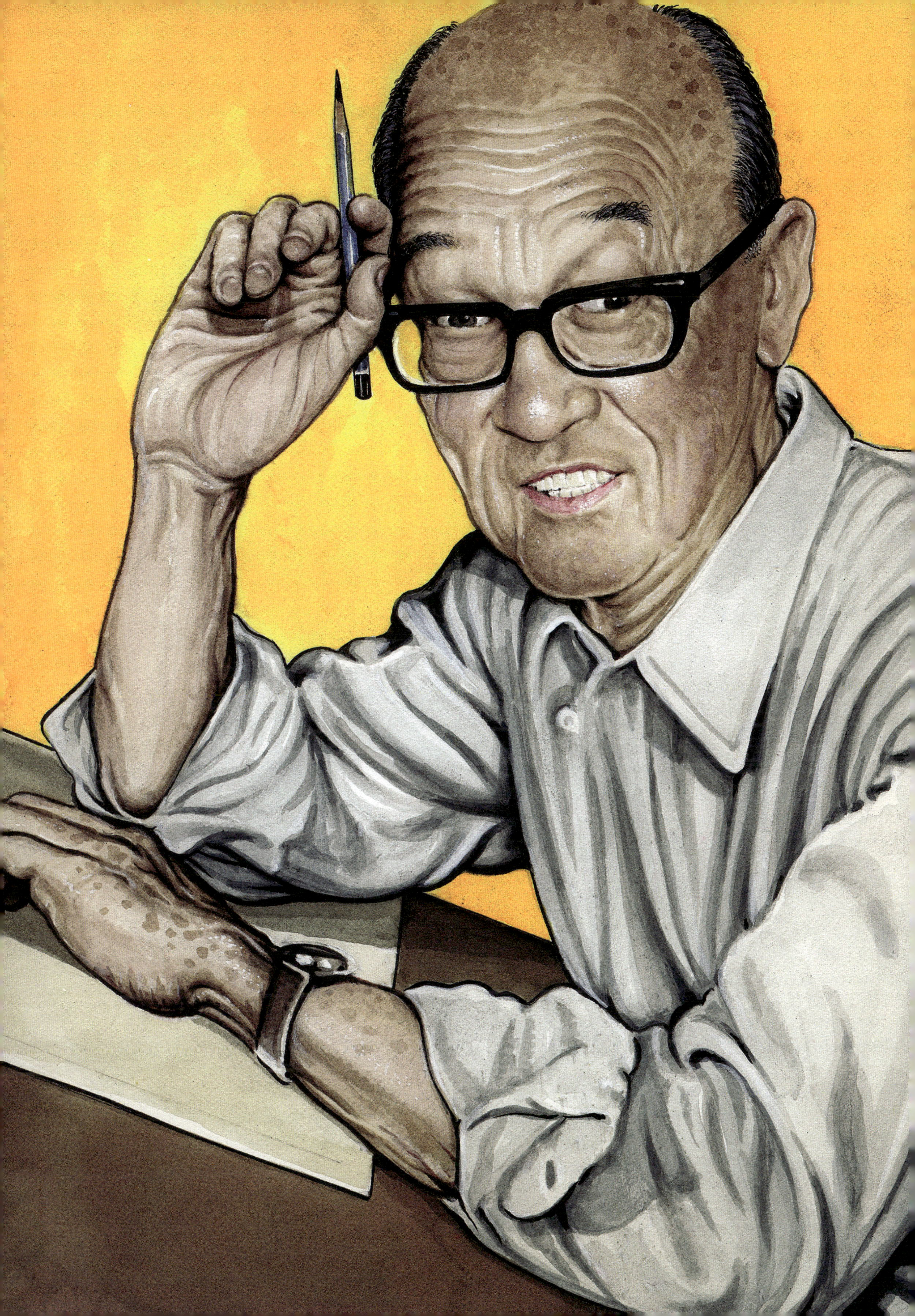

EVERETT KINSTLER

b. 1926

plate **50**

Everett Raymond Kinstler was born in New York. He attended the High School of Music and Art, but left in his second year to enter the comic book business as an apprentice inker for Cinema Comics in the early '40s. He later continued his studies at the Arts Students League and the National Academy of Design.

Kinstler's earliest comic book work, a ten-page story ("Captain Flight"), appeared in *Captain Flight Comics* #9, published by Four Star in 1945. He was also producing pen-and-ink illustrations for pulps such as *The Shadow* and *Doc Savage* for Street & Smith. His career was interrupted by a year in the US Army in 1945. After being honorably discharged, he studied at the School of Visual Arts while working on westerns for Avon Publications. He penciled and inked stories for *Jesse James* and *Dan Taylor, Boy Detective*, but by this time, he was also creating full-color paintings for Avon covers that were unusual for most comic book publishers at the time.

Kinstler eventually left the comic book and illustration world and became a highly regarded portrait artist. He painted the official White House portraits of Gerald Ford and Ronald Reagan. In 2005, he was commissioned by crooner Tony Bennett to paint a portrait of Donald Trump, which is (currently) hanging in Trump's office in Trump Tower.

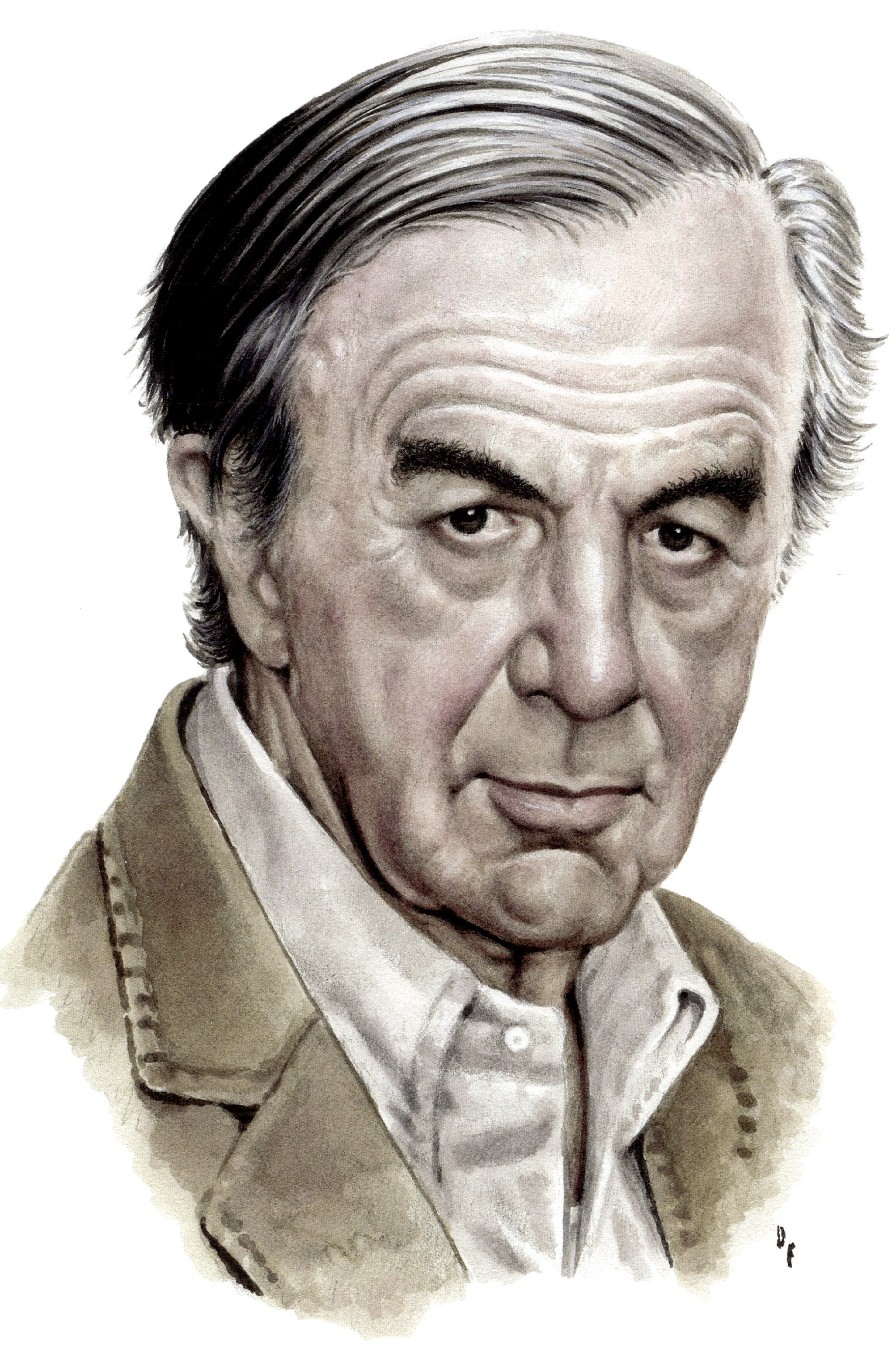

ROY KRENKEL

1918–1983

plate 51

Bronx-born Roy Gerald Krenkel studied at the Art Students League in New York before serving as a private in the US Army during World War II. After the war, Krenkel attended the Cartoonists and Illustrators School, where he became friends with Frank Frazetta and Al Williamson, with whom he would collaborate in the future.

By the early '50s, Krenkel was sharing a studio with Wallace Wood and inking Williamson's pencils for various Atlas and ACG titles. His earliest solo story was likely "I Was a P.O.W.," published November 1952, in *Youthful* magazines' *Attack!* Krenkel eventually made his way to EC, joining his old friends Frazetta and Williamson in creating stories for *Weird Science* and *Weird Fantasy.* Despite his peers' high regard, "Time to Leave" in *Incredible Science Fiction* was Krenkel's only solo story published in an EC title. Still, he kept busy by producing illustrations for pulp magazines like *Marvel Science Fiction* and *Space Science Fiction.*

In 1962, Krenkel's career flourished after Ace Books chose him to create covers and illustrations for their relaunched *Tarzan* paperback series. He would often call on his old friend, Frazetta, to lend a hand to meet deadlines. At Krenkel's urging, Ace enlisted Frazetta as a cover artist and the pair would often collaborate on each other's work.

By the mid-'60s, Warren Publications' black-and-white horror magazines *Creepy* and *Eerie* became Krenkel's most visible outlet as a comics artist.

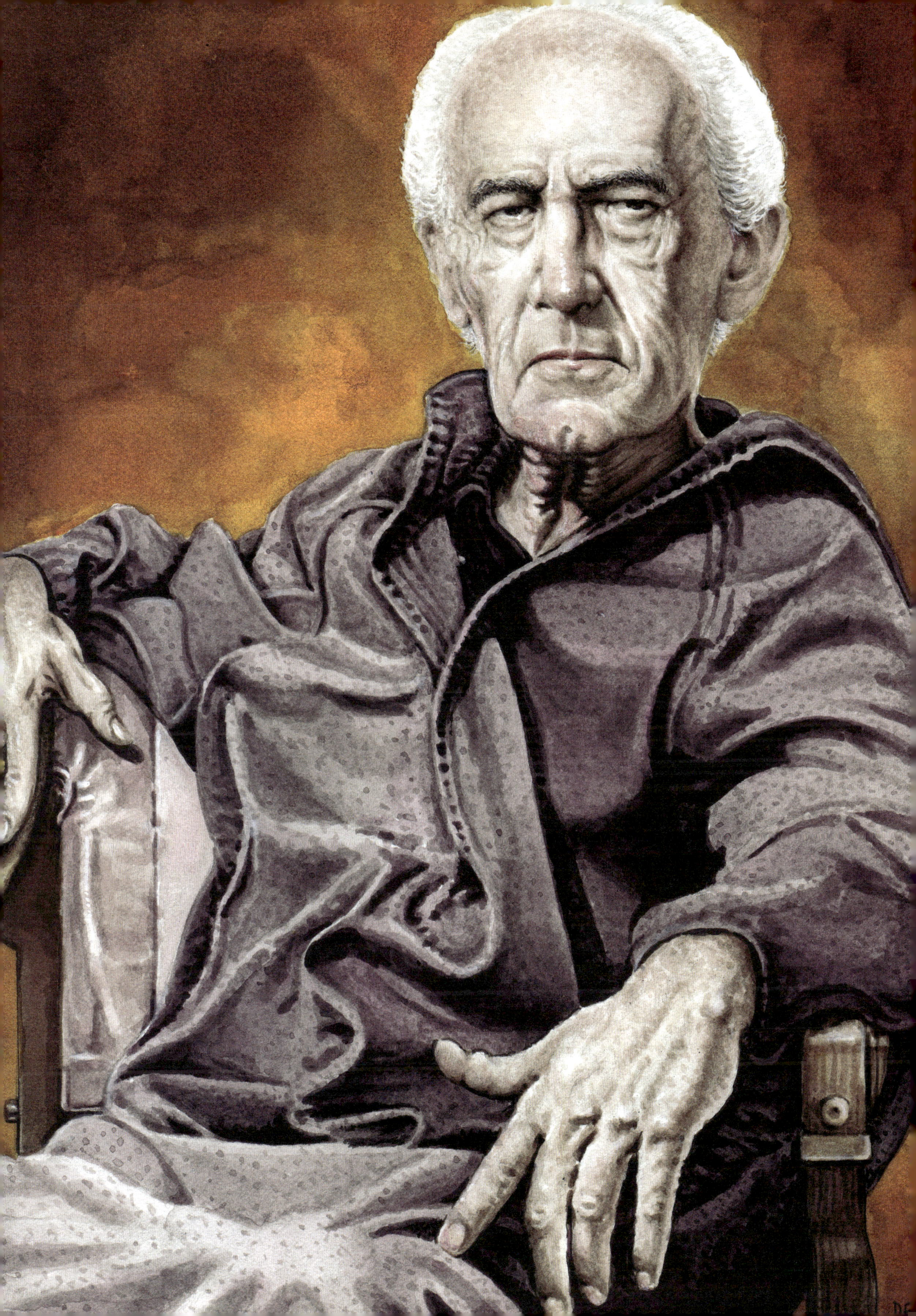

HARRY LAMPERT

1916-2004

plate 52

Born in New York, Harry Lampert started his artistic career at sixteen, inking animation cels for the Fleischer Studios' *Popeye* and *Betty Boop* cartoons. Lampert was a strike leader during the five-month labor action that led to the studio moving to Florida the next year. He started his comics career soon after. Some sources cite Lampert as being given the task of cutting up Jerry Siegel and Joe Shuster's sample comic strips, and turning them into a comic book story for Superman's 1938 debut in *Action* #1. His earliest confirmed work was penciling and inking a four-page humor story, "Movietown," for DC Comics' *Movie Comics* #4 in 1939. He made his biggest impact the following year when he collaborated with writer Gardner Fox to co-create the Flash, who was introduced in a fifteen-page origin story in *Flash Comics* #1. Despite the success of the Flash, he left the series after five issues.

Lampert drew the patriotic military characters Red, White, and Blue in several different titles, like *World's Finest Comic* and *All-American Comics*. He gravitated toward humorous work for most of his career, doing one-pagers and backup stories in titles such as *Buzzy* and *The Adventures of Bob Hope*. He also published gag cartoons in *Esquire* and the *Saturday Evening Post*, and served as an instructor at the School of Visual Arts in New York.

Lampert retired in 1976. An avid contract bridge player, Lampert wrote several books on the subject, including *The Fun Way to Advanced Bridge*.

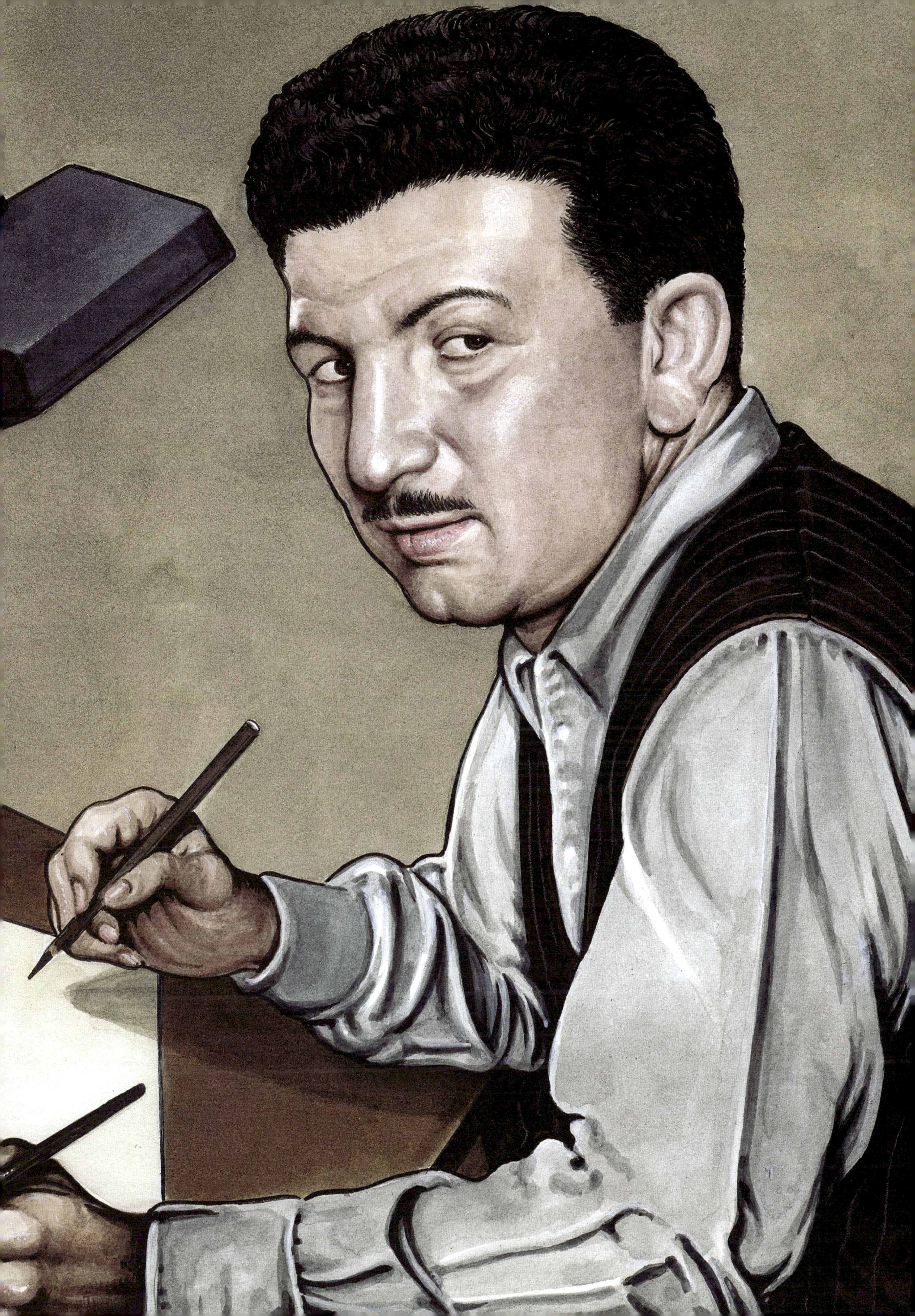

OSKAR LEBECK

1903–1966

plate 53

Oskar LeBeck was a twenty-seven-year-old stage designer when he left his native Berlin for the United States. LeBeck continued to hone his craft by designing Broadway productions for impresario Flo Ziegfeld.

A few years later, the versatile LeBeck was working as an industrial designer, while also writing and illustrating children's books for Grosset & Dunlap, including an abridged version of the *Wonderful Wizard of Oz.*

In 1938, LeBeck became art director and managing editor for Western Printing's comic book line, Dell. Even though Dell was primarily in the business of licensing popular characters from movies and cartoons, LeBeck's sensibilities were drawn from children's literature traditions. LeBeck hired former Disney animator Walt Kelly to write and draw a series based on Hal Roach's *Our Gang* shorts. Kelly's book outlasted the original films by several years. LeBeck hired writer/artist John Stanley to transform Marjorie Henderson Buell's *Little Lulu* from a *Saturday Evening Post* gag panel into a fully realized comic book. Initially part of Dell's *Four Color,* Stanley's *Lulu* was deemed worthy of its own stand-alone book after ten issues. LeBeck also launched *Famous Stories*, comic versions of classic literature like *Treasure Island* and *Tom Sawyer.*

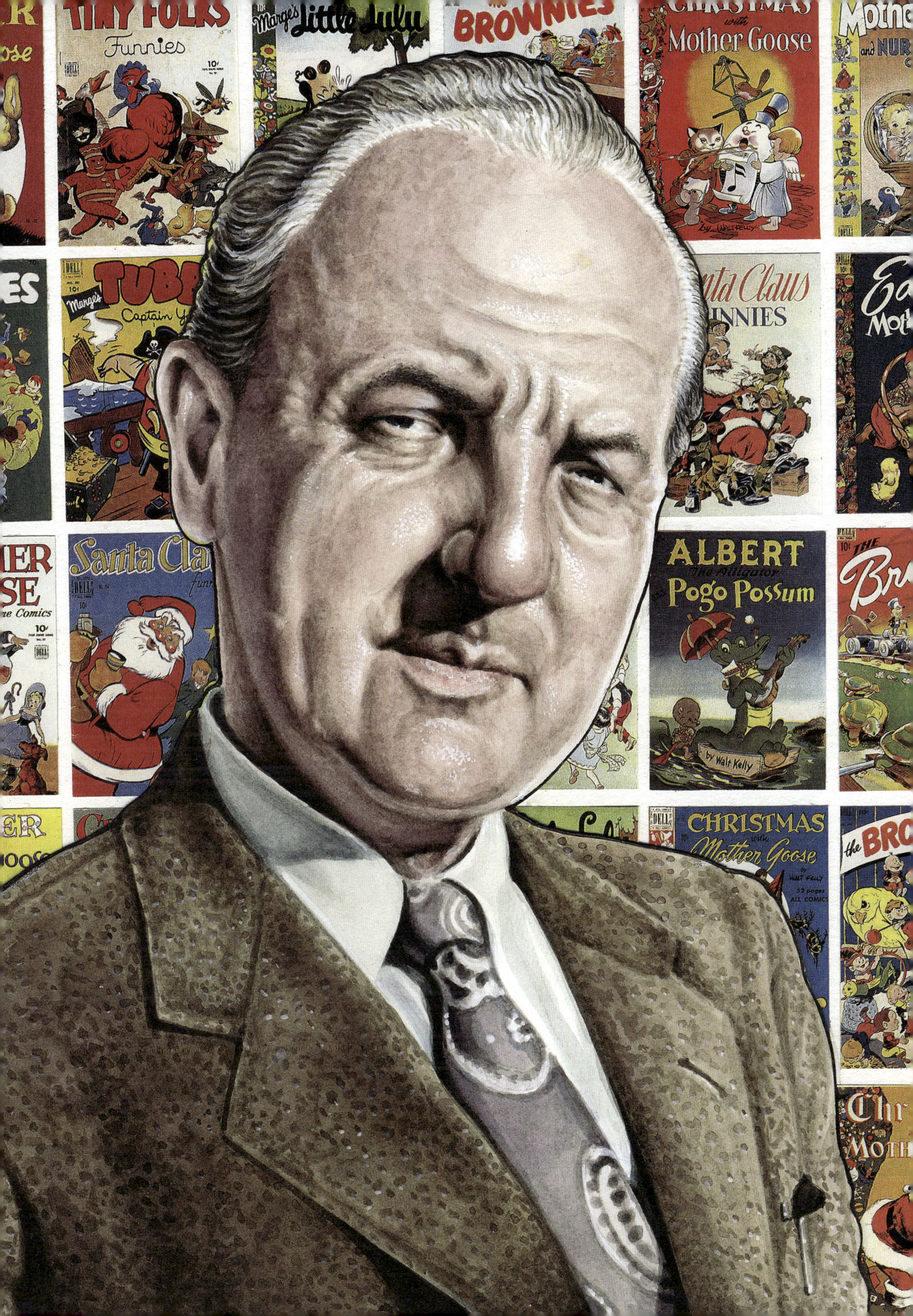
Funnies
Marge's Little Lulu
BROWNIES
CHRISTMAS with Mother Goose
Marge's
Funnies
INNIES
ALBERT The Alligator
Pogo Possum
by Walt Kelly
CHRISTMAS with Mother Goose
52 pages
ALL COMICS

LARRY LIEBER

b. 1931

plate 54

Born in New York, Larry Lieber graduated from George Washington High School and attended evening classes at Pratt Institute while working for publisher Martin Goodman's Magazine Management. Lieber's older brother, Stanley, had been an editor at the company's Timely Comics division for several years, using the name "Stan Lee." Larry Lieber's earliest published work was penciling and inking "Cop on the Beat" for *All True Crime* #44.

In 1951, Lieber joined the Air Force and spent the next four years in the military. After he was discharged, he rejoined his brother Stan's bullpen, drawing romance titles like *Love Romances* and *Love Tales*. He also had begun collaborating with his brother on scripts. In the early '60s, he often worked with artists Jack Kirby and Don Heck on the monster stories that dominated *Amazing Adventures* and *Strange Tales* before superheroes became Marvel's main product. As their popularity grew, he wrote Thor's origin story, working from Lee's plot, and went on to script the first eight issues. He performed similar duties for the earliest runs of *Iron Man* and *Ant-Man*.

Lieber said later that he preferred the freedom of drawing westerns over the high-profile superheroes that made Marvel's reputation. He drew the *Rawhide Kid* for nine years, starting in 1964. In 1980, he started penciling (and sometimes scripting) the syndicated comic strip version of *The Amazing Spider-Man*. Lieber has had a hand in producing the strip for more than thirty-five years.

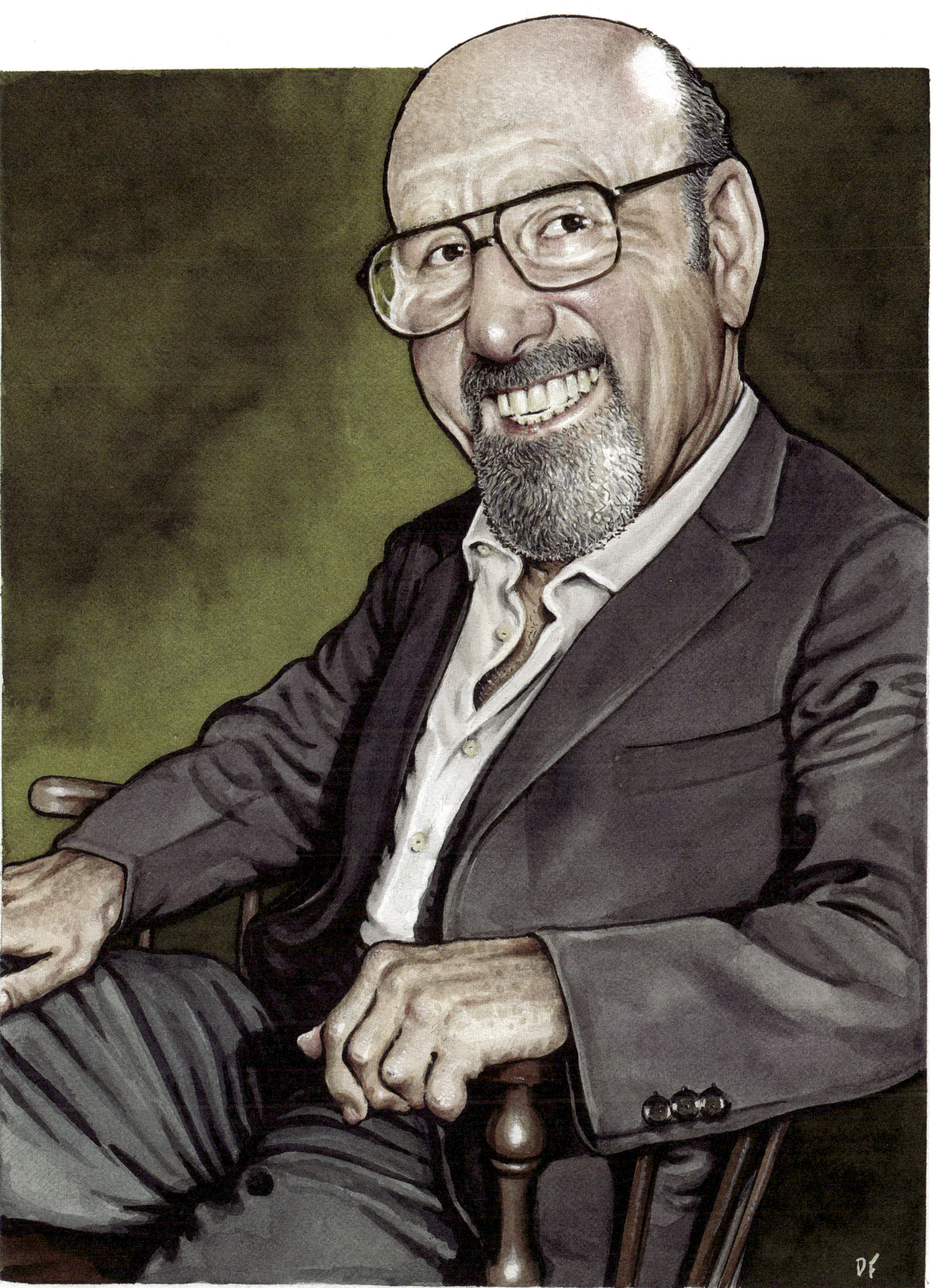

JACK LIEBOWITZ

1900-2000

plate 55

Jacob S. Liebowitz was born in Proskurov, Russia, and emigrated to the United States with his family when he was ten. Liebowitz graduated from New York University in 1925 with an accounting degree, and obtained a position managing finances for the International Ladies Garment Workers Union. After the market crash of 1929, Liebowitz left the I.L.G.W.U. for a position as the right-hand man with the union's printer, Harry Donenfeld. By 1934, Donenfeld and Liebowitz were publishing the lucrative *Spicy Detective Stories* and other risqué titles. In 1937, Donenfeld brokered a publishing deal with Major Malcolm Wheeler-Nicholson for a new company, Detective Comics, Inc. The company was bankrupt less than a year later, and the two partners bought out Wheeler-Nicholson's shares at auction.

In 1938, Donenfeld and Liebowitz launched *Action Comics* with Superman as the star attraction, and quickly acquired all the rights to the character from the young, naive creators, Jerry Siegel and Joe Shuster. The company flourished. The character Batman soon followed. In 1945, they bought out Max Gaines, their partner in another comic book publishing company, All-American Publications; this brought the Atom, Flash, Green Lantern, Hawkman, and Wonder Woman into DC/National's stable of characters.

They expanded the company's assets into radio, television, and film, and grew rich. DC Comics went public in 1961. Liebowitz remained president until the company became part of Warner Communications in 1968. Liebowitz retired in 1970, but remained an active member of the board of directors for many years.

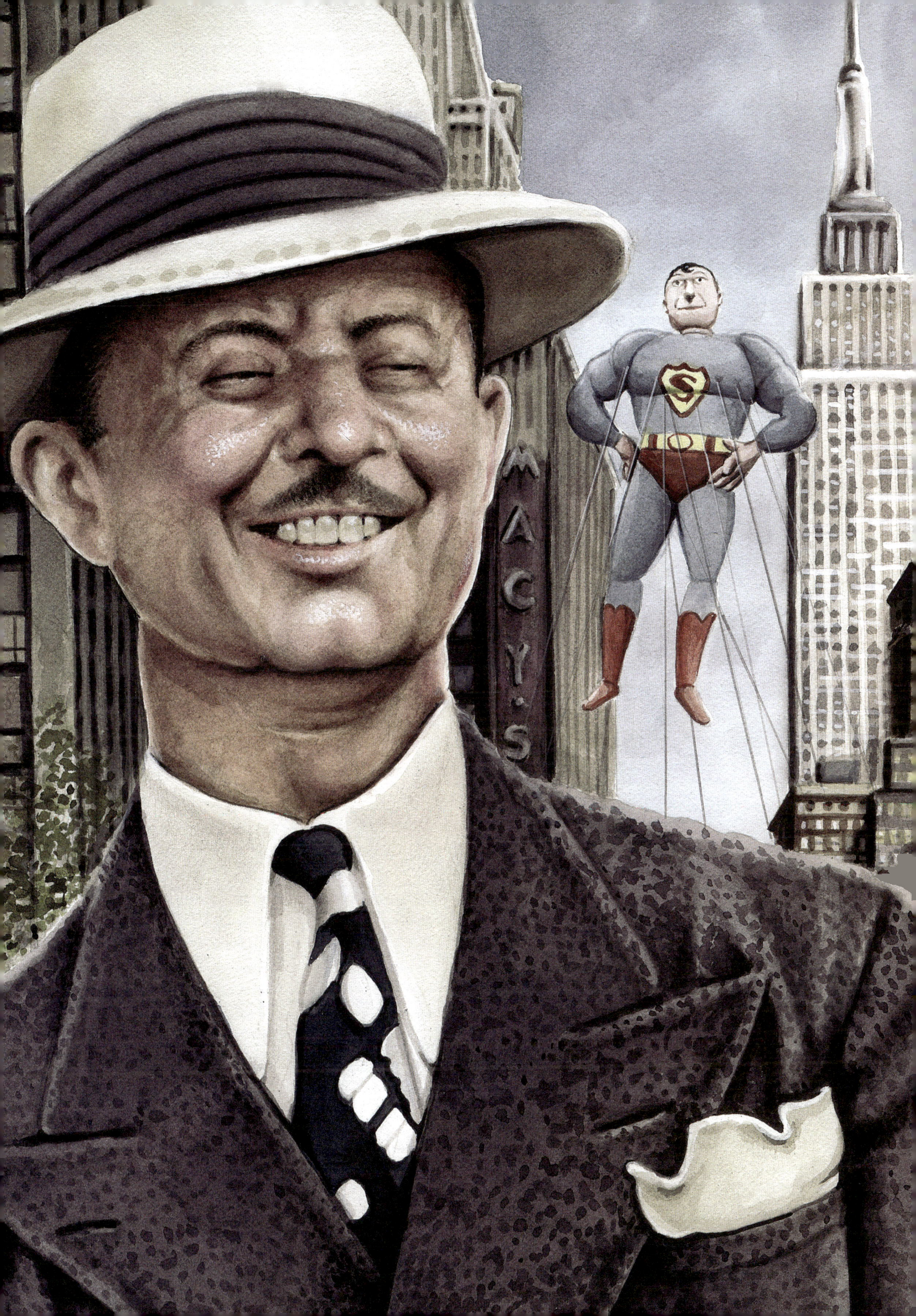
MACY'S

JOE MANEELY

1926-1958

plate 56

Born in Philadelphia, Joseph Maneely dropped out of high school in his sophomore year to enlist in the US Navy. After his discharge, Maneely returned to Philadelphia to study at the Hussian School of Art. After a stint in the art department of the *Philadelphia Bulletin,* Maneely began freelancing for comic book publisher Street & Smith in 1948, marking his comic book debut drawing "The Ragged Stranger" in *Top Secrets* #4. He spent two years at Street & Smith penciling and inking offbeat features like *Supersnipe* and *Ulysses Q. Wacky.* Maneely briefly ran his own Philadelphia-based comic book production shop, in partnership with two other artists.

Maneely started working for Stan Lee at Timely Comics in 1949. Lee admired his skill, and, especially, his speed. His pencils were the barest of lines and stick figures which he then inked into elaborately shaded and detailed final art. His first Timely work was "The Kansas Massacre of 1864" which appeared in *Outlaws and Sheriffs* #60.

After Timely became Atlas, Maneely became a staff artist, working on a number of horror, western, and science fiction titles from 1955 to 1957. A comic book slump cost him his staff job in 1957, and he freelanced for DC on titles like *House of Secrets* and *Tales of the Unexpected.*

In 1958, Maneely was killed when he slipped between the cars of a New Jersey commuter train.

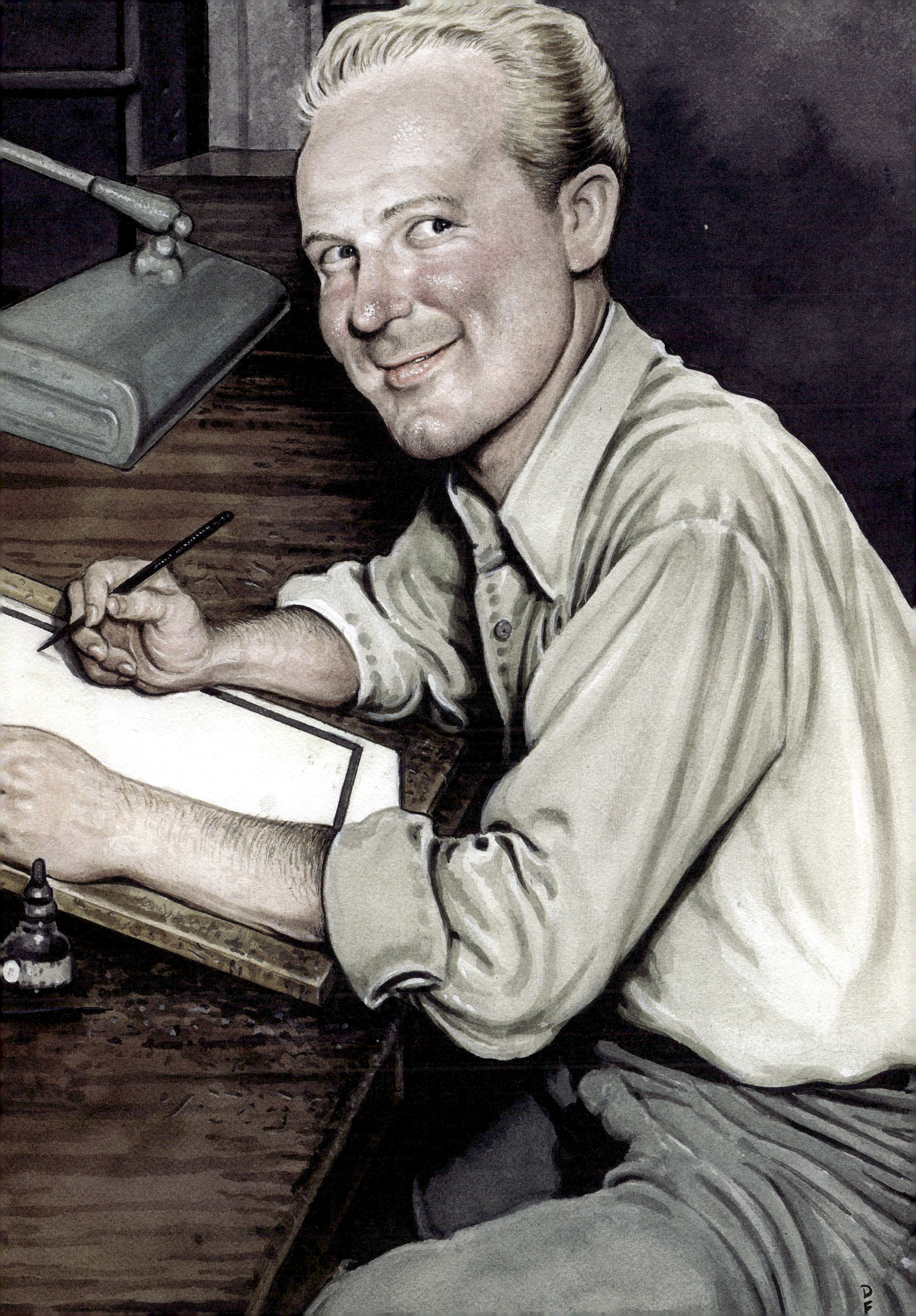

RUSS MANNING

1929-1981

plate 57

Russell George Manning was born in Van Nuys, California, and raised in Orcutt. He studied at the Los Angeles County Art Institute. In 1950, he had prepared some sample pages of a proposed *John Carter of Mars* comic book—but then the Korean War began, and his National Guard unit was deployed to Japan, where he spent the next two years.

After being discharged in 1952, Manning made his way to Western Publishing, where he contributed his first professional comic book work, an eight-page backup feature—"Brothers of the Spear"—in Dell Comics' *Tarzan* #39. The "Brothers of the Spear" feature ran until 1966, when he took over *Tarzan* from artist Jesse Marsh. He also worked across the Dell line, drawing westerns like *Roy Rogers, Wyatt Earp*, and *Annie Oakley*, while also showing up regularly in their extensive line of television adaptations, like *My Favorite Martian, Sea Hunt*, and 77 *Sunset Strip*. In 1963, he created *Magnus, Robot Fighter 4000 A.D.* The Gold Key series lasted until 1977 and has been revived several times.

Manning took over the *Tarzan* syndicated comic strip, drawing the daily and Sunday page from 1967 to 1972, and the Sunday page alone until 1979. His last significant work was writing and drawing the syndicated *Star Wars* comic strip from 1979 to 1980.

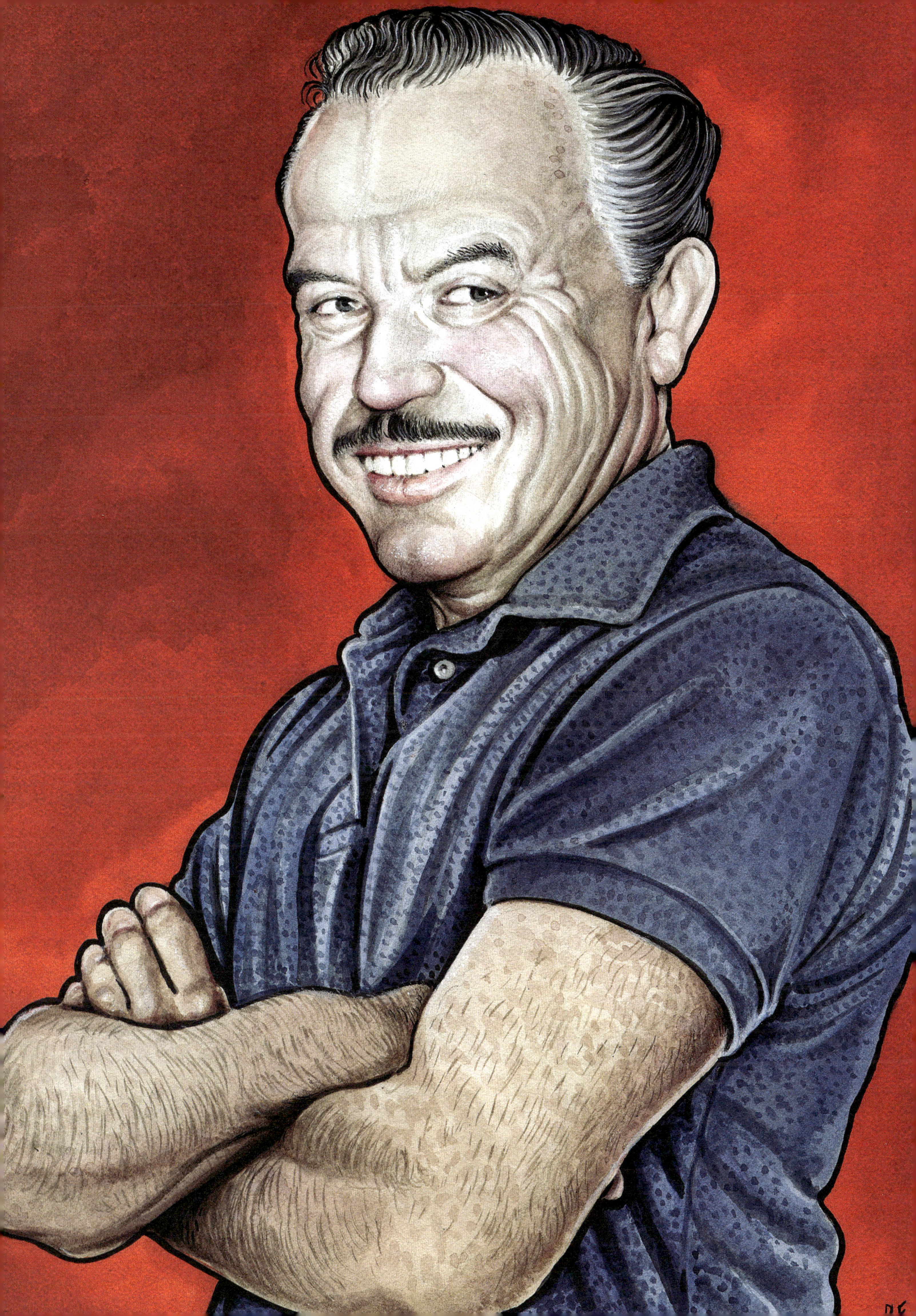

ELIZABETH MARSTON

1893–1993

plate
58

Elizabeth "Sadie" Holloway Marston was born in the Isle of Man and raised in Boston, Massachusetts. Holloway was a highly ambitious student, receiving degrees from Mount Holyoke College, Boston University, and Radcliffe College. She married William Moulton Marston in 1918. The newlyweds both joined the psychology department at Harvard. Elizabeth Marston is credited with inspiring her husband's research on deception that would later result in his inventing the polygraph.

William Marston was hired by Max Gaines at All-American Publications as an educational consultant in the early '40s. Marston wanted to create a new kind of superhero who would operate without using force and could elicit the truth not with violence, but understanding. Elizabeth Marston strongly suggested to her husband that the new superhero be a woman. Marston based the character both on his wife Elizabeth and the younger Olive Byrne, who lived with the couple in an open marriage. She was first called Suprema, which was soon changed to the liberated, powerful, modern "Wonder Woman."

Wonder Woman made her debut in *All-Star Comics* #8 in 1941, with art by H.G. Peter. Six months later, she was given her own title, *Wonder Woman*, which ran for twenty-five years. Elizabeth Marston died in 1993 on her one-hundredth birthday.

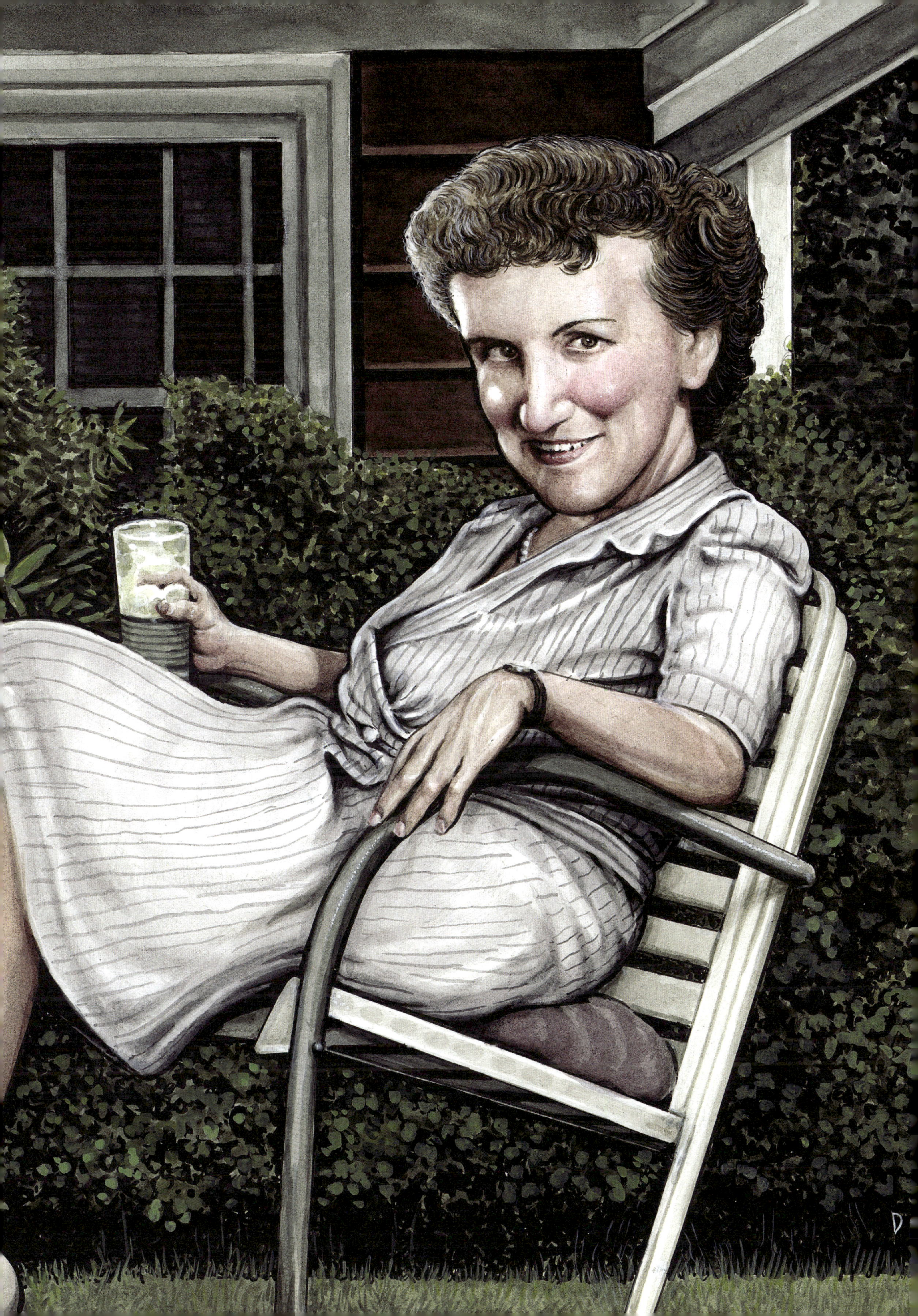

NORMAN MAURER

1926-1986

plate
59

Born in Brooklyn, Norman Albert Maurer started working in comic books while still a teenager.

Maurer's earliest credited work was in 1942, penciling and inking an eight-page story, "Back to Berlin," in Lev Gleason's *Boy Comics* #4. He also worked on Lev Gleason's *Daredevil Comics* and *Crime Does Not Pay*.

In 1947, Maurer married Joan Howard, daughter of Moe Howard of the Three Stooges. Two years later, he wrote and drew the first *Three Stooges* comic book (featuring Shemp Howard), for Jubilee Publications. In 1953, working with artist Joe Kubert, he created the first 3-D comic book for St. John (featuring Mighty Mouse); the 3-D process was developed by his brother Leonard. The team issued two 3-D *Three Stooges* comics (again, featuring Shemp) that same year.

Maurer became the manager of the Three Stooges in 1957, steering their careers, for better or worse, throughout their feature film revival of the 1960s. He also produced the syndicated *The New Three Stooges* cartoons in 1965–66.

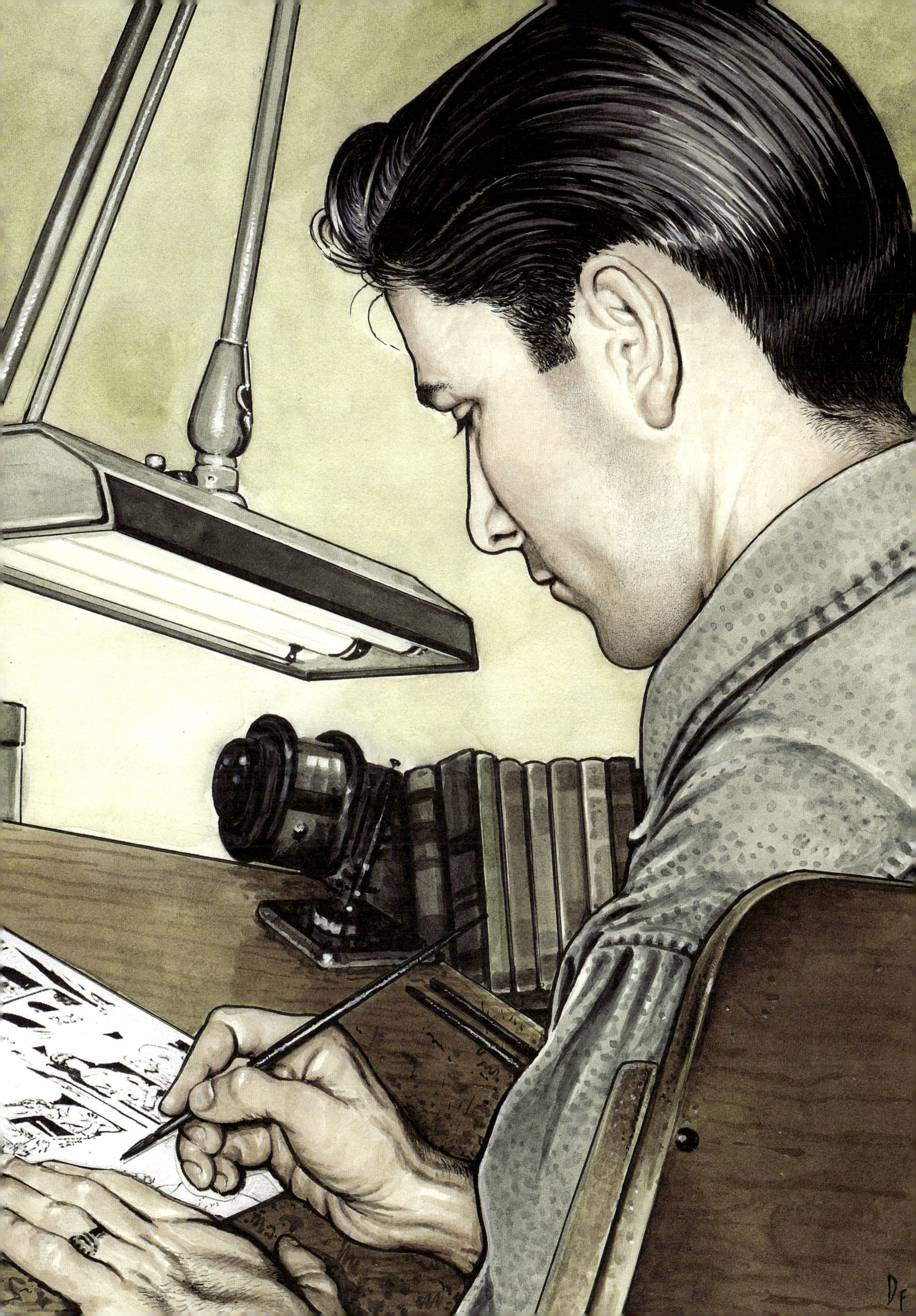

AL MCWILLIAMS

1916–1993

plate 60

Born in Greenwich, Connecticut, Alden Spurr McWilliams was the son of a chauffeur and a piano teacher. After graduating from high school in Greenwich, McWilliams attended the New York School of Fine and Applied Arts (now the Parsons School of Design). McWilliams first professional art experience was assisting Lyman Young on his newspaper strip *Tin Tyler's Luck.* By 1938, McWilliams was illustrating pulp magazines, as well as writing and drawing his own aviation-themed comic strip, *They Had What It Takes*, for *Flying Aces.* He made his comic book debut with the four-page "Capt. Frank Hawks—Air Ace" in Dell's *Crackajack Funnies.* Before enlisting in the US Army in 1942, McWilliams contributed to other Dell titles such as *Gangbusters*, *Space Cadets*, and *Flash Gordon.*

During World War II, McWilliams was awarded the Bronze Star Medal for serving in Normandy on D-Day. During the war, he wrote and drew a number of stories, returning to aviation themes for Quality Comics with "Spitfire" in *Crack Comics,* and "Secret War News" in *Military Comics.*

After his discharge, he returned to comics, handling art on the Steve Wood feature in Quality's *National Comics*. He finished out the decade drawing for a variety of comic book publishers while also supplying work to pulp magazines.

By the early 1950s, McWilliams was working increasingly for newspapers. He created, with Oskar LeBeck, the science fiction comic strip, *Twin Earths,* which ran from 1952–1963. By the mid-'60s, he was creating art for Warren's *Creepy.* In 1966, he created the art for Russ Jones Productions' graphic novel adaptation of *Dracula* for Ballantine Books.

His strip with John Saunders, *Dateline: Danger,* made its debut in 1968. It starred Danny Raven, one of the first African Americans prominently featured in a comic strip. McWilliams's art can also be seen in a number of Gold Key Comics television adaptations, like *Star Trek, The Man from U.N.C.L.E.*, and *I Spy.*

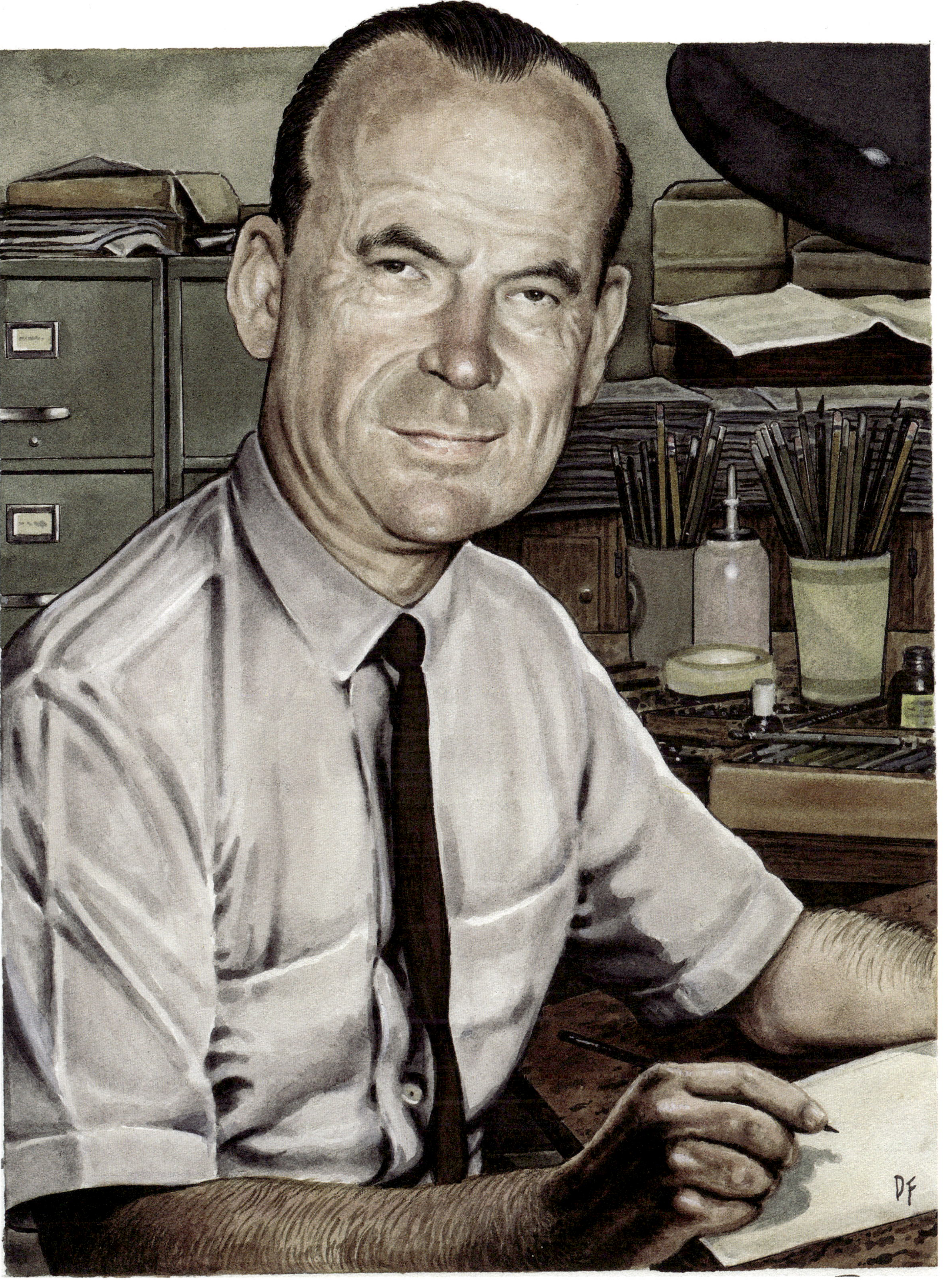
DF

SHELDON "SHELLY" MOLDOFF

1920-2012

plate 61

Sheldon "Shelly" Douglas Moldoff was born in Manhattan and raised in the Bronx. He was a self-taught artist, who learned his craft using a piece of chalk to draw comic strip characters on the sidewalk.

His first published art was a single-page, humorous filler, "Odds 'N' Ends," in Detective Comics' *Action Comics* #1 in 1938. His work was a familiar presence in titles like *All Star Comics*, where he drew Hawkman and Hawkgirl features. He was also a prolific cover artist during the Golden Age, including the very first appearance of the Green Lantern for *All-American Comics* #16 in 1939.

His career was interrupted by the draft in 1944, and he spent two years in the military. When he returned, he freelanced for various publishers; he drew several Captain Marvel Jr. stories for Fawcett, and EC's *Moon Girl* for its five-issue run, starting in 1947.

In 1953, Moldoff became one of DC's primary Batman artists, alongside Dick Sprang and Win Mortimer. Working uncredited, he would "ghost" Bob Kane for the next fourteen years. During his tenure, he was responsible for co-creating memorable Batman characters like Poison Ivy, Batgirl, and Ace the Bat-Hound.

He later worked creating storyboards on Bob Kane's animated TV series *Courageous Cat and Minute Mouse*.

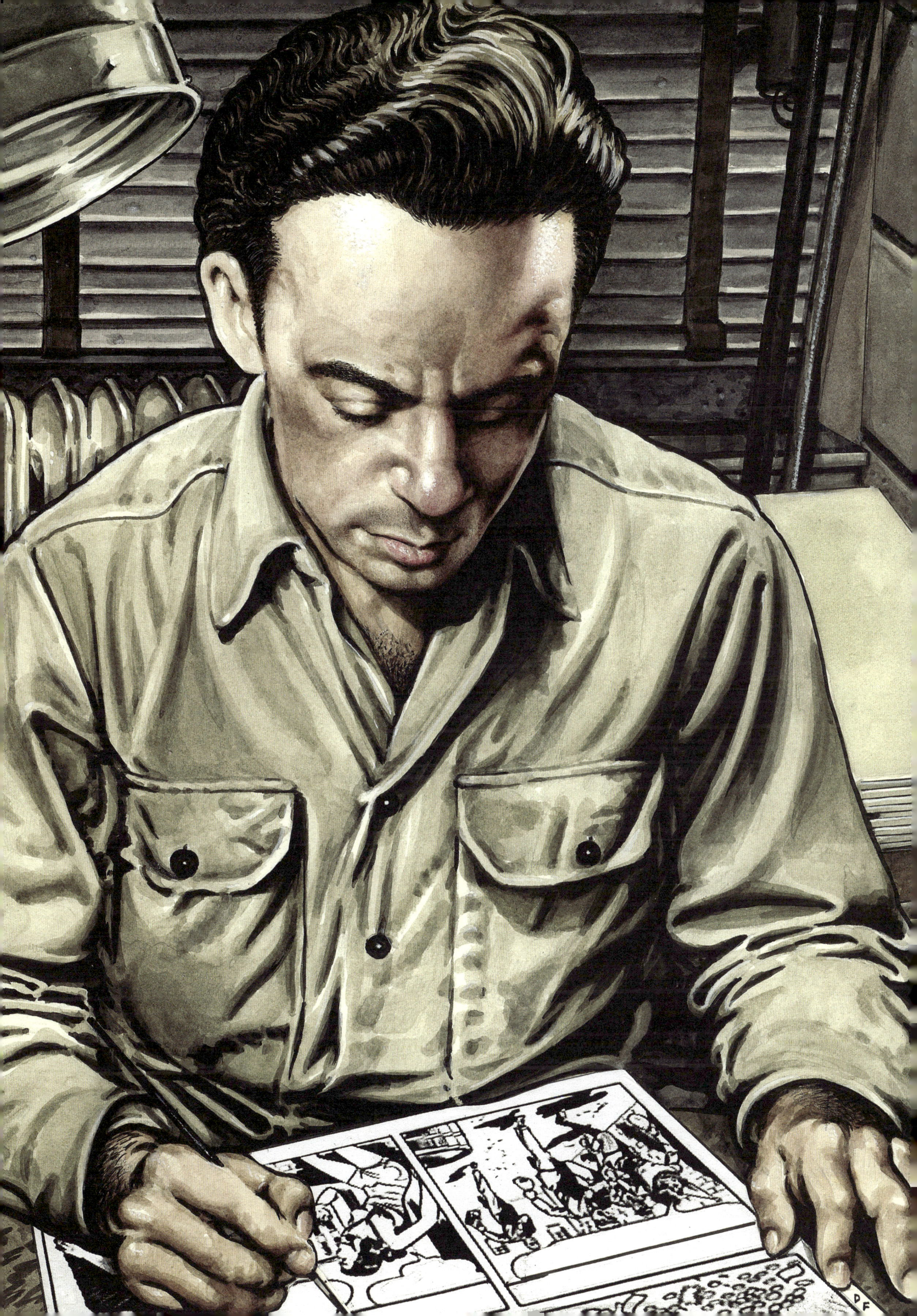

JIM MOONEY

1919-2008

plate 62

James Noel Mooney was born into a wealthy family in Mount Vernon, New York. His father made his fortune raising Arabian horses, and lost it all when the Great Depression began. A wealthy uncle became his benefactor, and bankrolled his tuition at the the Otis Art Institute in Los Angeles.

In 1938, he drew the cover for the first issue of Forrest J. Ackerman's fanzine, *Imagination*. The same year he sold an illustration to pulp magazine *Weird Tales*. It was then that he decided to head for New York to break into the comic book business.

Mooney's first comic book assignment was "Enter: The Moth," a seven-page story in Fox Comics' *Mystery Men Comics* #9, in 1940. After working for nine months at Fiction House, he arrived at Timely Comics, where he met editor Stan Lee. His initial collaboration with Lee was drawing Funny Animal stories based on *Terrytoons* animated shorts. After the market for talking animals dried up, he began his long association with DC Comics in 1946.

His first job at DC was "ghosting" for Bob Kane, replacing Dick Sprang, yet another uncredited Batman artist. Later, also at DC, he would draw *Supergirl* from 1959 to 1968. For Supergirl, he co-created Streaky the Supercat and Supergirl's pet horse, Comet.

Mooney rejoined Stan Lee at Marvel in 1968 to ink John Romita's pencils on *The Amazing Spider-Man*, as well as doing the same for John Buscema's *The Mighty Thor.*

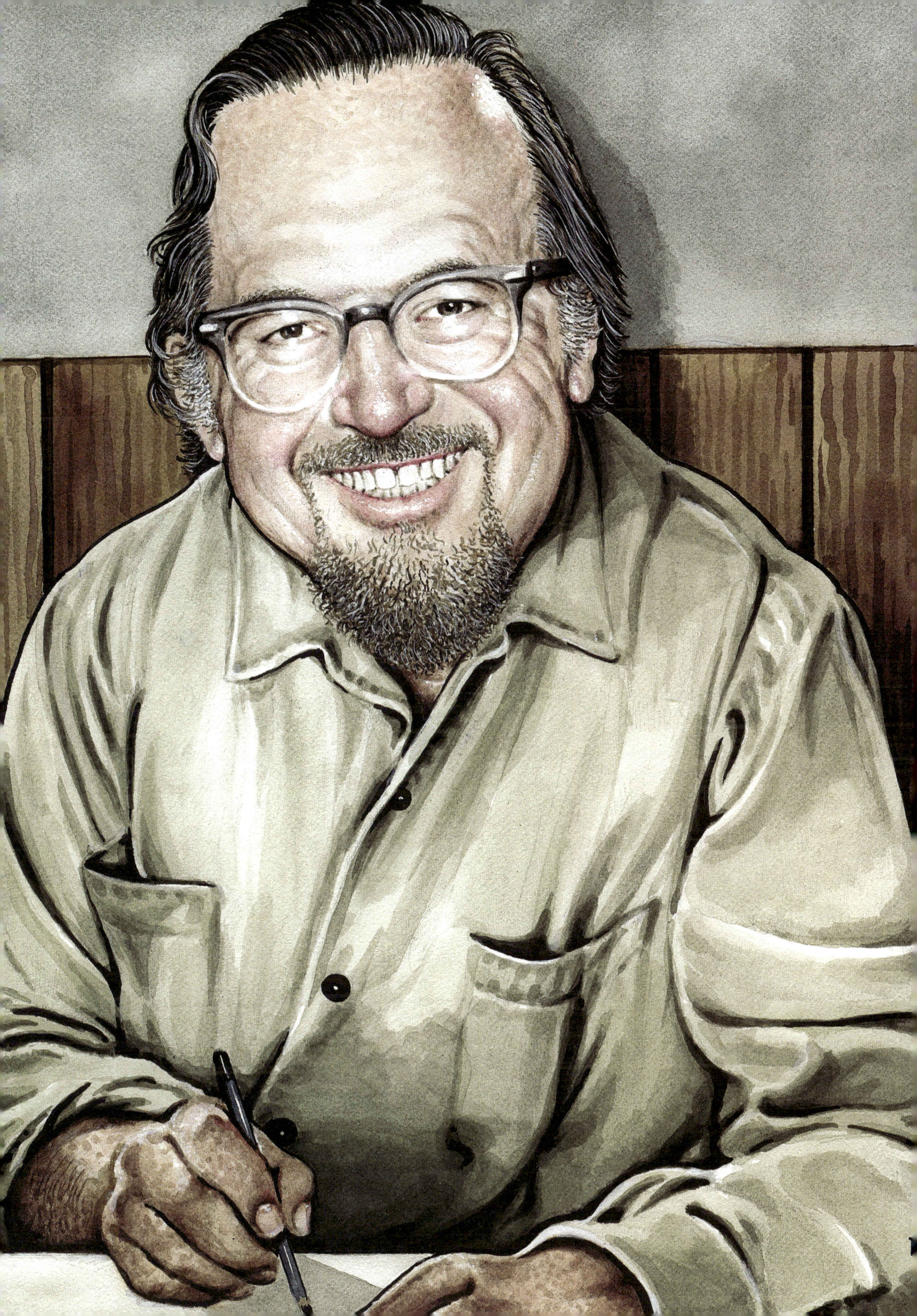

GRAY MORROW

1934-2001

plate
63

Dwight Graydon "Gray" Morrow was born in Fort Wayne, Indiana, where he graduated from Northside High School. In 1954, Morrow attended the Chicago Academy of Fine Arts for three months before accepting a position at Chicago's Feldkamp-Malloy art studio. He lasted only a few months before moving to New York City in 1955.

In New York, Morrow got assignments from two different publishers, who each went out of business before his work saw print. Artists Al Williamson and Wallace Wood hired him to create layouts and backgrounds. Williamson later helped Morrow land inking assignments from Atlas Comics. His first published penciling was a four-page story, "The Field of Battle," in Atlas Comics *Battlefront* #41. He was drafted into the US Army in 1956, and spent the next two years in South Korea.

After the war, Morrow worked for *Classics Illustrated,* adapting literary work like Jules Verne's *Master of the World.* In 1964, his "Bewitched!" appeared in *Creepy* #1, the first of many stories to appear in Warren Publishing's black-and-white magazine line (which would soon expand to include *Eerie* and *Blazing Combat*). He also worked in animation as a layout artist for two seasons of Ralph Bakshi's animated Spider-Man series, starting in 1967. In 1971, he co-created Man-Thing as a backup feature in Marvel Comics' first black-and-white magazine, *Savage Tales* #1. Morrow's work took a turn toward more adult fare with his work on *Orion,* originally introduced in the pages of *Heavy Metal.* A lifelong fan of Edgar Rice Burroughs, Morrow spent eighteen years drawing the *Tarzan* Sunday strip. In the late '90s, Morrow was diagnosed with Parkinson's disease. By 2001, he was unable to draw and he died of a self-inflicted gunshot wound.

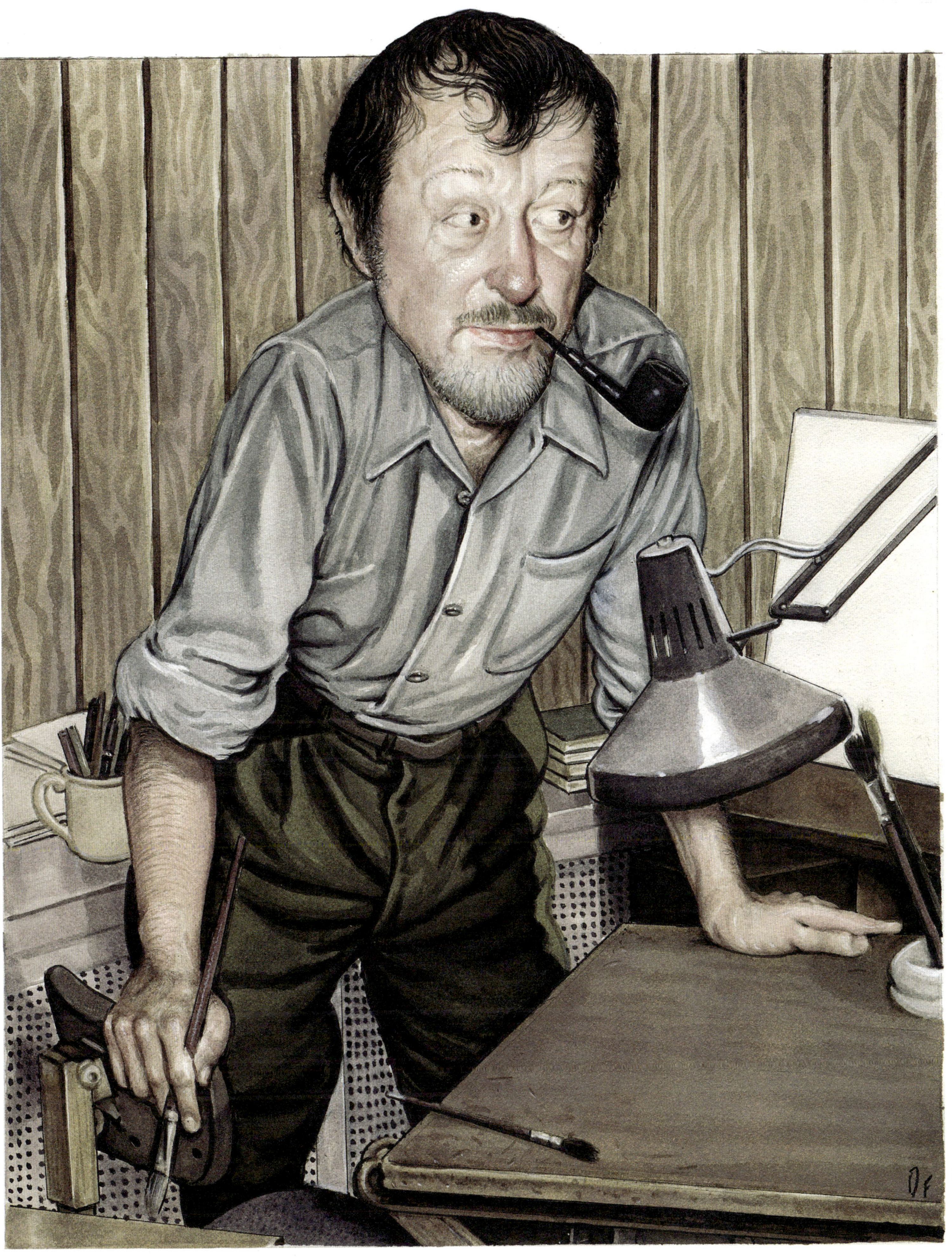

WIN MORTIMER

1919–1998

plate 64

James Winslow Mortimer was born in Hamilton, Ontario, Canada. Mortimer started his career early, assisting his father after school at a local poster printer. Mortimer studied at the Art Students League of New York before enlisting in the Canadian army at the start of World War II. After the war, Mortimer designed posters for the Canadian Ministry of Information before returning to New York in 1945. DC Comics hired Mortimer as a staff artist and assigned him his first published comic book work, penciling and inking "Batman Goes Broke" for *Detective Comics* #105. The following year, he became DC's premier cover artist, creating dynamic and unique covers for *Batman, Adventure Comics, Action Comics*, and many others. His covers for the Batman/Superman anthology *World's Finest* often bordered on the absurd, featuring Batman and Superman playing basketball, roller-skating, or riding a seesaw. Mortimer's whimsical side was also readily apparent in his work on DC's 1952 series *The Adventures of Dean Martin and Jerry Lewis.*

For six years, starting in 1949, Mortimer replaced Wayne Boring as the artist on the daily Superman comic strip. He left DC for the most part in 1956 to draw another strip, *David Crane*, for the next four years. In 1961, he started work on the *Larry Bannon* strip for the *Toronto Star.* Mortimer returned to comic book work as a freelancer in the early '70s, drawing fifty-seven issues of the Spider-Man children's comic, *Spidey Super Stories*, as well as working for Gold Key on *Twilight Zone* and *Boris Karloff Tales of Mystery.*

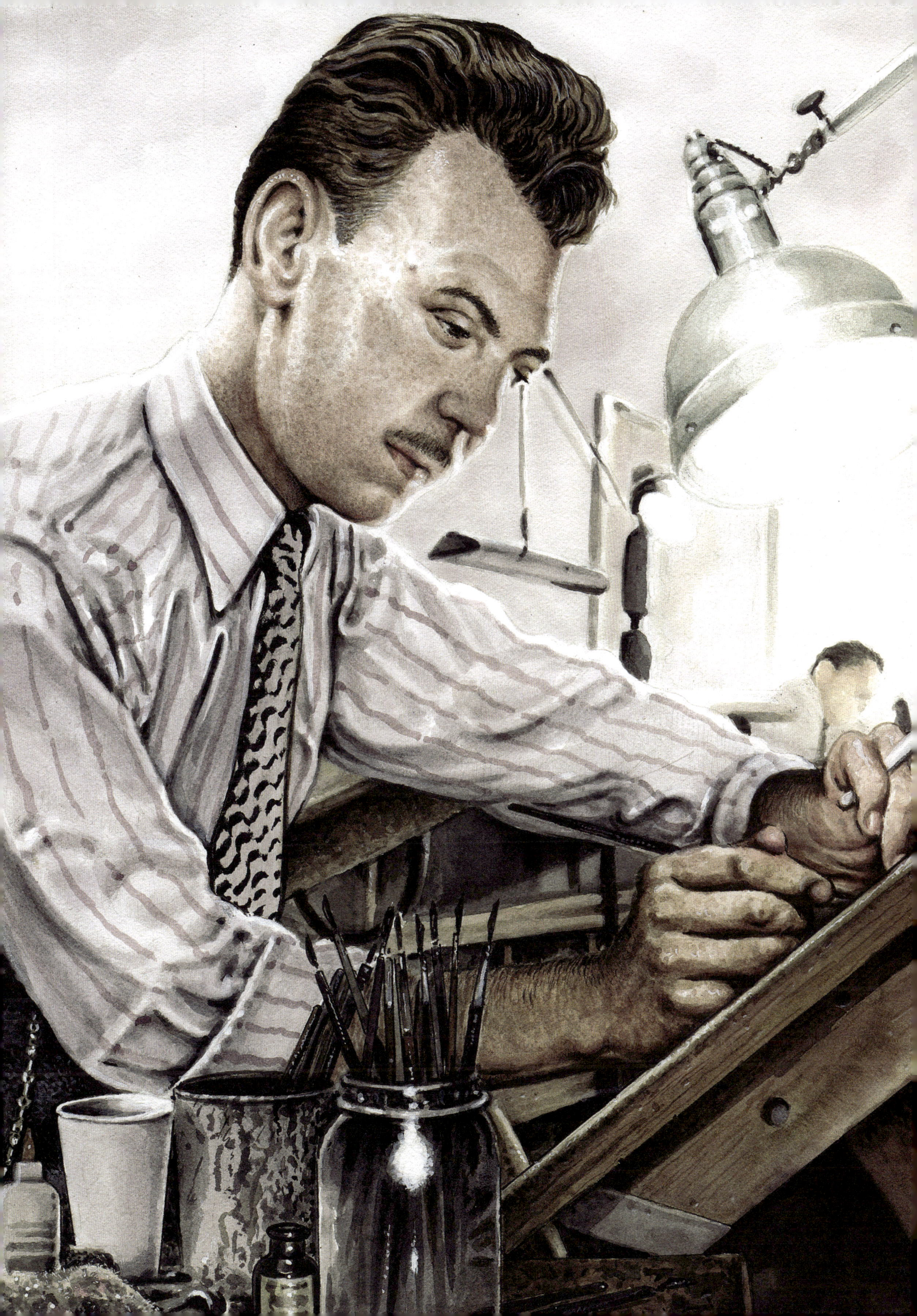

MARTIN NODELL

1915-2006

plate 65

Philadelphia-born Martin Nodell attended the Art School of Chicago before moving to New York to continue his education at Pratt Institute. Nodell's first comic book work was freelancing for Fox Comics and Ace Comics under the pen name Mart Dellon. In 1940, while waiting for a train, inspiration struck him when he noticed a subway worker walking the track with a signal light. Nodell pitched his concept for the Green Lantern to All-America Publications' Max Gaines, who assigned *Batman* writer Bill Finger to script the story. The Green Lantern made his debut in *All-American Comics* #16. Nodell drew the character for seven years before departing for Timely Comics in 1947. At Timely, he contributed to *Marvel Tales, Marvel Mystery Comics,* and *Captain America's Weird Tales,* a horror-themed, last-ditch attempt to breathe life into the Golden Age of comics.

With the comic book business in decline, Nodell turned to advertising work. In 1950, he joined the Leo Burnett advertising agency as an art director and was part of the team that designed the Pillsbury Doughboy. In 1952, he penciled a story for Avon Comics, *City of the Living Dead*, but would remain largely absent from the comic book world for forty years.

In 1996, at the age of eighty, Nodell came out of retirement to pencil a story for Dark Horse's *Harlan Ellison's Dream Corridor Quarterly* #1.

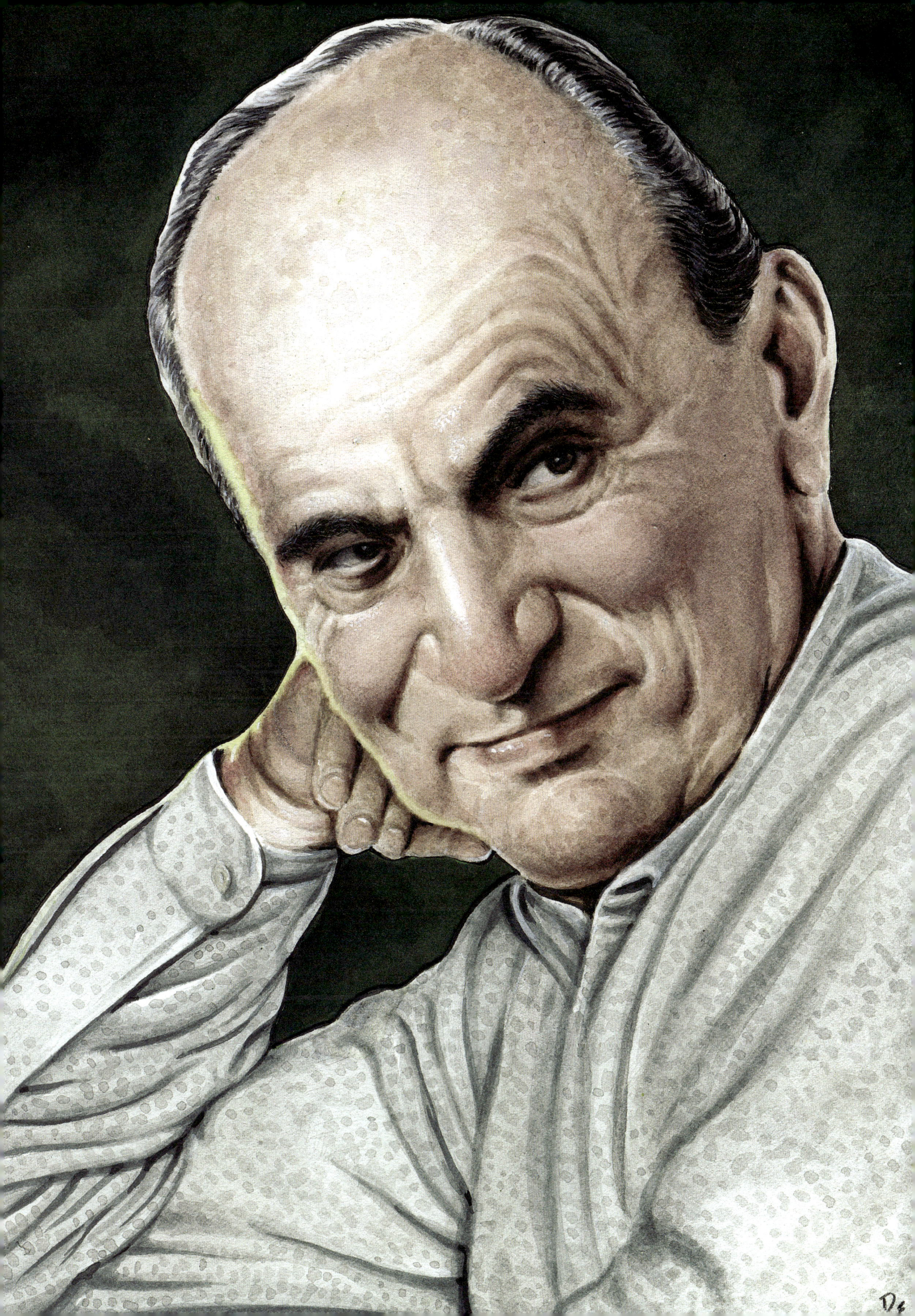

PAUL NORRIS

1914-2007

plate
66

Paul Leroy Norris was born in Greenville, Ohio. In 1934, Norris studied at Midland Lutheran College in Nebraska, where he was art director of the college yearbook. He left school before graduating to work on a comic strip his cousin had sold to a syndicate. Before Norris could get the strip ready, the syndicate went out of business. He worked in an electric-motor plant, and continued his studies at the Dayton Art Institute.

Norris moved to New York in 1940, and, within a year, had published his earliest, confirmed comic book work, an eight-page story, "The Sandman at Sea," in DC Comics' *Adventure Comics* #65. In 1941, Norris and Mort Weisinger created Aquaman, introducing the character in an eight-page origin story, "The Submarine Strikes," in *More Fun Comics* #73. Norris would draw Aquaman for only a handful of issues before taking over the scripting and art duties on *Secret Agent X-9* for King Features Syndicate in 1943. Three months after starting work on the strip, he was drafted into the US Army.

One of his comic strips in an army newspaper caught the eye of the top brass, who assigned him to illustrate propaganda leaflets to drop from planes over Japan.

In 1946, after the war, Norris returned to King Features to draw Sunday pages for *Jungle Jim*. By 1950, he had returned to DC Comics, penciling and inking stories for *Adventure Comics* and *Star Spangled Comics*. Starting in the early '50s, he worked extensively for Dell and Gold Key, drawing *Tom Corbett, Space Cadet*, *Tarzan*, and *Magnus, Robot Fighter*.

Norris took over the comic strip *Brick Bradford* in 1952, and stayed with it for thirty-five years, until his retirement.

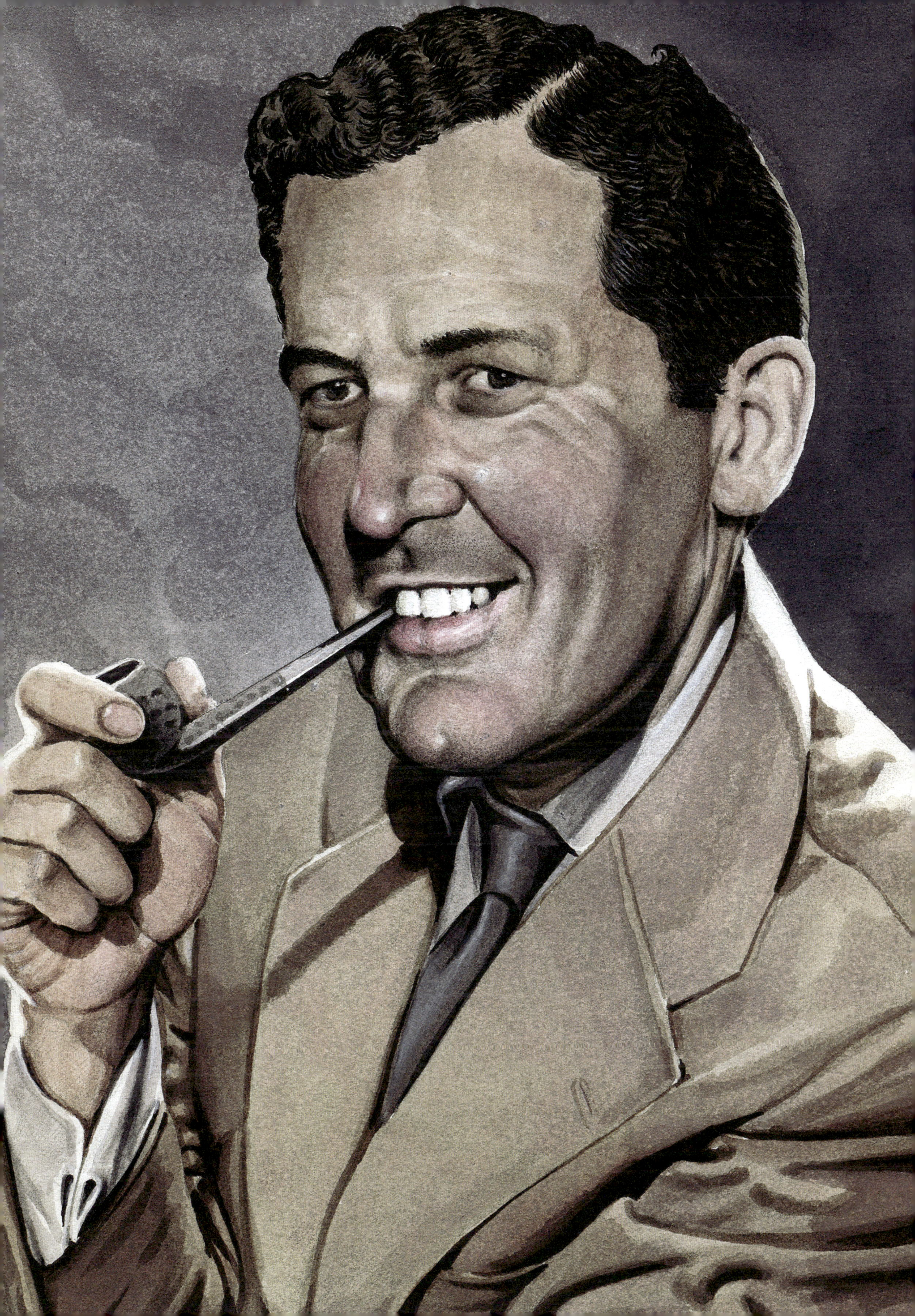

IRV NOVICK

1916-2004

plate
67

Irving Novick was born in New York and attended the National Academy of Design. Novick joined Harry "A" Chesler's comic book production line in 1939. His earliest published work was a five-page story, "Vendetta with Von Schiller," in MLJ's *Top Notch Comics* #1. Before MLJ decided to concentrate on their *Archie* titles, Novick was the company's main artist on most of their superhero books, like *Shield-Wizard Comics* and *Pep Comics*, both of which featured his co-creation, the patriotic hero *The Shield*. The Shield was the first flag-draped superhero, landing on newsstands a full year before Timely's Captain America. His last work for MLJ was the seven-page Betty and Veronica story, "All Washed Up!," *Archie Comics* #33 in 1950.

Novick worked in advertising and on a newspaper version of *The Scarlet Avenger* before landing briefly at DC Comics in the early '50s, drawing covers and stories for *Our Army at War*, and occasional romance titles. He turned to advertising work again in the '60s, but, toward the end of the decade, returned to DC for long runs on *Batman*, *The Flash*, and *The Brave and the Bold*. He's credited with restoring Batman's sense of mystery, which had been stripped away by the influence of the 1966 television incarnation.

Pop artist Roy Lichtenstein's painting "Whaam!" is a virtual line-by-line recreation of a Novick panel from *All-American Men of War* #89. Lichtenstein's "Blam!" was appropriated from several Russ Heath panels from the same issue. Lichtenstein's twelve-cent investment into that particular comic book paid off very nicely for him, but not for Novick and Heath.

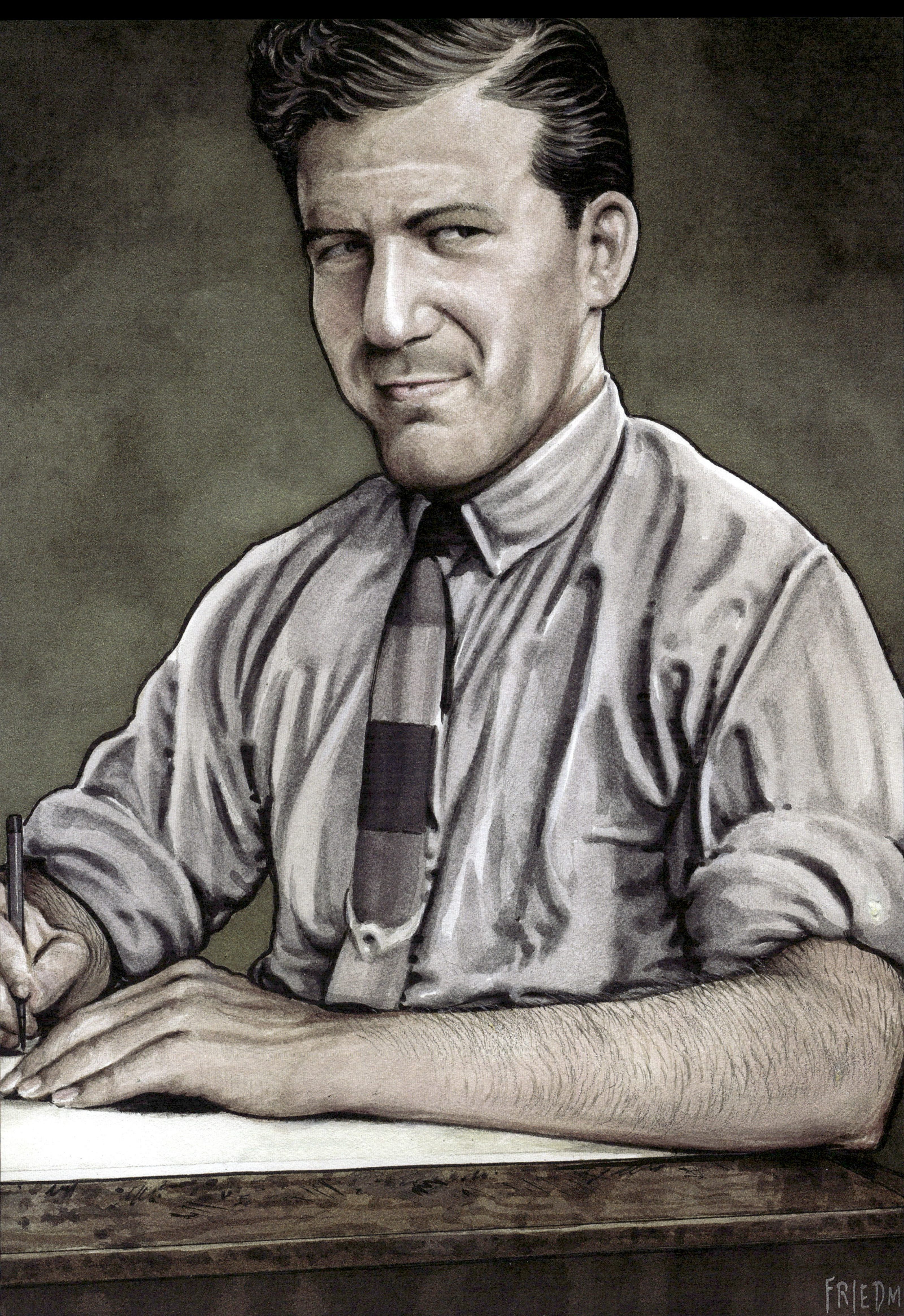

BEN ODA

1915-1984

plate 68

California-born, Japanese American Ben Oda graduated from Chouinard School of Fine Arts in Los Angeles. Oda's apprenticeship at Walt Disney Studios was cut short in 1941 when he was drafted into the US Army at the beginning of World War II. Oda trained as a paratrooper, but spent the war years stateside in Fort Sheridan, Illinois, where he wrote and drew a comic strip, *Donald Doc,* for the camp newspaper.

After the war, Oda's early lettering jobs for Hillman Periodicals' *Airboy* and *Real Clue Crime Stories* caught the attention of Joe Simon and Jack Kirby, whose staff letterer had recently died. He would work long into the night for Simon and Kirby — as well as a list of clients unmatched by anyone else in the comic book and comic strip industry. Oda had keys to the homes of many of his freelance clients, and it was not unusual for him to show up unannounced at the home of a syndicated cartoonist in the middle of the night, letter the day's work, and leave quietly.

In addition to inking words inside balloons and captions, Oda's work on logos and title pages has had a lasting influence. For EC, he designed most of the logos for the New Trend comics, and as Harvey Kurtzman's go-to letterer, designed the original *Mad* comic book logo and *Mad*'s interior title lettering. For Warren Publishing, Oda created the logos for *Eerie*, *Creepy*, and the often-imitated *Famous Monsters of Filmland* logo. The influence of his jagged horror lettering lives on in a thousand heavy metal band logos and horror movie posters. Oda's newspaper work included Will Eisner's *The Spirit*, *Dondi, Terry and the Pirates*, *Flash Gordon*, *Little Orphan Annie*, and *Rip Kirby.*

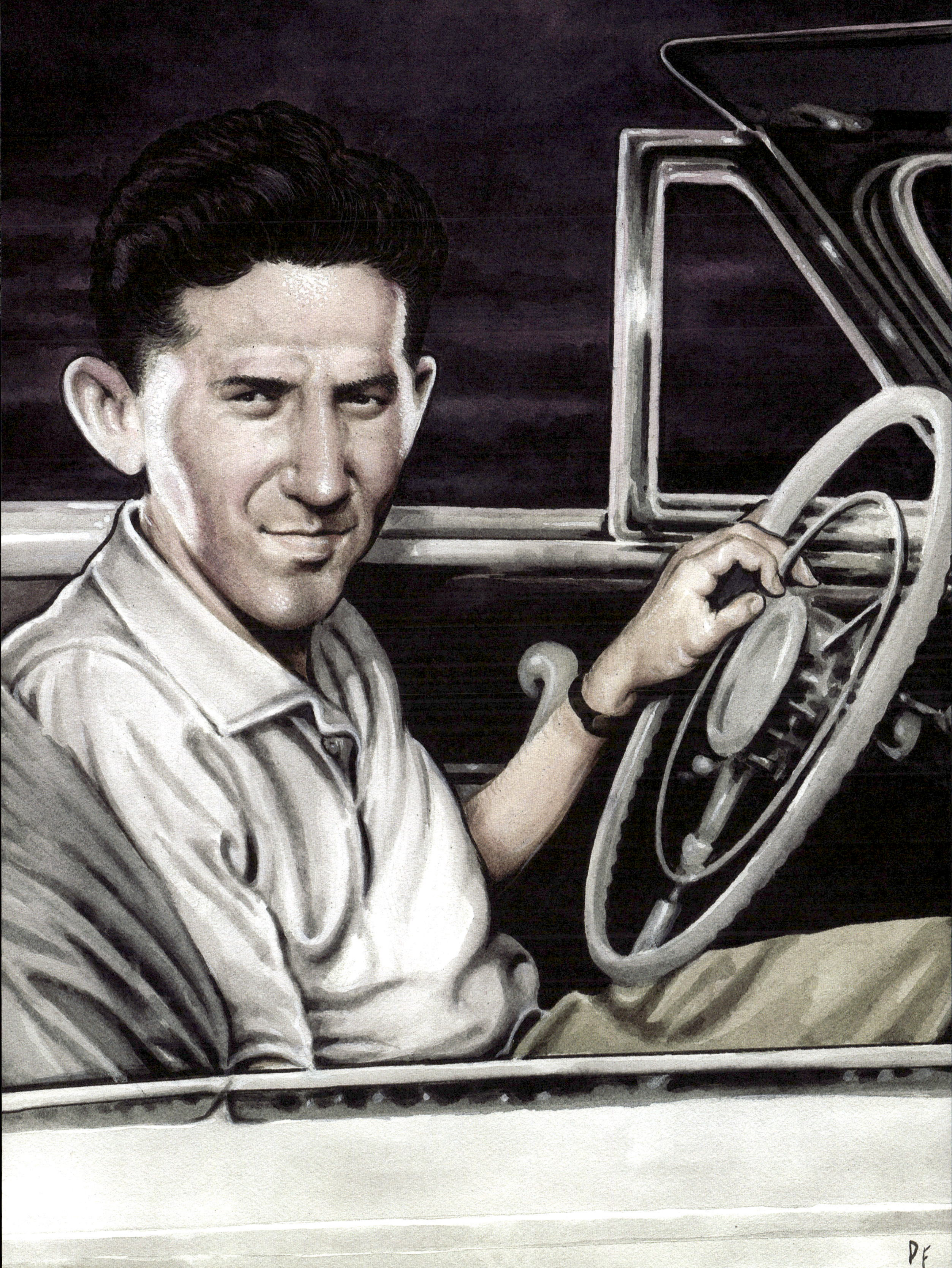

BOB OKSNER

1916-2007

plate
69

Born in Paterson, New Jersey, Oksner attended New York University with the intention of getting a law degree. Oskar's legal career took a backseat after he became editor of the campus humor magazine. Oskar switched gears, taking classes at the Art Students League of New York and Columbia University. In 1940, his first published story, "Mayhem at the Midget Race Track," appeared in *Marvel Mystery Comics* #11. He also worked on *Marvel Boy* and *The Adventurer* for Timely Comics.

In 1945, Oksner began drawing the syndicated comic strip *Miss Cairo Jones* for two years. The sexy strip caught the attention of DC Comics' Sheldon Mayer, who hired him to work on the teenage title *Leave it to Binky*. Oksner soon carved out a unique place for himself at DC Comics, creating celebrity and television themed comic books like *The Adventures of Dean Martin and Jerry Lewis* (followed by *The Adventures of Jerry Lewis*), *The Many Loves of Dobie Gillis*, *Sgt. Bilko*, and others.

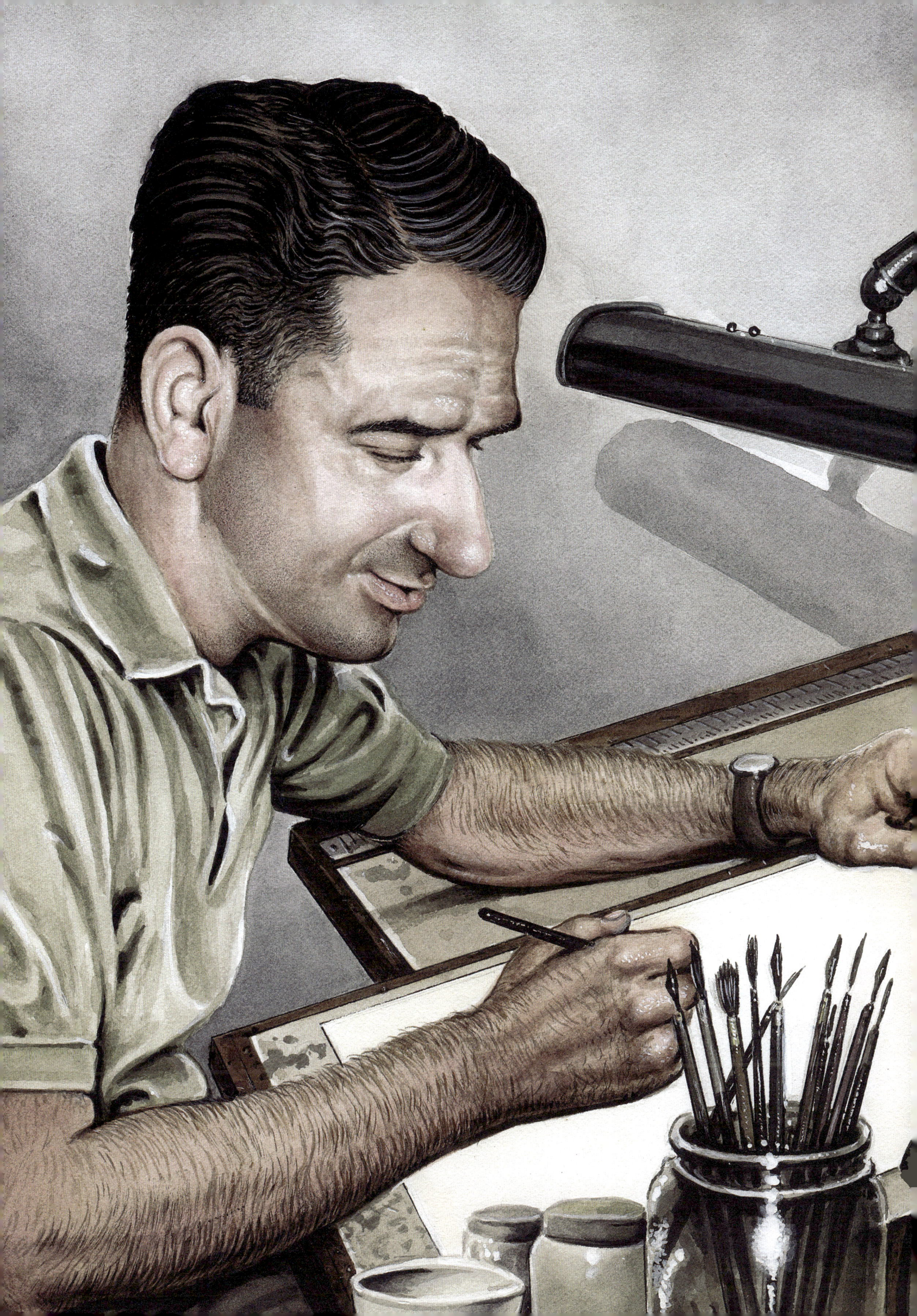

GLADYS PARKER

1910-1966

plate 70

Born in North Tonawanda, New York, Parker began submitting cartoons to magazines before she graduated high school. When she was eighteen, Parker left for New York to study fashion illustration. Parker received her earliest known credit in 1928, when she briefly took over *May and June,* a Graphic Syndicate comic strip originated by Harold McGill several years earlier.

Parker spent the next decade on several different comic strips for various distributors. In 1928 she created *Gay and Her Gang.* The strip was a stylish and modern look at flappers, but was gone within a year. The next year, she took over Ethel Hay's single-panel *Flapper Fanny*, updating the property with fashion-forward drawings and humor.

In 1939, Parker created the comic strip *Mopsy.* The title was inspired by Rube Goldberg's offhand comment that Parker's hair "looked like a mop." Mopsy was always stylishly attired, even when the wartime strip had her working in a munitions plant or at a hospital as a nurse. *Mopsy* would eventually be published in three hundred newspapers. The Sunday version often featured paper dolls alongside the strip. Mopsy appeared in St. John Publications' *Pageant of Comics* #1 in 1947. Two years later, St. John gave *Mopsy* her own comic book, a title which ran till 1953. Parker ceased production of the strip when she retired in 1965.

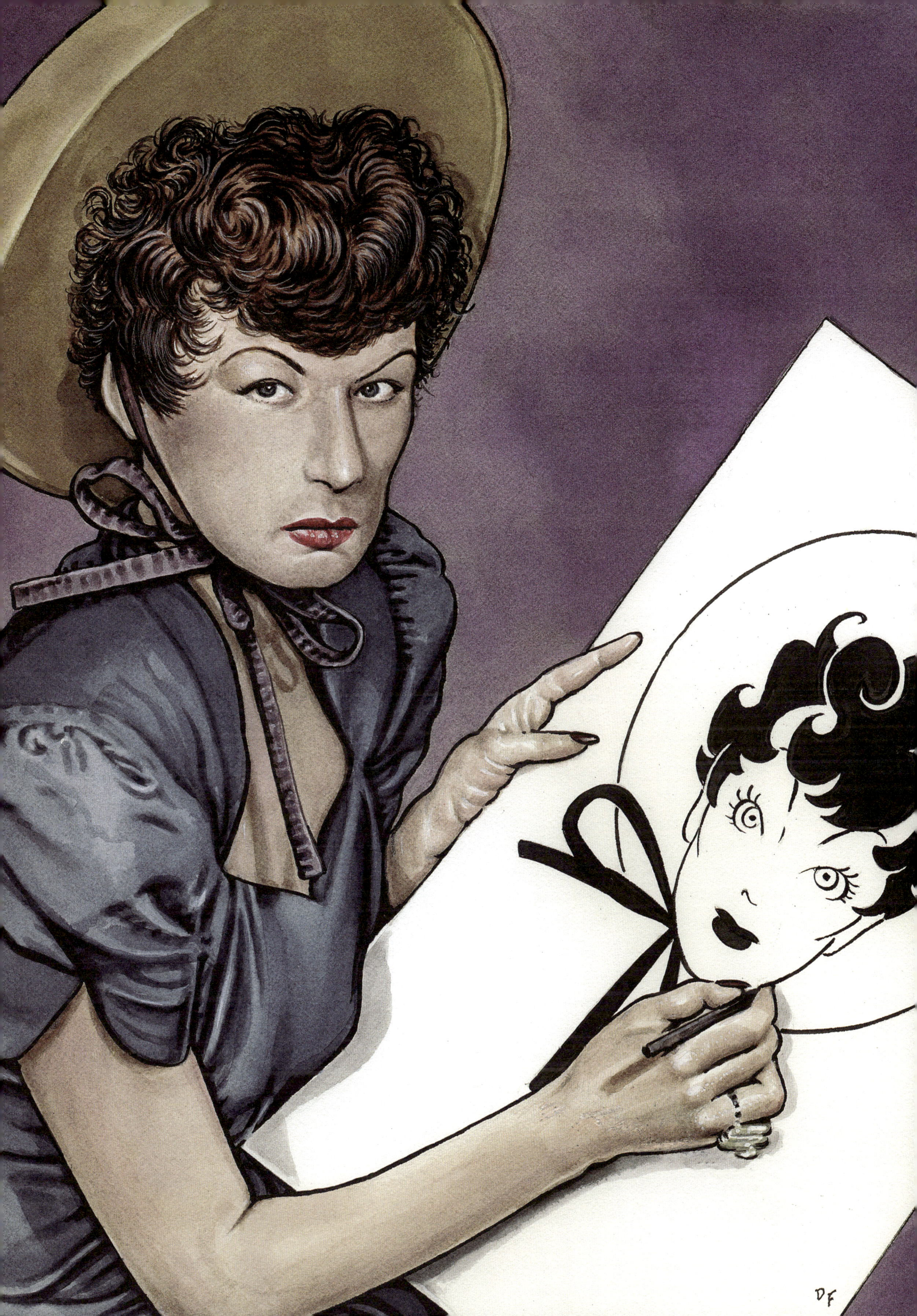
DF

H.G. PETER

1880-1958

plate
71

Harry George Peter was born in San Rafael, California, and started his illustration career working for the *San Francisco Chronicle* before moving to New York with his future wife and fellow artist, Andronica Fulton, in 1907. Peters got a late start in the comic book trade. His first published work was a 1941 biography of General George Marshall for *True Comics* #4. The same year, the sixty-year-old Peter was hired to create the art for the first female superhero, William Moulton Marston's Wonder Woman, which made its debut in All-American Publications' *All Star Comics* #8.

The success of Wonder Woman led to the establishment of the Marston Art Studio in 1944, devoted to producing Wonder Woman comic books and an ongoing daily comic strip featuring the Amazon warrior. As lead artist, Peter did most of the penciling and primary inking before passing his work on to a handful of largely female assistants. He continued to work on Wonder Woman for eleven years after Marston's death in 1947.

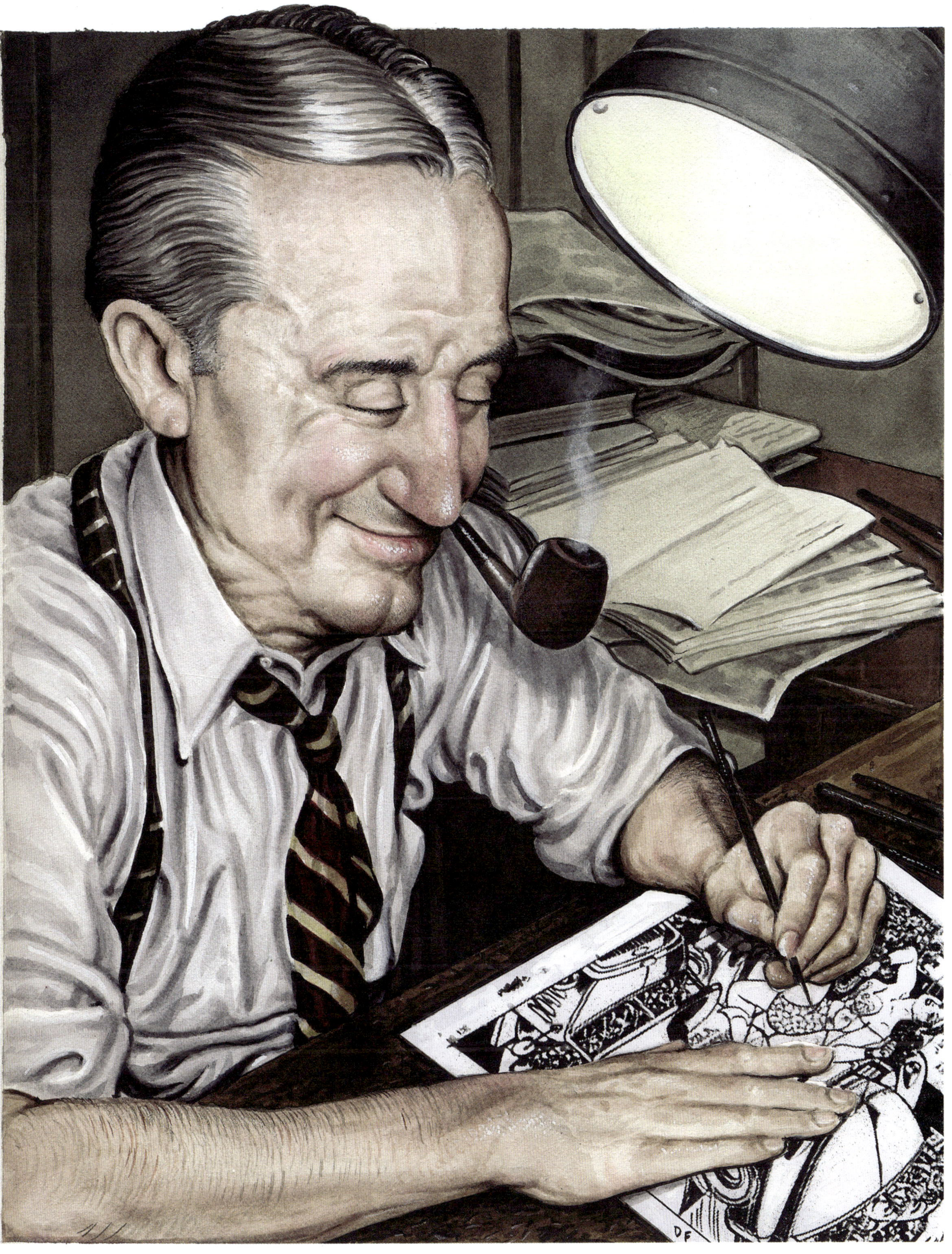

AL PLASTINO

1921-2013

plate
72

Alfred John Plastino was raised in the Bronx and attended the School of Industrial Art in Manhattan. While still in high school, Plastino was already working as an illustrator for *Youth Today* magazine. His entry into comic books was assisting Bill Everett on *Sub-Mariner.* By 1941, he had completed his first published comic book work, penciling and inking a Dynamic Man story for the second issue of *Dynamic Comics.* Prior to being drafted during World War II, he worked for Harry "A" Chesler's shop and freelanced for Fawcett Publications. His work appeared in books like *Blue Bolt Comics*, *Scoop Comics*, and *Captain America*.

While serving in the US Army, Plastino's artistic knack for drawing realistic aircraft landed him an assignment with military contractor Grumman Aerospace. He eventually made his way to the Pentagon, designing military posters and technical manuals.

In 1948, Plastino showed some Superman samples to editors at DC Comics. After some initial haggling over page rates, he began his lengthy career at DC.

Despite resistance to the DC "house style" of Wayne Boring, Plastino settled nicely into his role as one of the key artists of mid-century Superman titles. In his three decades at DC, he had a hand in introducing or co-creating Supergirl, the bottle city of Kandor, Braniac, and many others. In 1963, he collaborated with the White House on "Superman's Mission for President Kennedy," which promoted the president's physical fitness initiative. After Kennedy's assassination, they expected the book to be canceled, but it was issued the next year at the request of President Lyndon Johnson. When Jack Kirby's likeness of Superman in *Superman's Pal Jimmy Olsen* failed to meet the standards of DC editors, Plastino was enlisted to create "on model" revisions that were pasted over the Kirby originals.

Plastino also served as artist on the *Batman* and *Superman* newspaper strips and took over the *Nancy* Sunday strip when Ernie Bushmiller died. In the 1970s, *Peanuts* creator Charles Schulz was in the midst of renegotiating his contract with United Feature Syndicate and the distributor feared he would walk. Plastino was hired to create an inventory of *Peanuts* strips to be used as a contingency plan.

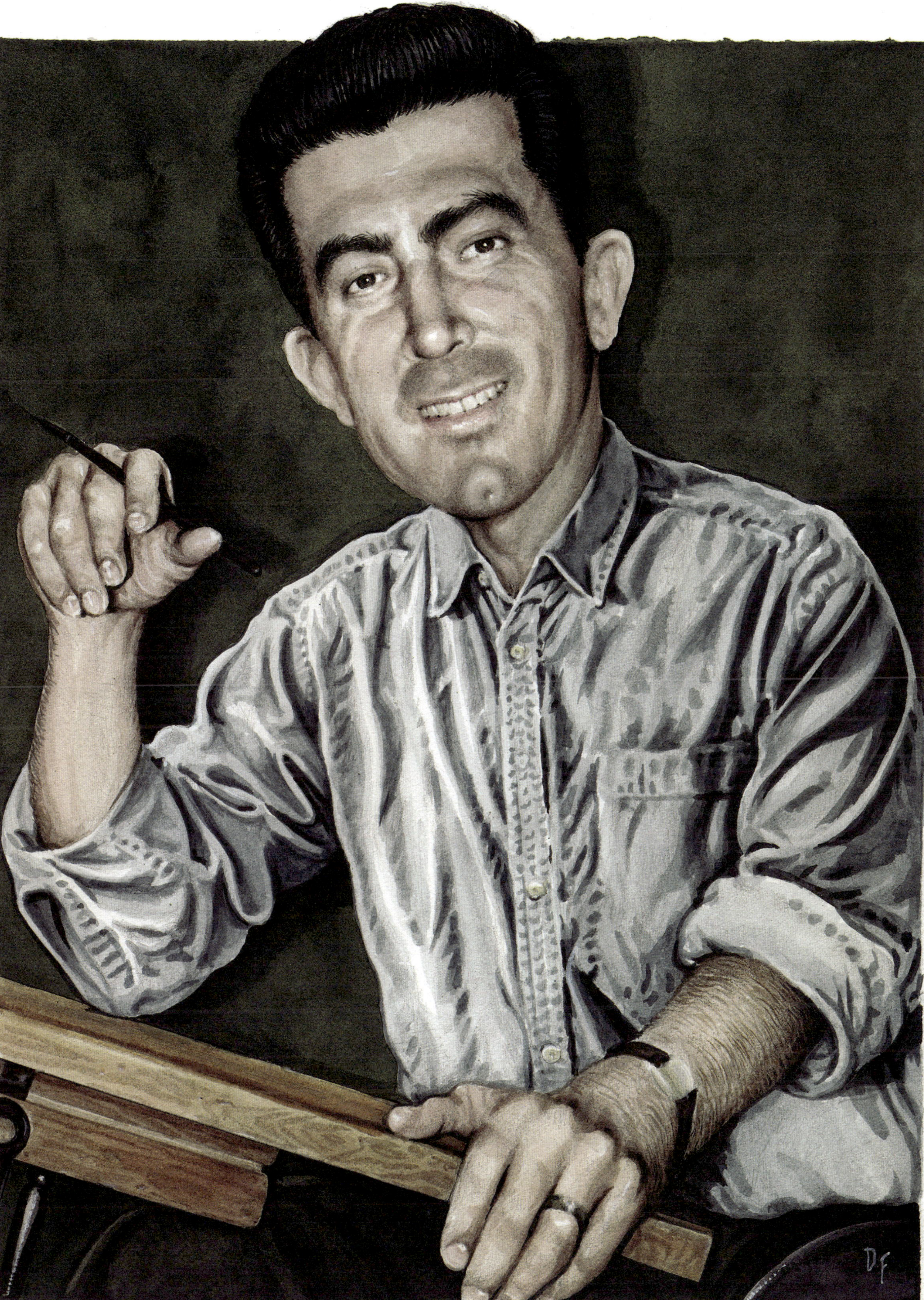
DF

PAUL REINMAN

1910–1988

plate **73**

Joseph Paul Reinmann (later, Reinman) was born in Germany and emigrated to New York in 1934. He had no formal art training, but had worked as a sign painter and window display designer in Germany. In New York, he worked as an assistant designer at a neon sign shop, and as a designer of matchbook covers. Eventually, he started freelancing as a pulp magazine illustrator before breaking into comic books; he worked at MLJ Comics in the early '40s.

Reinman's earliest known published work was penciling and inking a seven-page story, "Extortion for a Bail-Out," seen in Timely's *The Human Torch* #2. He contributed to MLJ titles *Hangman Comics, Jackpot Comics*, and *Shield-Wizard Comics.* During the '40s, he was especially active at DC Comics precursor All-American Comics, becoming one of the primary Green Lantern artists.

For Atlas Comics, he drew numerous war stories for titles like *Battlefield* and *War Comics*. When Atlas became the superhero-oriented Marvel, Reinman inked over Jack Kirby's pencils in the 1962 debut issue of *The Incredible Hulk* and the first five issues of *The X-Men*.

Reinman remained active in comic books through the mid-'70s.

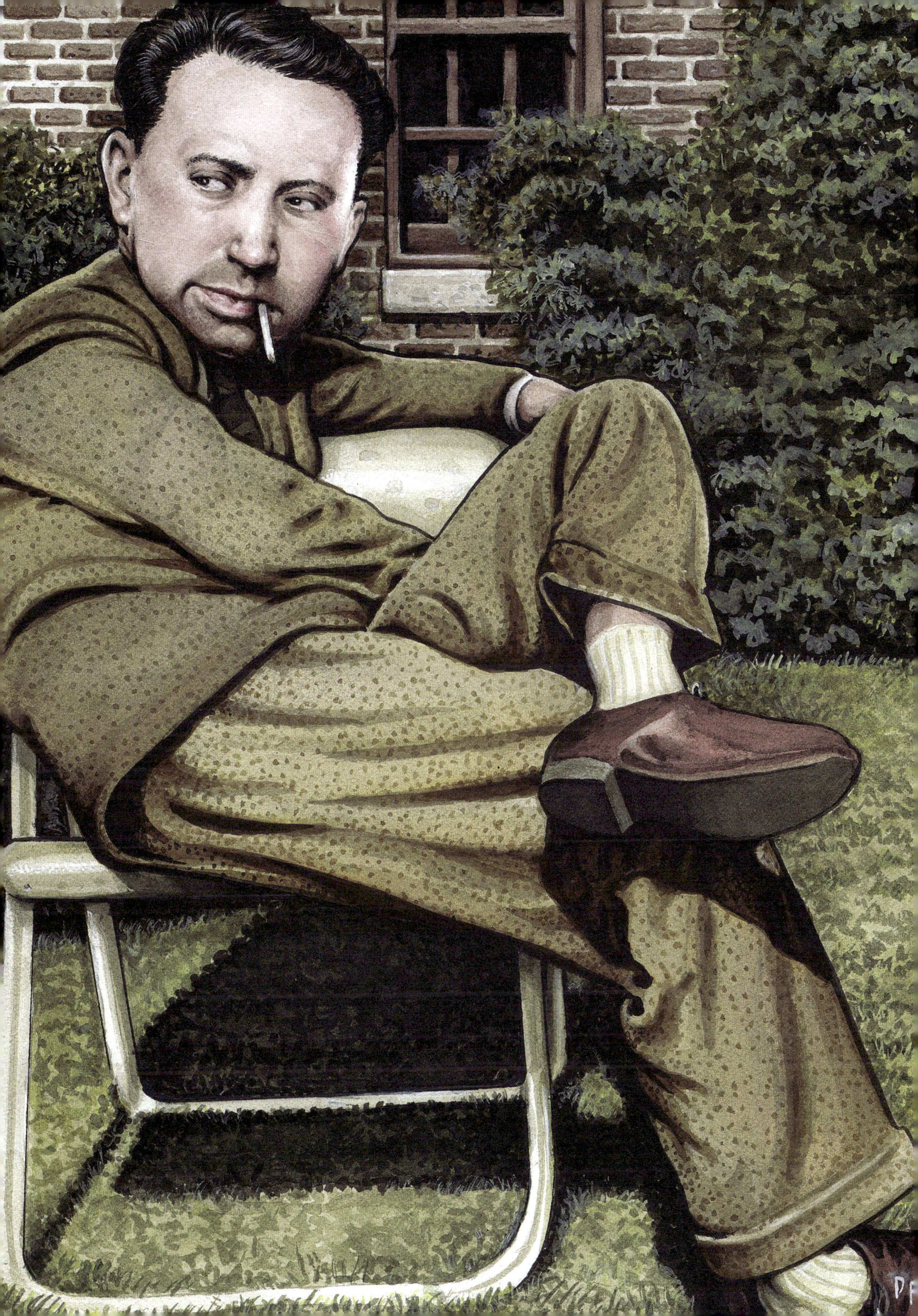

FRED RHOADS

1921-2000

plate
74

Fred Rhoads was born in Shamokin, Pennsylvania. After two frustrating years studying illustration in New York, Rhoads joined the Marines in 1942. While serving, he was assigned to the *Leatherneck* magazine where he published his own comic strip, *Gizmo and Eightball,* starting in 1943. While stationed in Washington, he met fellow Marine and cartoonist Fred Lasswell, who had taken over Billy DeBeck's *Barney Google and Snuffy Smith* after DeBeck's death. When the war ended, Rhoads became Lasswell's assistant.

Rhoads joined Harvey Comics in 1954 to adapt George Baker's newspaper strip *Sad Sack* into a monthly comic book. He softened Baker's adult-oriented *Sad Sack* to appeal to a younger readership.

Rhoads drew Harvey's *Sad Sack* for more than twenty years, until Harvey abruptly ceased sending him assignments in 1977. When he applied for unemployment compensation, he was told that his status as an independent contractor left him ineligible for benefits. He spent the next few years in a protracted court battle with Harvey. An Arizona court ruled in his favor, awarding him more than two million dollars, but an appeals court threw out the decision in 1984. Rhoads said the legal battle left him bankrupt. He spent his last years drawing editorial cartoons for the *Tucson Citizen.*

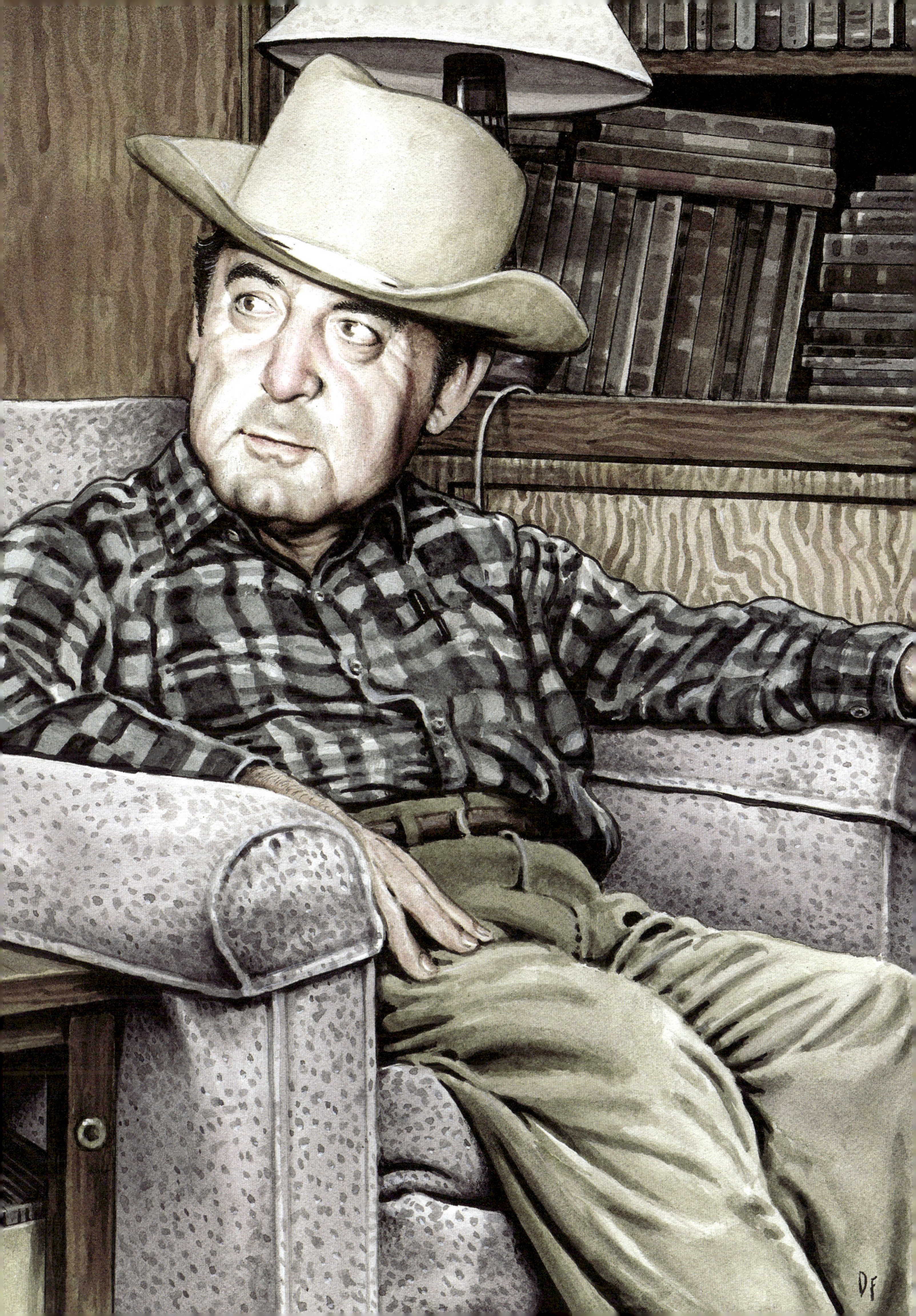

GUS RICCA

1910-1982

plate 75

Gasparo "Gus" Ricca started his career as an illustrator for *Liberty*, *Esquire*, and *Collier's* in the '30s.

Ricca went to work for Harry "A" Chesler's studio in 1940. His earliest confirmed work appears in Fawcett's *Slam-Bang Comics* #1; it's an eight-page story, "The Legacy of Tony Bond." The cover is also by Ricca. Although he contributed interior art to Chesler's Dynamic Comics, St. John Publishing, American Comics Group, and others, cover art would become his strong suit. While serving as art director of Dynamic from 1944 to 1946, his crazed covers for *Punch Comics*, *Dynamic Comics*, and *Scoop Comics* were equal parts macabre and morbid, and usually had little relationship to the stories inside. He also provided covers and single-page gags for *Mirth of a Nation* and *Yankee Magazine,* a series of digest-sized books published by Remington Moore and packaged by the Chesler studio.

Ricca's psyche troubled even Dr. Frederic Wertham, whose book, *Seduction of The Innocent,* compared his art in *Red Seal Comics* #16 to the work of the Marquis de Sade.

Ricca's last known work was in 1953, a five-page story, "Menace from Beyond," in St. John's *Strange Terrors*.

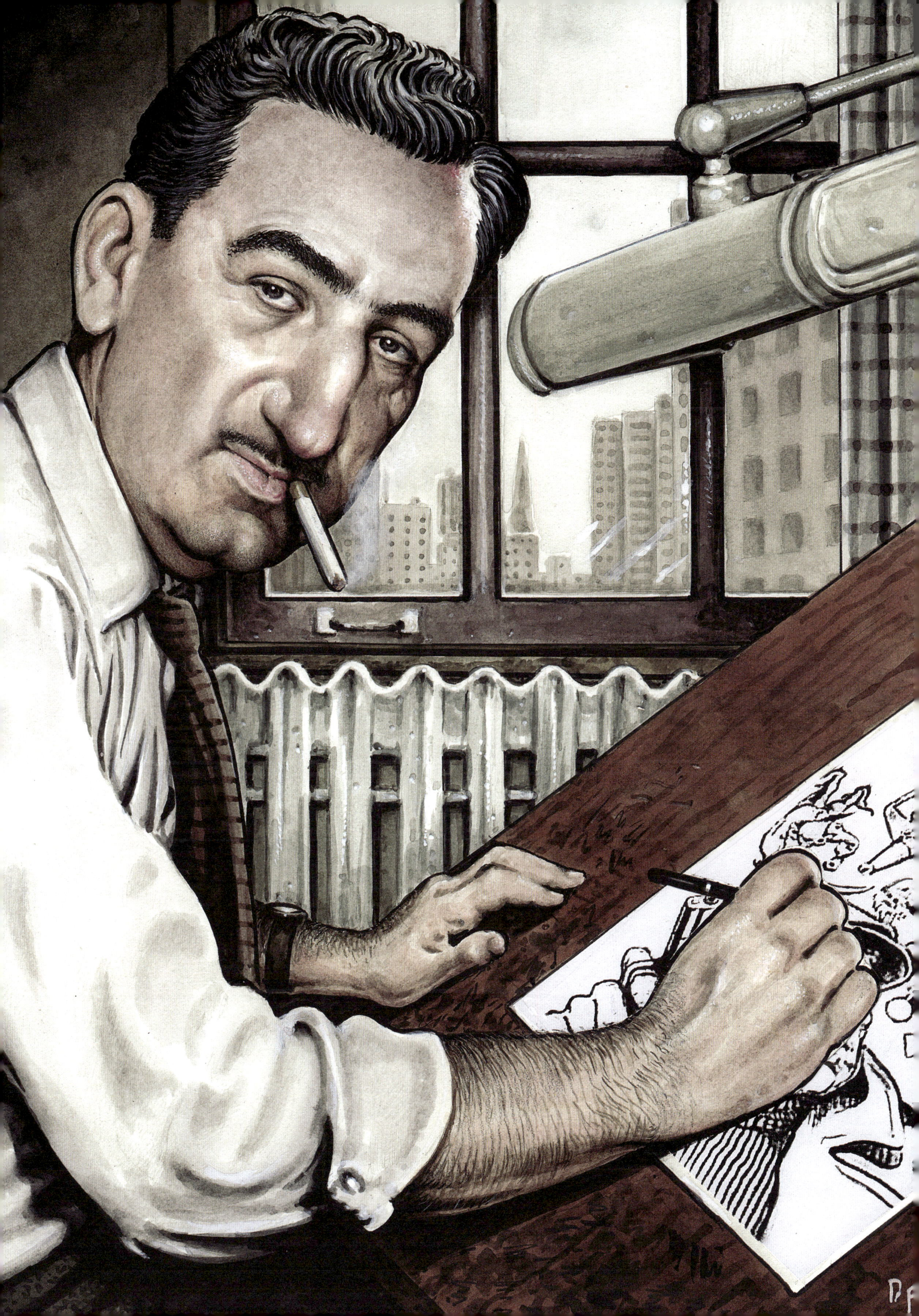

FRANK ROBBINS

1917–1994

plate 76

Franklin Robbins was born in Boston and showed artistic promise early on. When he was only nine, Robbins won a scholarship to study at Boston's Museum of Fine Arts. By the time he was eighteen, he had an impressive list of credentials, including assisting Edward Trumbull on murals for the National Broadcasting Company, and working as an illustrator for RKO Pictures.

In 1939, AP Newsfeatures asked twenty-two-year-old Robbins to take over the syndicated comic strip *Scorchy Smith* when artist Noel Sickles left amidst a financial dispute. After five years, he left to create his own aviation-themed strip, *Johnny Hazard*. He worked on *Johnny Hazard* for the next thirty-three years.

Early in his career, *Scorchy Smith* was reprinted in *Famous Funnies*, and Johnny Hazard appeared in his own comic book from Standard Comics in the late '40s. Aside from these two exceptions, Robbins had avoided comics for most of his career. However, in 1968, he made his debut as a comic book writer on *Superman's Girl Friend, Lois Lane* #83. He continued scripting flagship titles like *Superboy*, *Superman*, and *Detective Comics*. Robbins drew several issues of DC's revival of *The Shadow* before making the move to Marvel Comics in 1977.

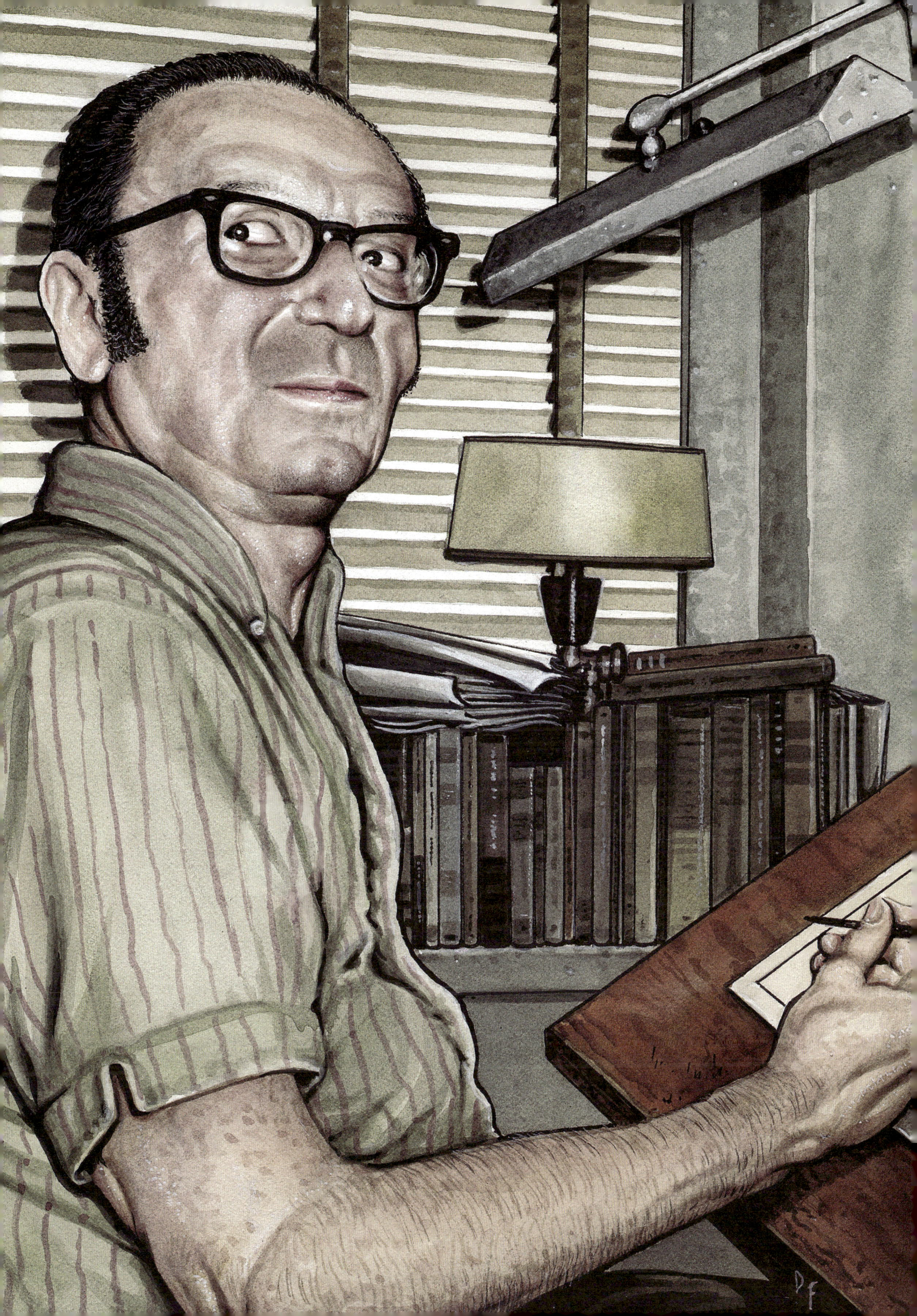

JOHN ROMITA

b. 1930

plate 77

John V. Romita was born in Brooklyn and graduated from the School of Industrial Art. He started drawing at an early age, carefully copying Joe Shuster panels from *Action Comics* #1.

In 1949, a chance encounter on the subway with inker Lester Zakarin led to Romita penciling an uncredited, ten-page story for Timely. Zakarin and Romita worked as a team again on Trojan Comics' *Crime-Smashers* and other titles, before he was drafted into the US Army in 1951. He was stationed in New York, and frequently dropped by Stan Lee's office at Atlas. His pencils and inks on "Out of My Mind" in *Astonishing* #7, published by Atlas in 1951, was probably his earliest solo work. In 1953, he worked on the short-lived revival of Captain America, drawing the six-page "Back from the Dead" in *Young Men* #24. Romita kept freelancing for Atlas on horror, romance, and war stories, until the company ran into financial troubles and shut down in 1957. He moved over to DC Comics the following year, and spent the better part of a decade working almost exclusively on romance titles. Romita had planned to leave DC for an advertising gig when Stan Lee offered to match the advertising agency's offer, and gave him the flexibility to work from home.

His first job at the new Marvel Comics was inking over Jack Kirby's pencils on *Daredevil* #12 in 1966. After seeing his work on a Daredevil story featuring Spider-Man, Lee picked Romita to succeed the departing Steve Ditko in *The Amazing Spider-Man* #39. The title became the company's top seller within a year of his taking over the title. He drew the series for almost fifty issues, and became Marvel's official art director in 1972.

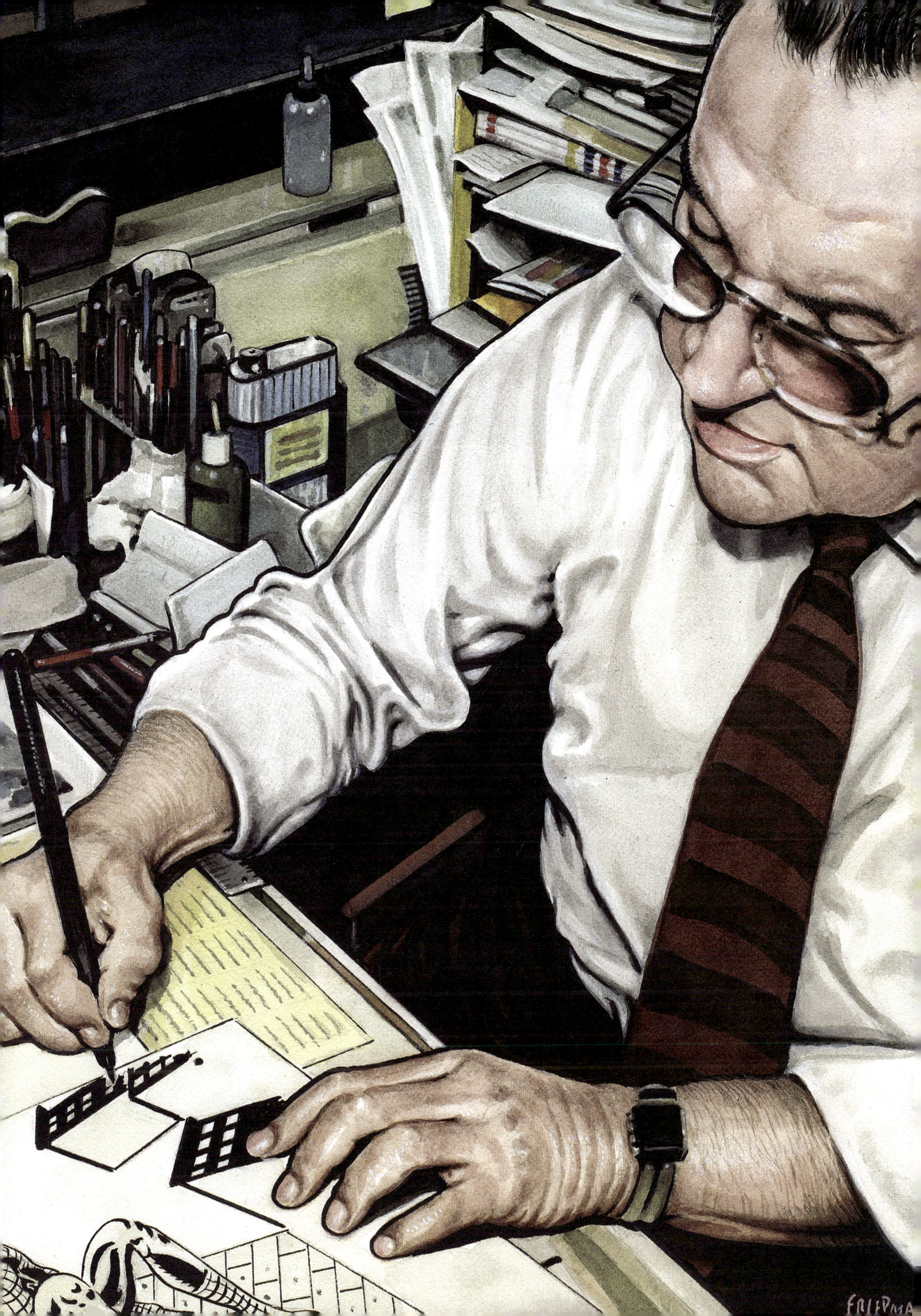

JOHN ROSENBERGER

1918–1977

plate 78

Born in Queens, New York, John Francis Rosenberger started drawing while confined to bed for two years with scarlet fever. In 1938 he began studying art at Pratt Institute.

In 1942, shortly after marrying comic book colorist Peggy Chapellier, he was drafted into the US Army. He was stationed in Washington DC and assigned the task of editing military magazine the *Specialist*.

In 1953, inspired by his war years, Rosenberger and writer Robert Bernstein created *Sands of the South Pacific* for Toby Press. Intended as an original series, the book only lasted a single issue. In the mid-'50s, his work was featured regularly in the pages of American Comics Group titles, like *Adventures into the Unknown*, *Forbidden Worlds*, *My Romantic Adventures*, and others.

He started the '60s at Archie Comics working on *The Fly* and a revival of *The Shadow*. Rosenberger and Bernstein also created the *Adventures of the Jaguar* for Archie. He started working for DC Comics on romance titles in 1963, and two years later drew his first superhero story—featuring Wonder Woman and Supergirl—for *The Brave and the Bold* #63. He continued at DC for a decade, working on *Superman's Girl Friend Lois Lane*, *Wonder Woman*, and a long list of romance titles.

Rosenberger left DC in 1974 and spent a year penciling *The Phantom* newspaper strip. He was already ill with cancer in 1975 when he accepted an assignment penciling *Wonder Woman* #217. He only completed four pages of the book before turning it over to another artist.

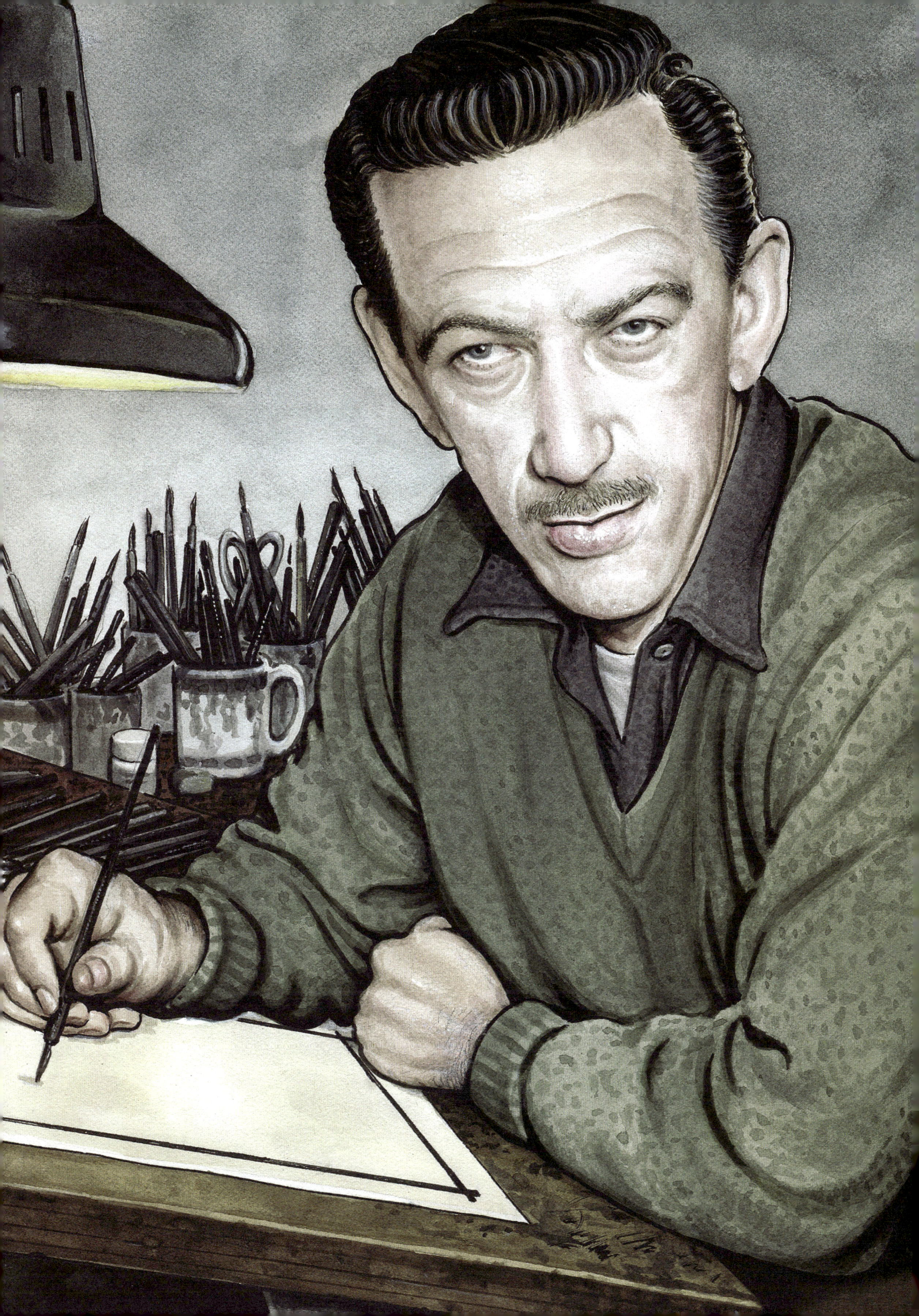

KURT SCHAFFENBERGER

1920-2002

plate 79

Kurt Schaffenberger and his family left their farm in the German village of Zella-Mehlis for West Hartford, Connecticut, where his father became a toolmaker for the Royal Typewriter Company.

Schaffenberger graduated from Pratt Institute in New York, and, in June of 1941, joined Jack Binder's studio in New Jersey. His first professional work was filling in backgrounds on a Captain Marvel story. Before World War II interceded, he contributed to other Fawcett titles like *Bulletman* and *Ibis.*

After the war (and a stint in the Office of Strategic Services), he returned to comics, working on Fawcett's Marvel Family line, notably taking over Mac Raboy's *Captain Marvel Jr.* in 1944.

In 1957, Otto Binder brought Schaffenberger to DC, where he spent the next thirty years contributing to various Superman-related titles. He spent a decade as lead artist on *Superman's Girl Friend, Lois Lane,* where his clean, crisp style became a fan favorite.

In 1970, DC severed ties with Schaffenberger after he organized artists to protest poor working conditions. He worked briefly on Marvel romance titles before leaving comics to focus on commercial illustration. His exile ended in 1972, when DC brought him back for the relaunch of Captain Marvel.

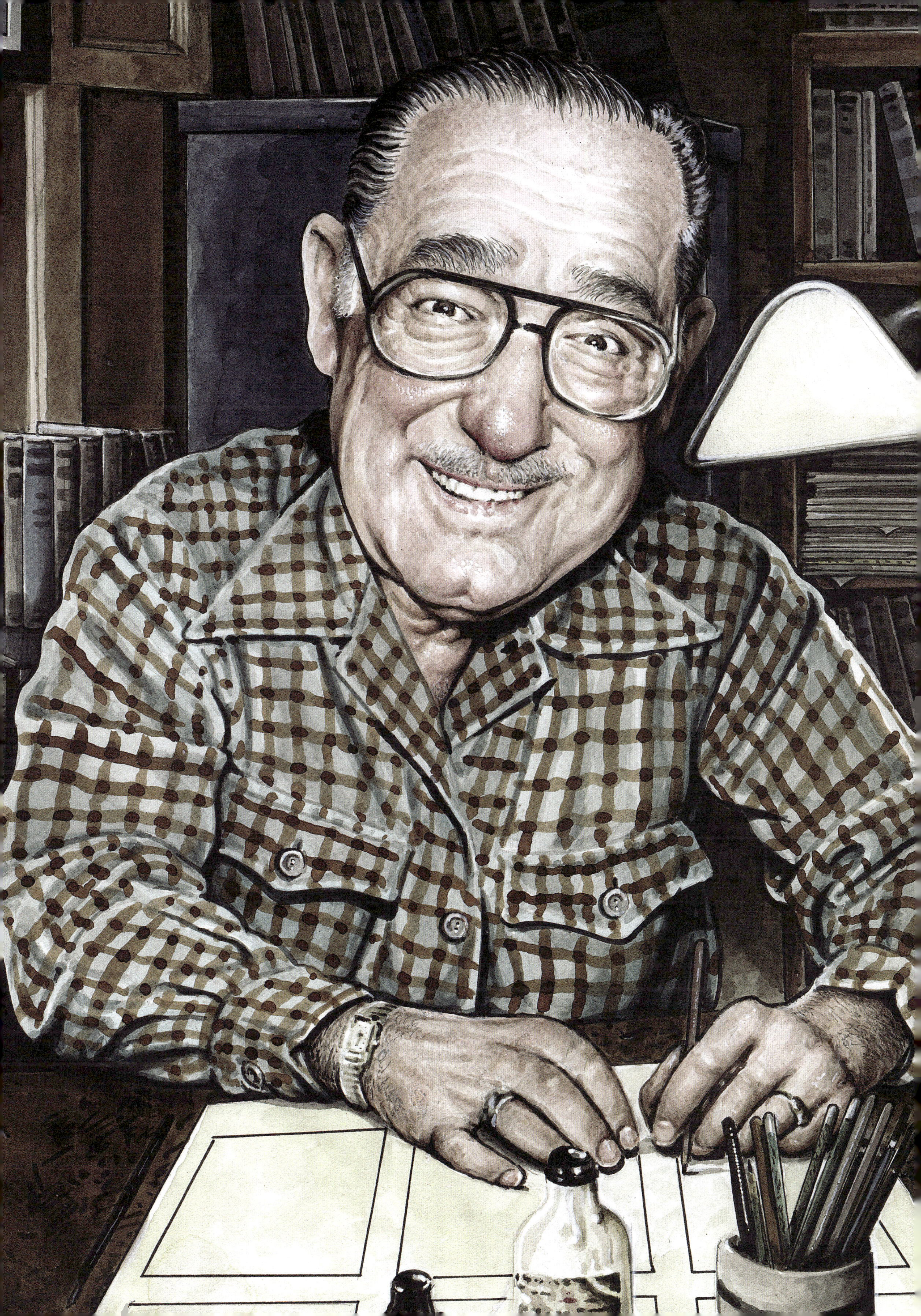

IRA SCHNAPP

1892–1969

plate 80

Born in Austria, Ira Schnapp emigrated to the United States with his family when he was eighteen. Trained as an engraver and stonecutter, Schnapp utilized those skills shortly after his arrival in the States. In 1914, Schnapp designed and hand-carved the post office motto ("Neither snow nor rain nor heat nor gloom of night stays these couriers from the swift completion of their appointed rounds") on the facade of New York's main post office across from Penn Station. He did similar work for facade of the main branch of the New York Public Library. Before entering the world of comic book publishing, he also designed lobby cards for movie theaters and silent movie titles.

By 1934, Schnapp was working as a designer for pulp magazines. In 1938, he began his long association with DC Comics. For his first logo for *Superman* #6, he refined Joe Shuster's original lettering into the gently curved, perspective logo that has been adapted for comics, film, and television projects ever since. Schnapp also designed the familiar DC logos for *Green Lantern, The Flash, Aquaman,* and *Justice League of America,* among many others. He was also responsible for designing the familiar stamp-like logo of the Comics Code Authority that began appearing on virtually every mainstream comic since 1958. Sadly, Ira Schnapp was rarely credited for his work. He retired to Florida in 1968.

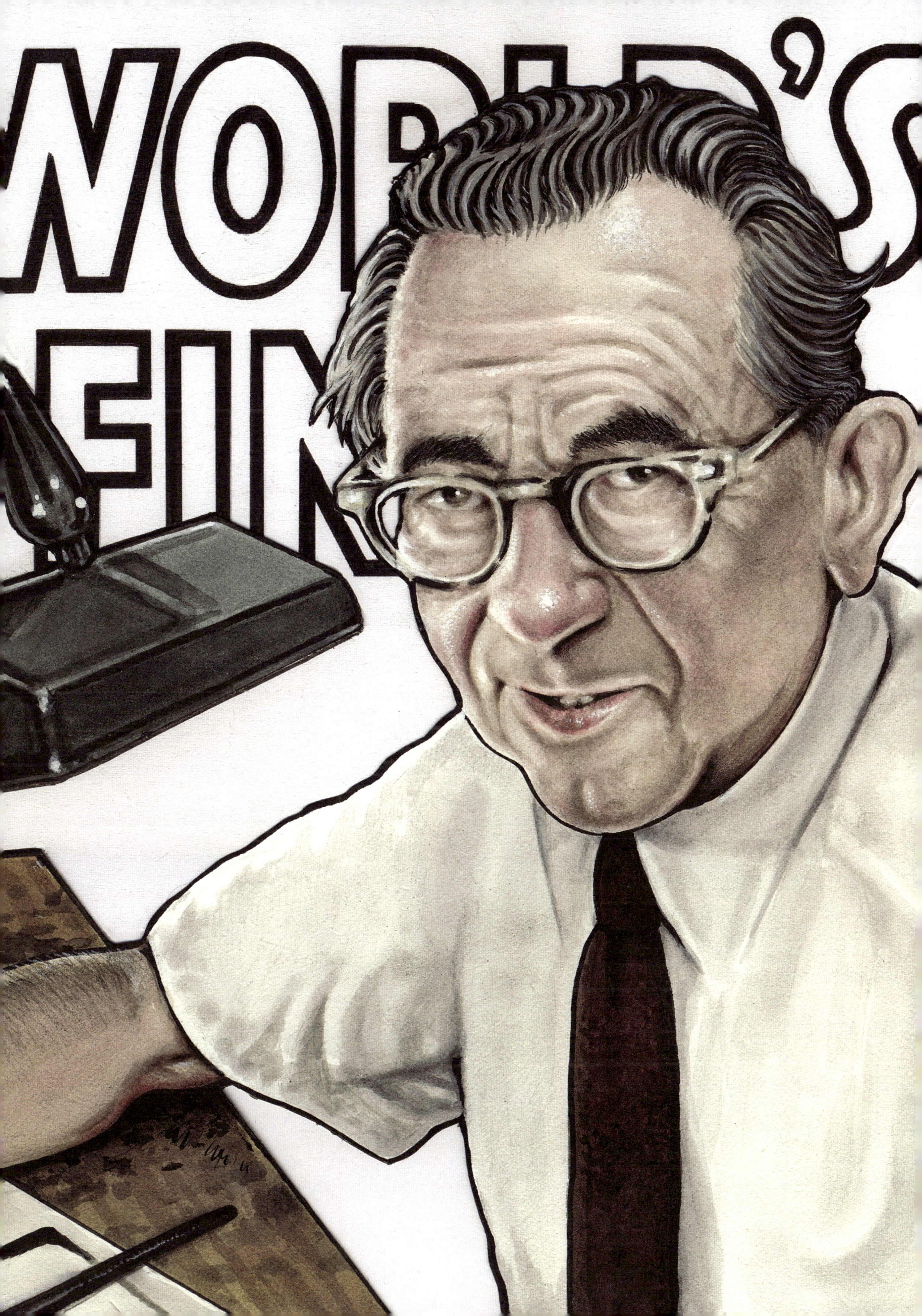

JULIUS SCHWARTZ

1915-2004

plate 81

Julius "Julie" Schwartz was born in the Bronx and graduated Theodore Roosevelt High School at age sixteen. Schwartz attended City College of New York.

In 1931, Schwartz contacted fellow science fiction enthusiast Mort Weisinger after seeing Weisinger's name in the letters column in *Amazing Stories*. By 1932, Schwartz and Weisinger, along with another future editor, Forrest J. Ackerman, would publish one of the earliest science fiction fanzines, *Time Traveler*.

Schwartz and Weisinger joined forces again two years later, forming Solar Sales Service, a literary agency devoted exclusively to representing science fiction and fantasy writers. He and Weisinger became author Ray Bradbury's first agents. Schwartz was an active member of early fandom, helping to organize the first science fiction convention in 1939.

Schwartz became an editor at All-American Comics in 1944, shortly before the company was purchased by National Periodicals and became DC Comics. He would remain there as editor for the next forty-five years.

In 1956, Schwartz helped breathe new life into the then moribund superhero genre, presiding over Robert Kanigher and Carmine Infantino's update of the Flash in *Showcase* #4. By the end of the decade, he used the same template to bring back other Golden Age characters, such as Green Lantern, Hawkman, and the Atom.

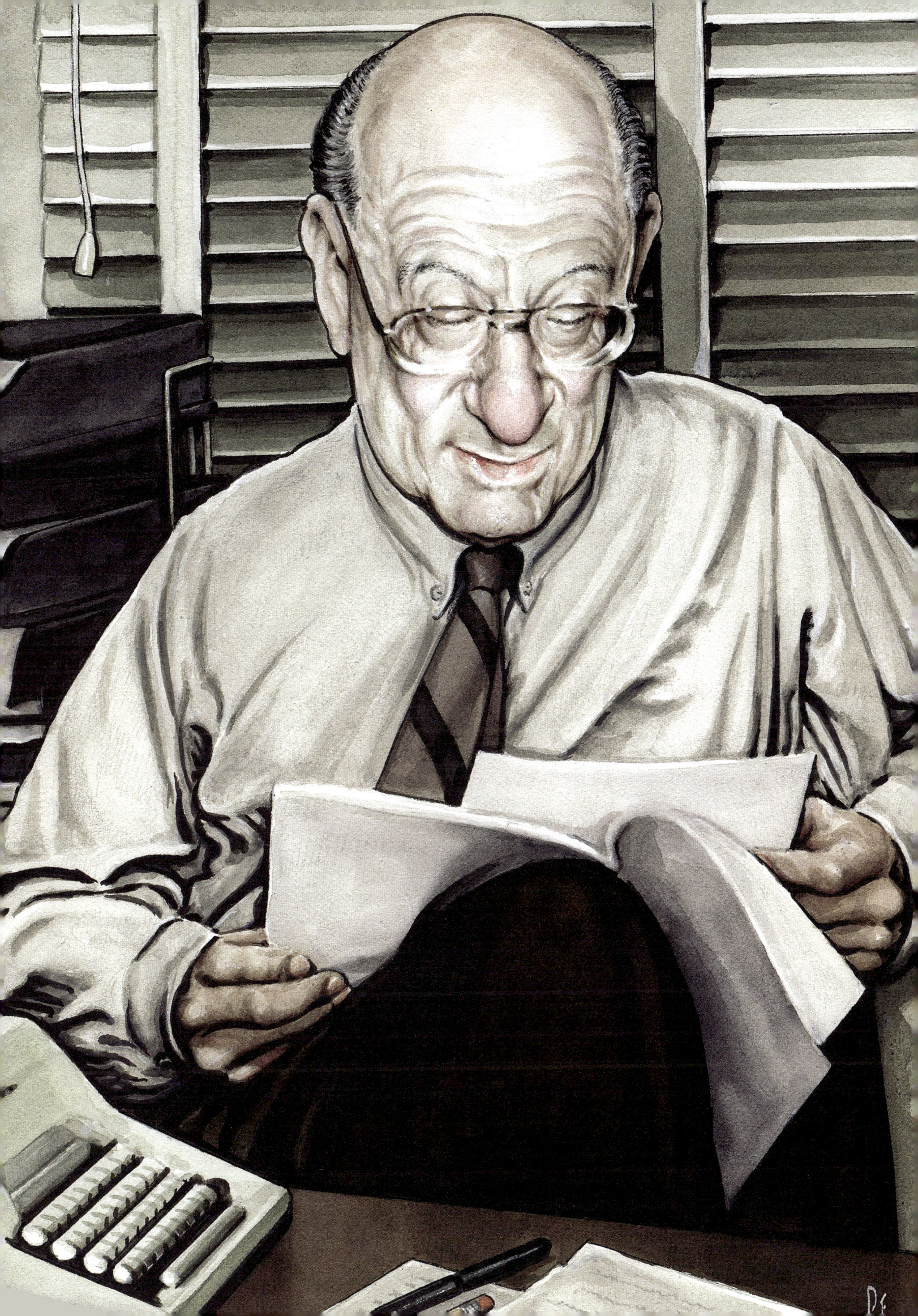

MIKE SEKOWSKY

1923–1989

plate **82**

Michael Sekowsky was born in New York and attended the High School of Art and Design. He got his start working uncredited as an inker and occasional penciler on gag cartoons and one-page fillers. His earliest signed work is penciling for an eight-page story, "A Fight to the Death," in Timely's *Mystic Comics* #7 in late 1941.

For most of the '40s, Sekowsky was a frequent contributor to Timely's teen-oriented humor comics, with long runs on *Willie Comics*, *Georgie Comics*, and *Patsy Walker*. He also worked on *The Human Torch* and *Captain America*. In the '50s, his work could be seen on everything, from war titles like *Young Men on the Battlefield* to romance books, like *My Own Romance*. In the mid-'50s, he contributed to Dell's ubiquitous television tie-ins like *Captain Kangaroo*, *The Life of Riley*, and *Peter Gunn*.

He also began working for DC Comics in the early '50s, initially on romance and science fiction titles. He is credited with drawing the debut of Adam Strange in *Showcase* #17 in 1958, and co-creating the Justice League of America in 1960.

In 1968, Sekowsky and writer Denny O'Neil were given the task of modernizing the twenty-seven-year-old title *Wonder Woman*. Sekowsky traded Wonder Woman's leggy, patriotic costume for a pantsuit and mod go-go boots. Wonder Woman surrendered her powers, learned martial arts, and became involved in espionage and running a fashion boutique.

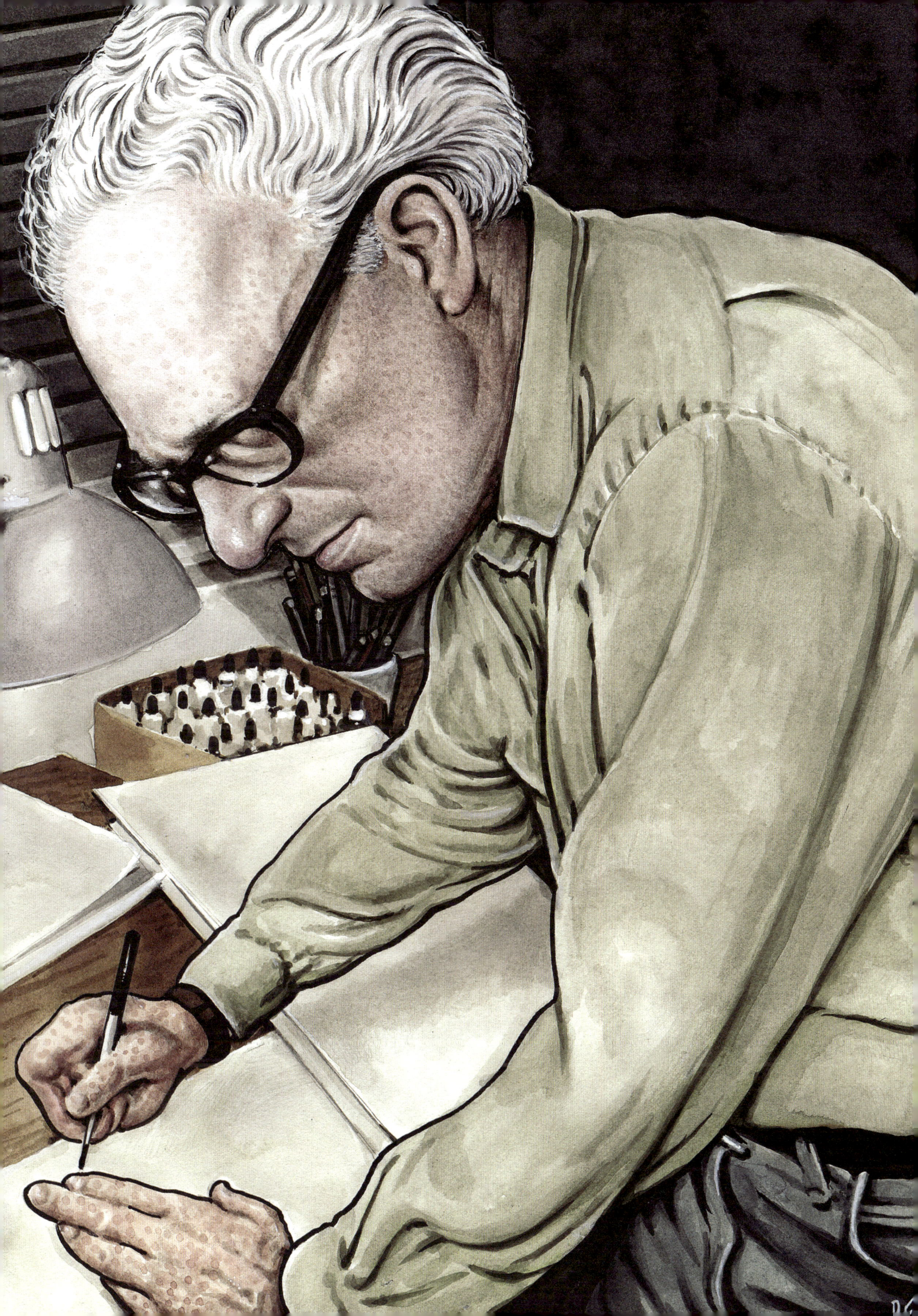

JOE SINNOTT

b. 1926

plate
83

Born in Saugerties, New York, Joe Sinnott grew up with a love for adventure comics, especially *Terry and the Pirates*. Sinnott spent three years in the US Army and, in 1949, took advantage of the GI Bill. He made his way to New York's Cartoonists and Illustrators School. He was still a student when he published his first professional comic book work, a five-page filler, "Trudi," that appeared in St. John Publications' *Mopsy* #12. He began assisting his Cartoonist and Illustrators instructor, Tom Gill, who drew adaptations of TV westerns *The Lone Ranger* and *Cheyenne* for Dell Comics. Soon after, Gill was inking over Sinnott's pencils on Atlas Comics titles like *Kent Blake of the Secret Service*.

Starting in 1951, Sinnott spent the next six years working with Stan Lee at Atlas, easily moving among western, horror, and the occasional romance title. Sinnott appeared in *Arrowhead*, *War Comics*, *Adventures into Terror*, and many others. When Atlas began having financial troubles and assignments slowed down, he did freelance illustration work for an encyclopedia publisher, and the Catholic school periodical *Treasure Chest*.

As Atlas transformed into Marvel Comics, Sinnott paired off with Jack Kirby on several western and horror tales. Kirby and Sinnott's first published collaboration was "Doom Under the Deep" in *Battle* #69 in April 1960. Although he was still working on occasional projects for publishers Charlton and Dell, Sinnott would be an almost constant presence at Marvel, starting with *Fantastic Four* #44 in 1965. He would spend the next thirty years working for the company.

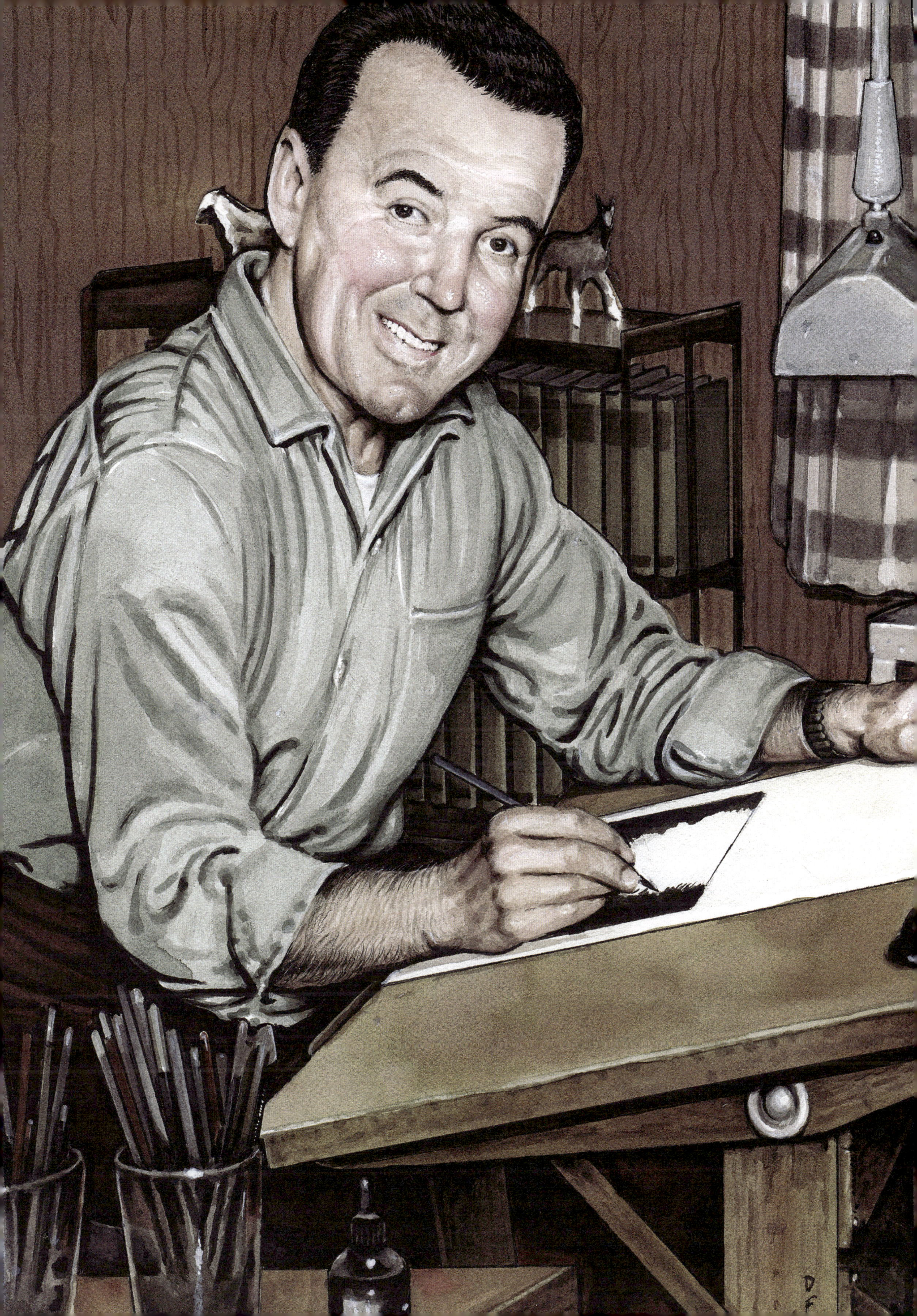

DAN SPIEGLE

b. 1920

plate 84

Dan Spiegle was born in Cosmopolis, Wisconsin, and lived in Hawaii before settling down and attending high school in California. After leaving the US Navy in 1946, Spiegle attended Chouinard Art Institute. Spiegle was picked by actor Bill Boyd to illustrate the syndicated comic strip version of his alter ego, *Hopalong Cassidy*. He drew the strip for the next six years.

Spiegle's first comic book work was an advertisement for Wheaties cereal in *Walt Disney's Comics and Stories*, published by Dell in 1952. His earliest confirmed story was in 1956. He penciled and inked the eight-page "The Bushwacker," published in Dell's *Annie Oakley and Tagg* #7.

Spiegle's career at Dell gained momentum quickly. He started drawing lighthearted westerns based on film and television properties, like *Gene Autry* and *Spin and Marty*. Soon, he was adapting everything from *My Favorite Martian*, to *The Parent Trap*, to Jerry Lewis's film *Don't Give Up the Ship*, in Dell's monthly anthology series, *Four Color*. For Gold Key, he worked on *Space Family Robinson*, *Magnus Robot Fighter 4000 A.D.*, and *Tarzan*. He also excelled at drawing comic book versions of Saturday morning cartoons, like Hanna-Barbera's *Scooby Doo*.

Spiegle remained active in comic books until well into his 70s.

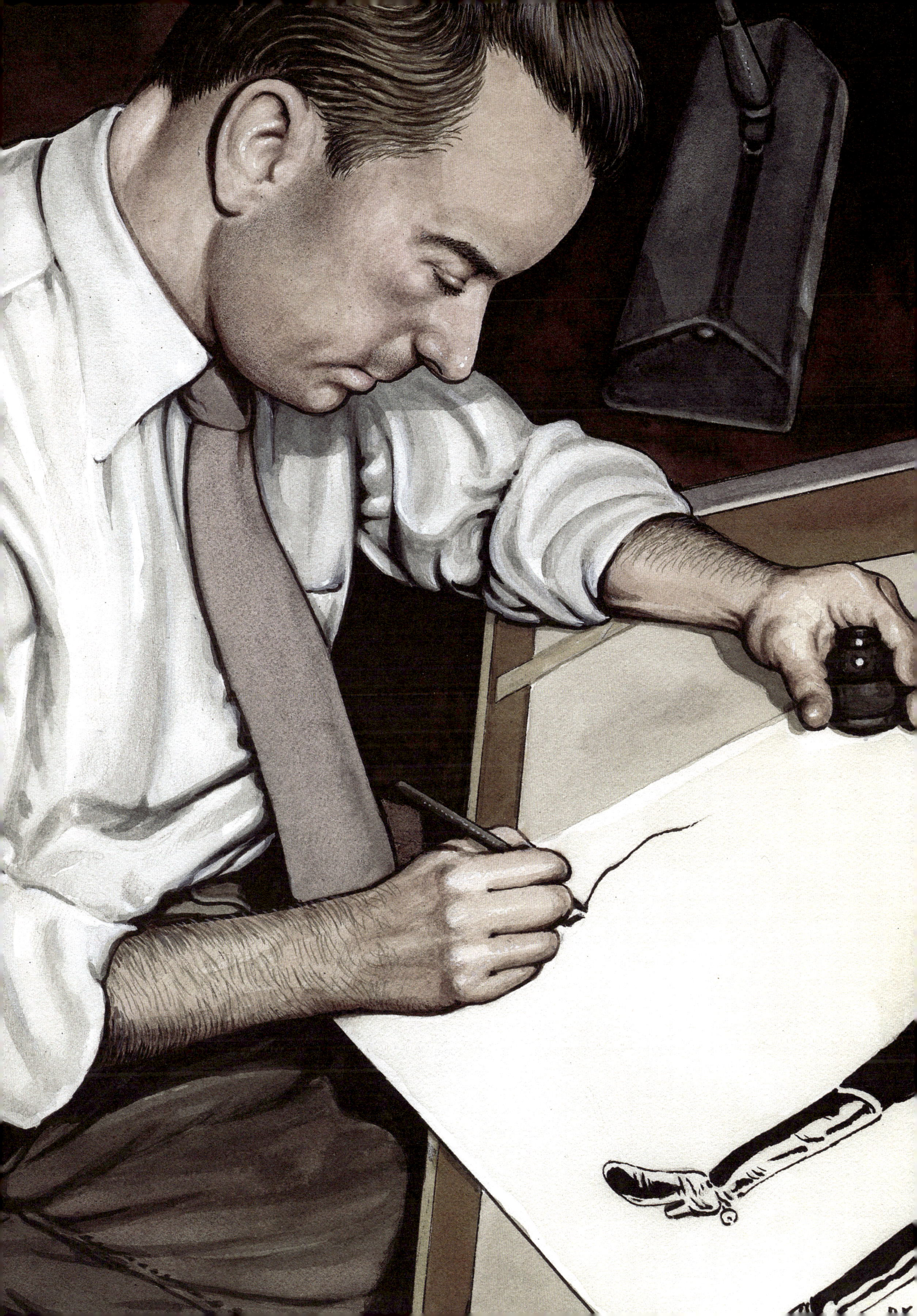

MICKEY SPILLANE

1918-2006

plate 85

Frank Morrison Spillane was the son of a Brooklyn bartender. Even before graduating from Erasmus Hall High School, Spillane managed to sell an occasional pulp story—but earned considerably more from his part-time job as a lifeguard.

After a brief stint at Fort Hays State College in Kansas, Spillane returned to New York and found work writing and editing comic books at Lloyd Jacquet's Funnies Inc. Jacquet was putting together artists and writers to create books for publishers like Martin Goodman's Timely. Spillane could churn out a comic book script in a single day, a job that typically took lesser mortals a week. Spillane scripted gritty and violent stories for *Sub-Mariner*, *Captain America*, and *Human Torch*, and also penned many of the two-page text stories comic books required to qualify for mass mailing rates by arcane Post Office regulations.

Shortly after the bombing of Pearl Harbor, Spillane joined the Army Air Force, and spent the war years stateside as a flight instructor. After the war ended, Spillane returned to Brooklyn and began his own comic book production operation. In 1946, bored with the constraints of creating stories for superheroes, Spillane created tough-talking private eye Mike Danger. When Danger failed to attract the interest of publishers or newspaper syndicates, Spillane announced he would use the character in a novel. Less than twenty days later, Spillane finished *I, the Jury*, which featured a dark and violent P.I., now rechristened Mike Hammer. Spillane's books, featuring Hammer and others, went on to sell more than 200 million copies. He's forever immortalized in the Paddy Chayefsky TV play, *Marty*, with the line "Boy, that Mickey Spillane can write."

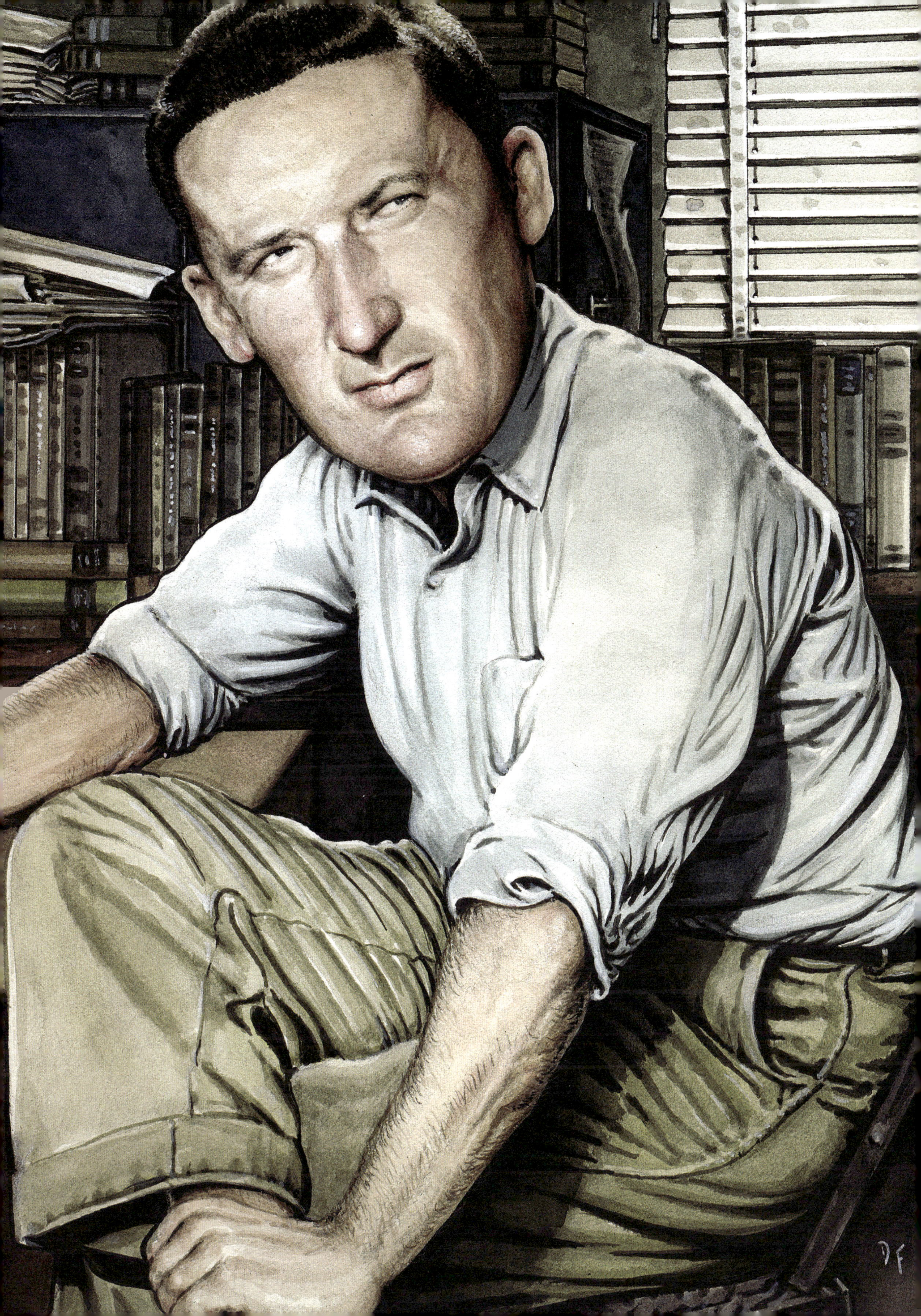

CHIC STONE

1923-2000

plate 86

New York native Charles Eber Stone studied at the School of Industrial Art and broke into comic book business in 1939 at age sixteen with an apprenticeship at the Eisner & Iger shop. By 1940, he was penciling and inking backup stories like "Jeep Joins the Army" in Timely's *U. S. A. Comics* #6. He also drew romance and crime for titles like Ace Magazine's *Real Love* and *Men Against Crime*.

Shortly after a stretch at Charlton drawing *My Little Margie*, Stone switched careers as the comic book business went into decline in the mid-'50s. He drew storyboards and worked for an advertising agency, eventually moving to Hollywood to become the art director of *Modern Teen* magazine.

Stone rejoined comics in 1963, drawing horror and romance titles for American Comics and DC. A chance meeting with Stan Lee in 1964 led to him becoming Jack Kirby's primary inker on Marvel centerpieces like *Journey into Mystery*, *Fantastic Four*, and *The Avengers*. He teamed up with Kirby for most of the '60s, leaving in 1971 to work on Skywald Publishing horror magazine *Psycho*, as well as Archie Comics' superhero imprint Red Circle. Stone returned to Marvel several times over the next two decades.

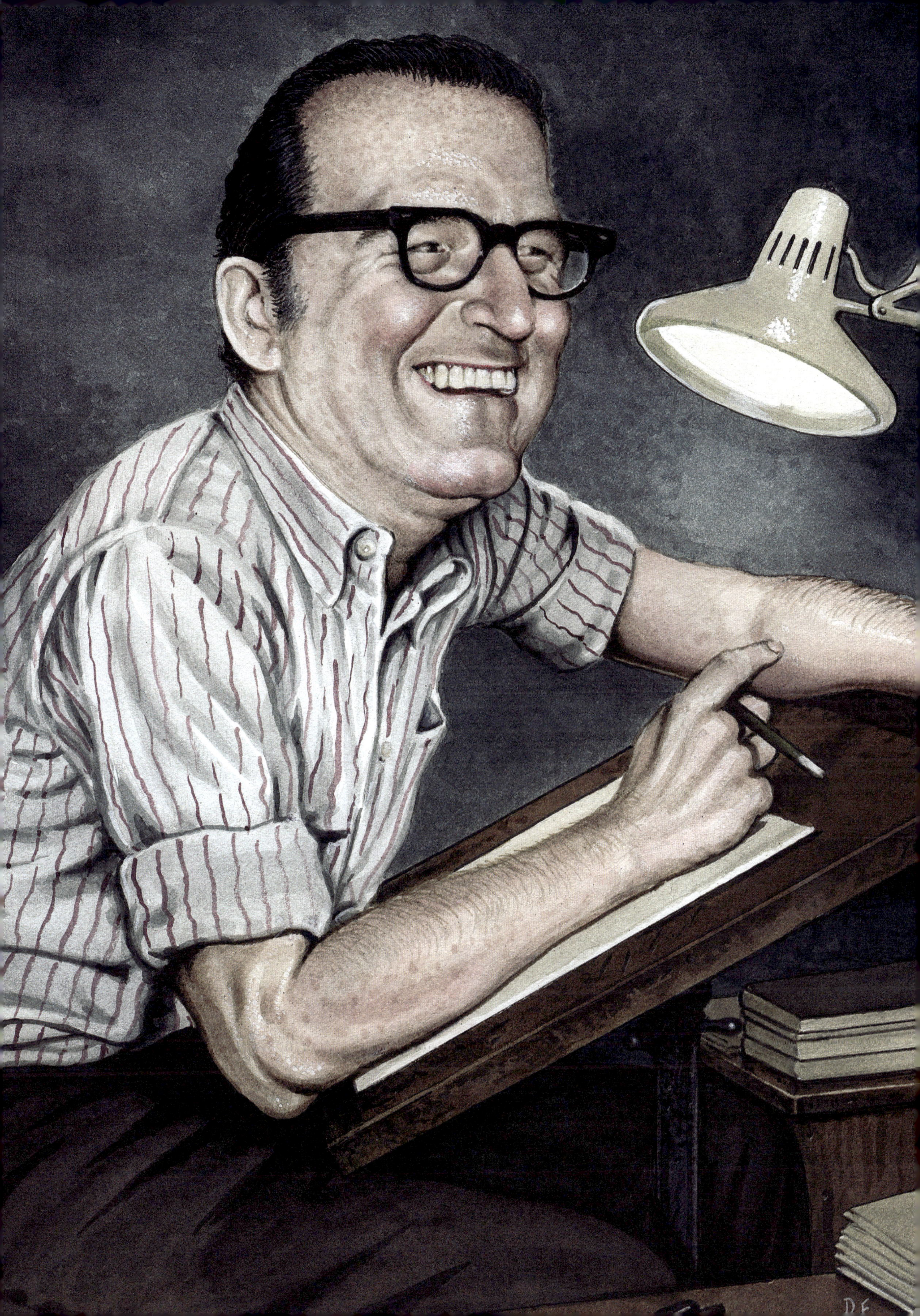

VIN SULLIVAN

1911-1999

plate 87

Vincent Sullivan was born in Brooklyn. National Allied Publications' Major Malcolm Wheeler-Nicholson hired Sullivan in 1934 to work as an assistant editor on an anthology comic book, *New Fun Comics / More Fun*. By 1937, Sullivan was creating artwork and handling several other titles, including *Detective Comics*, which featured a sinister Asian villain on its very first cover, and *Adventure Comics*, while preparing to launch a new title, *Action Comics*.

Jerry Siegel and Joe Shuster had worked for Sullivan on features like *Slam Bradley* and *Doctor Occult*. The two were in the process of shopping around an idea for a syndicated strip that Sullivan thought might be a good fit for *Action Comics*.

Sullivan paid Siegel and Shuster $130 for their thirteen-page story "Superman" and made it the lead feature in *Action* #1. The following year, Superman became the first comic book character to get his own title when *Superman* #1 hit the stands.

After the huge success of Superman became apparent, Sullivan asked artist Bob Kane to come up with something along the same lines. Kane's Batman, (scripted by Bill Finger), appeared in *Detective Comics* #27 and quickly became a sensation.

Sullivan left the company for upstart Columbia Comics in 1943. In 1947, Siegel and Shuster created their short-lived comeback character, Funnyman, for Sullivan, who was working as a comics editor for Magazine Enterprises.

Sullivan exited the comic book business for good in 1958. In 1998, sixty years after he helped launch an industry, the eighty-seven-year-old Sullivan attended his first comic book convention.

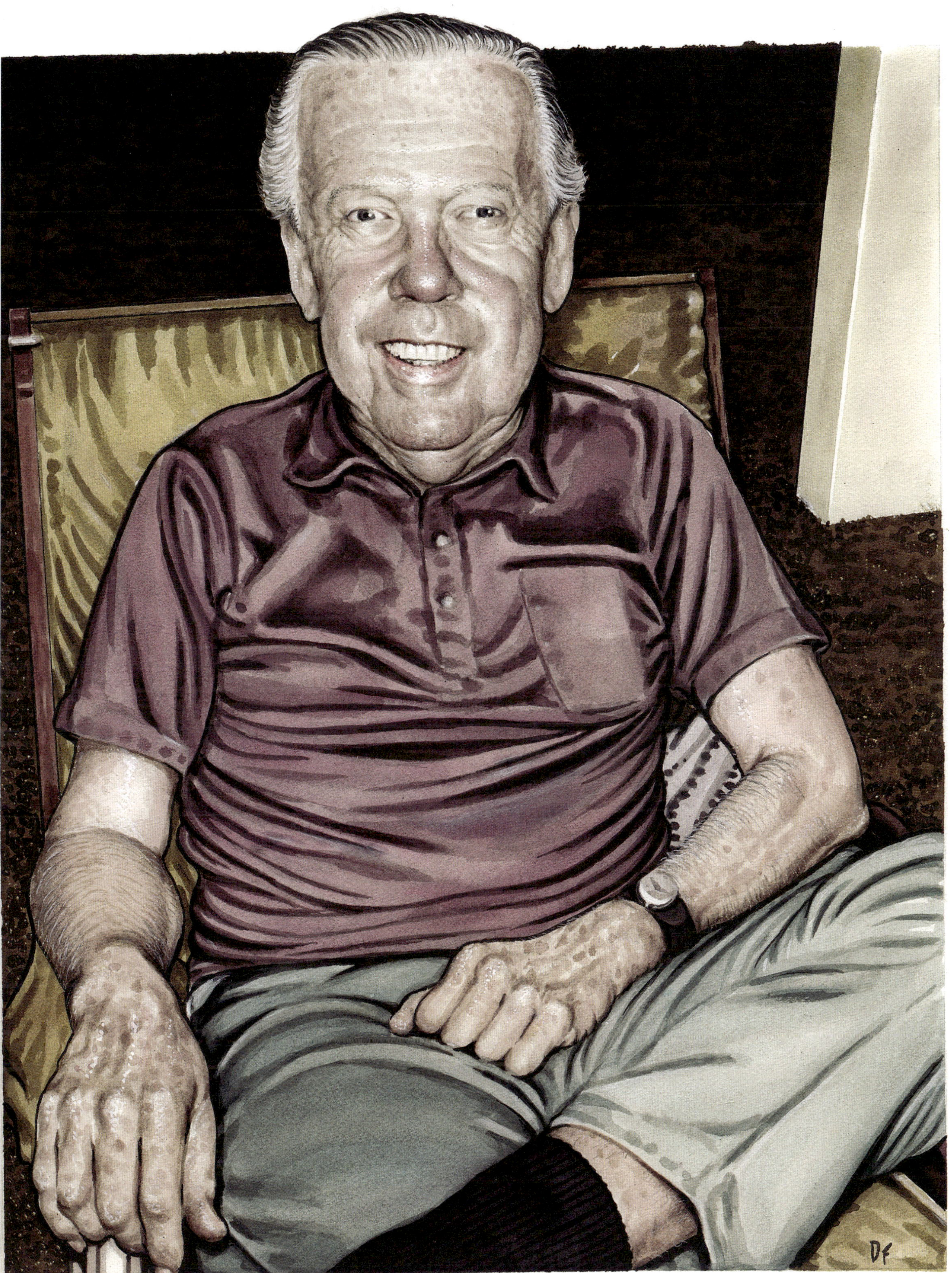

CURT SWAN

1920-1996

plate 88

Born in Willmar, Minnesota, Curt Swan worked at a Sears and Roebuck warehouse after graduating high school. He spent two years in the National Guard before joining the US Army in 1940. Swan eventually found himself in Europe, drawing maps and illustrations for the military newspaper *Stars and Stripes*. After the war, a *Stars and Stripes* colleague who had worked at DC Comics suggested Swan contact editor Whitney Ellsworth. After a brief meeting with Ellsworth, Swan left with a job drawing *Boy Commandos* for $18 a page.

Swan penciled his first *Superman* story in 1949. In 1955, he replaced artist Wayne Boring, who had been squabbling with editor Mort Weisinger over money. He created a modern, mid-century version of the Man of Steel, toning down his angular, lantern jaw and bringing some grace to his previously rigid flying scenes. His Superman became a particular fan favorite, and was said to be the model for Richard Donner's 1978 *Superman* film.

Swan's last Superman story was a nostalgic 1986 collaboration with Alan Moore, *Whatever Happened to the Man of Tomorrow?*

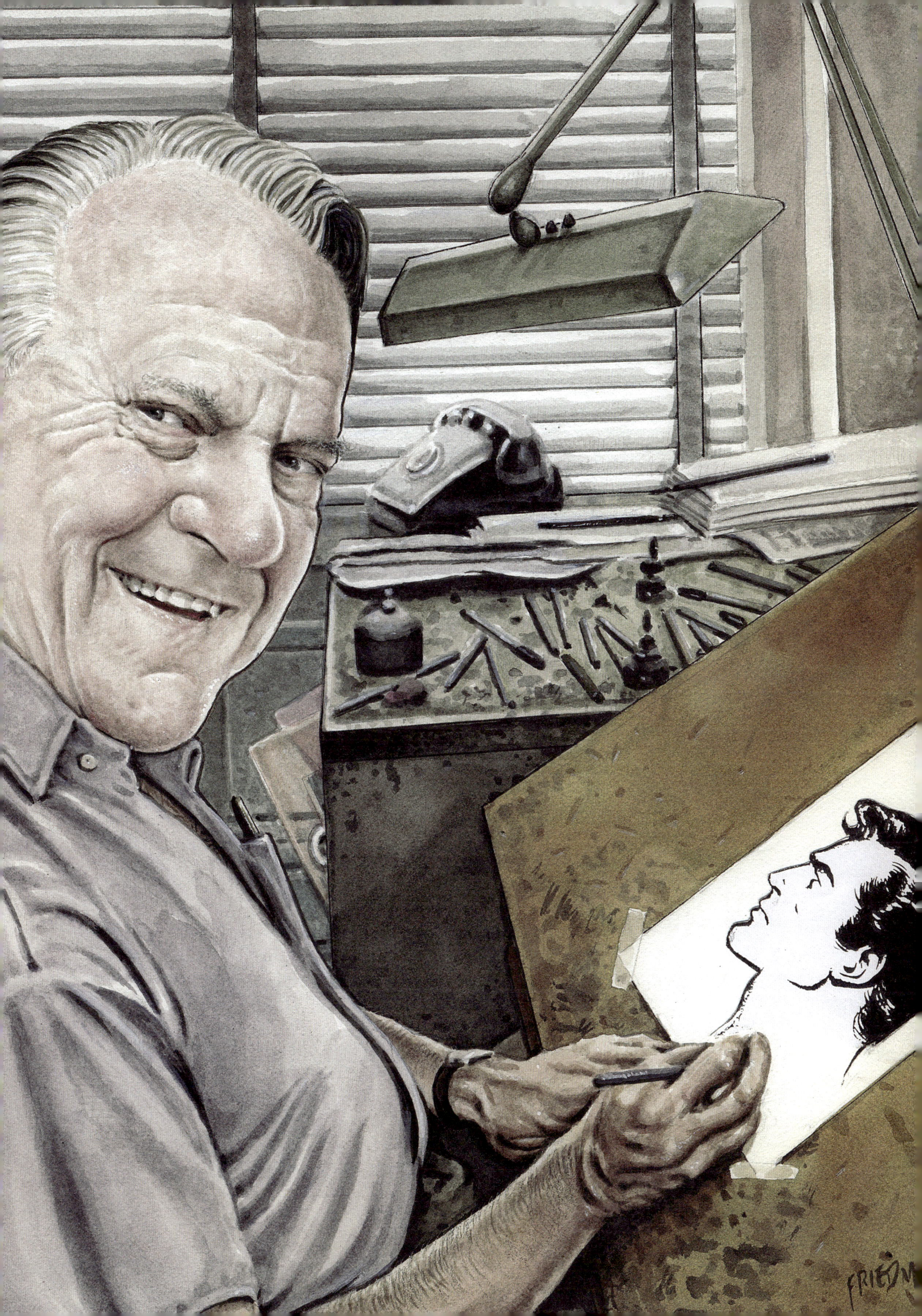

MARC SWAYZE

1913–2012

plate 89

Marcus Desha Swayze was a native of Monroe, Louisiana. Swayze came to comic books with a master's degree from Louisiana University, where he also taught art classes. Swayze's first professional comics work was in 1939, as an assistant on Russell Keaton's syndicated newspaper strip *Flyin' Jenny.* Swayze joined Fawcett Comics in 1942, drawing and writing for *Captain Marvel Adventures* and *Whiz Comics* and co-creating Mary Marvel. During World War II, he was drafted into the US Army. While stationed in Fort Oglethorpe, Georgia, Swayze found time to entertain the troops, playing guitar alongside Bing Crosby on two occasions. During his army service, he continued to write scripts for *Captain Marvel.*

After the war, Swayze rejoined Fawcett as a freelancer, working from his home in Monroe, Louisiana, contributing art and scripts to *Mary Marvel* and the *Phantom Eagle.* When his mentor, Russell Keaton, became ill, he took over art duties on Keaton's *Flyin' Jenny* Sunday page. Keaton died soon after and Swayze, with writer Glenn Chaffin, tried to keep the property alive, but the postwar years proved a tough market for the aviator-themed comic strip. Swayze left comics books for good after a brief stint at Charlton in the late 1950s.

In 1994, at age eighty-three, Marc Swayze made his debut as columnist for Roy Thomas's magazine *Alter Ego,* chronicling his comic book career in *We Didn't Know It Was the Golden Age!*

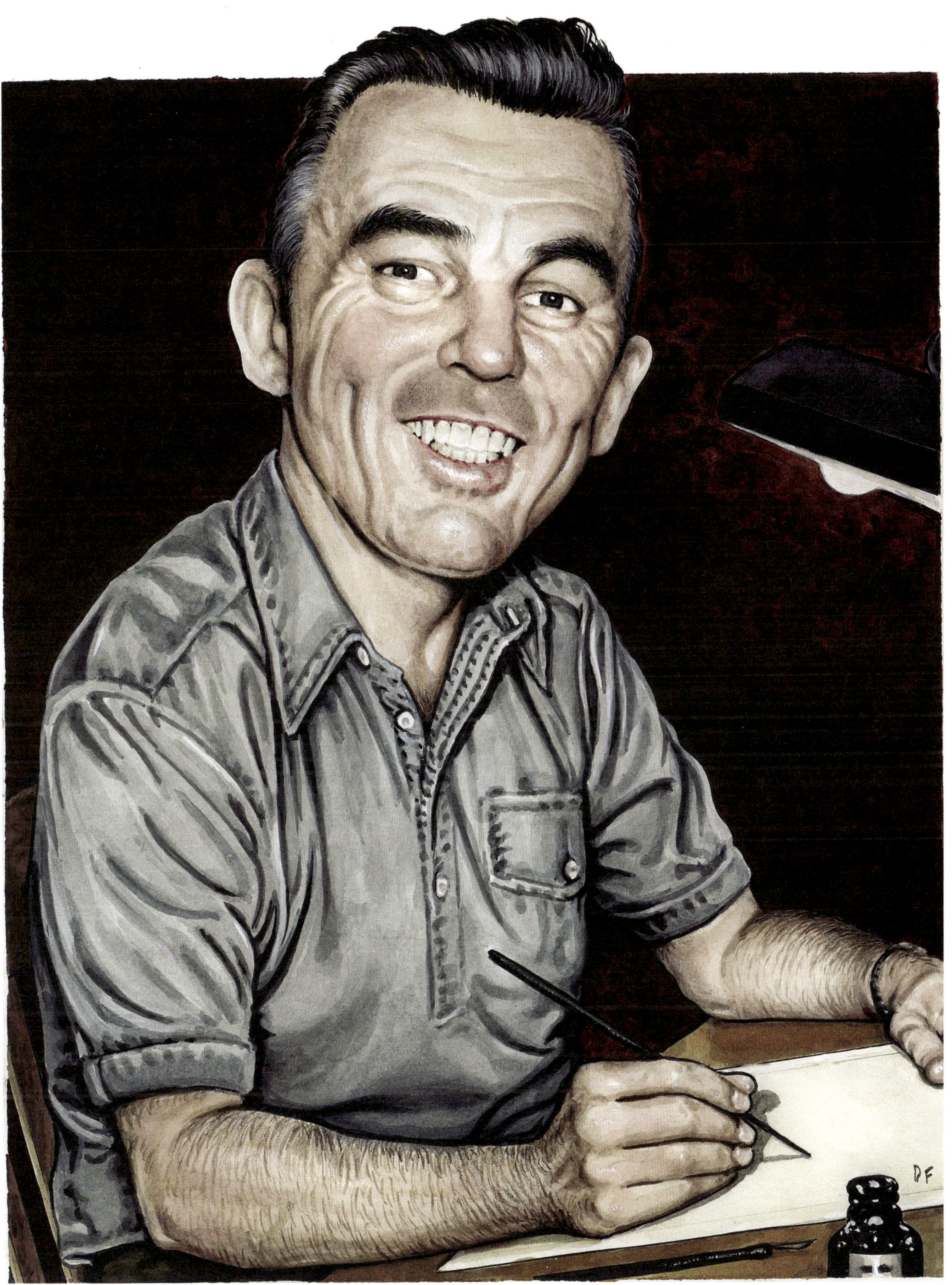
DF

JOHN TARTAGLIONE

1921-2003

plate 90

Born in Brooklyn, John Tartaglione attended the Pratt Institute and the Traphagen School of Fashion.

Tartaglione's earliest signed work was penciling and inking a six-page crime story, "The Mad Monk," published in Timely's *Amazing Detective Cases* #6 in 1951. Soon after, he started making frequent appearances in Timely's romance books like *Love Romances*, *My Own Romances*, and *My Love Story*. With Timely in disarray near the end of the decade, he started working on romance titles for Charlton, as well as *Classics Illustrated* adaptations like "Tom Brown's School Days." His work can also be seen in Dell adaptations of *Jason and the Argonauts*, *Beach Blanket Bingo*, and *Dr. Kildare*.

Tartaglione carved out a special niche for himself when he illustrated the biographical comics *John F. Kennedy Life Story* and *Lyndon B. Johnson* for Dell Comics in 1964. Soon after, he landed back at the Marvel bullpen, working mostly as an inker on titles like *Daredevil*.

In 1982 Marvel enlisted him to draw *The Life of Pope John Paul II*, which went on to sell millions of copies worldwide. In 1984, he was chosen for another ambitious one shot, *Mother Teresa of Calcutta*.

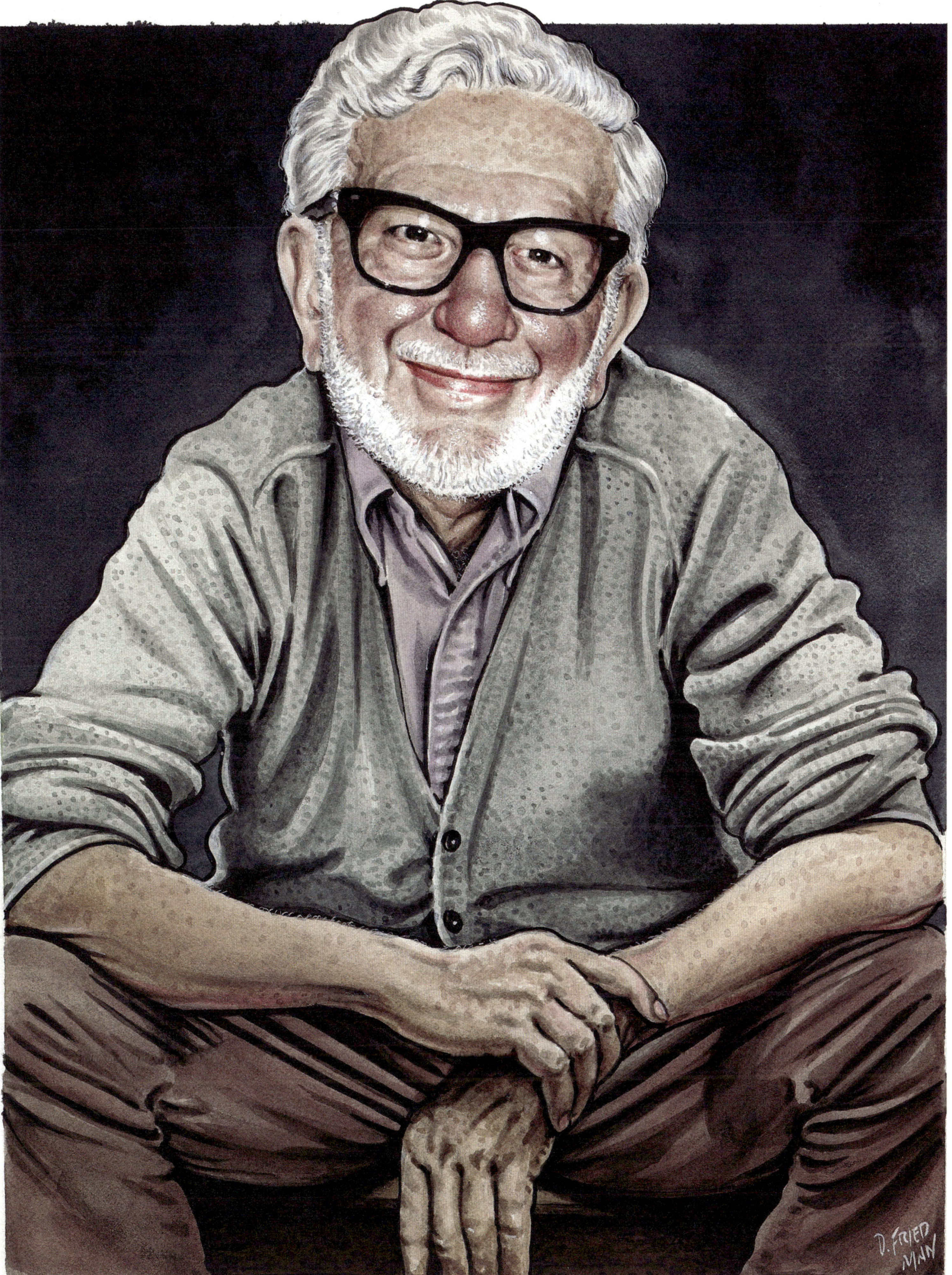

ANGELO TORRES

b. 1932

plate 91

Born in Santurce, Puerto Rico, and raised in New York City, Angelo Torres graduated from the School of Industrial Art in 1951. After spending two years in the Army, Torres studied at the Cartoonists and Illustrators School. Torres's earliest comic book work was assisting Al Williamson on EC titles like *Valor,* alongside Roy Krenkel and Frank Frazetta. Torres penciled and inked a solo story, "An Eye for an Eye," that was slated for publication in EC's *Incredible Science Fiction* #33, but the Comics Code Authority deemed it unfit for print. "An Eye for an Eye" was finally published sixteen years later in Nostalgia Press's EC comics hardcover *Horror Comics of the 1950's.*

After the demise of EC's horror line, Torres contributed to *Classics Illustrated* special issues, and various mystery and horror titles for Atlas. Torres became a mainstay of Warren Publishing's horror line, starting with the first issue of *Creepy* in 1965 and continuing in *Eerie* and *Blazing Combat.* While Torres's early work was noted for his attention to detail and historical accuracy, he was also adept at humor and caricature, as seen in his work for *Mad* imitator *Sick.* In 1968, Torres made his first appearance in *Mad* magazine, where he would spend the next twenty-five years as one of the Usual Gang of Idiots, mainly illustrating TV show parodies.

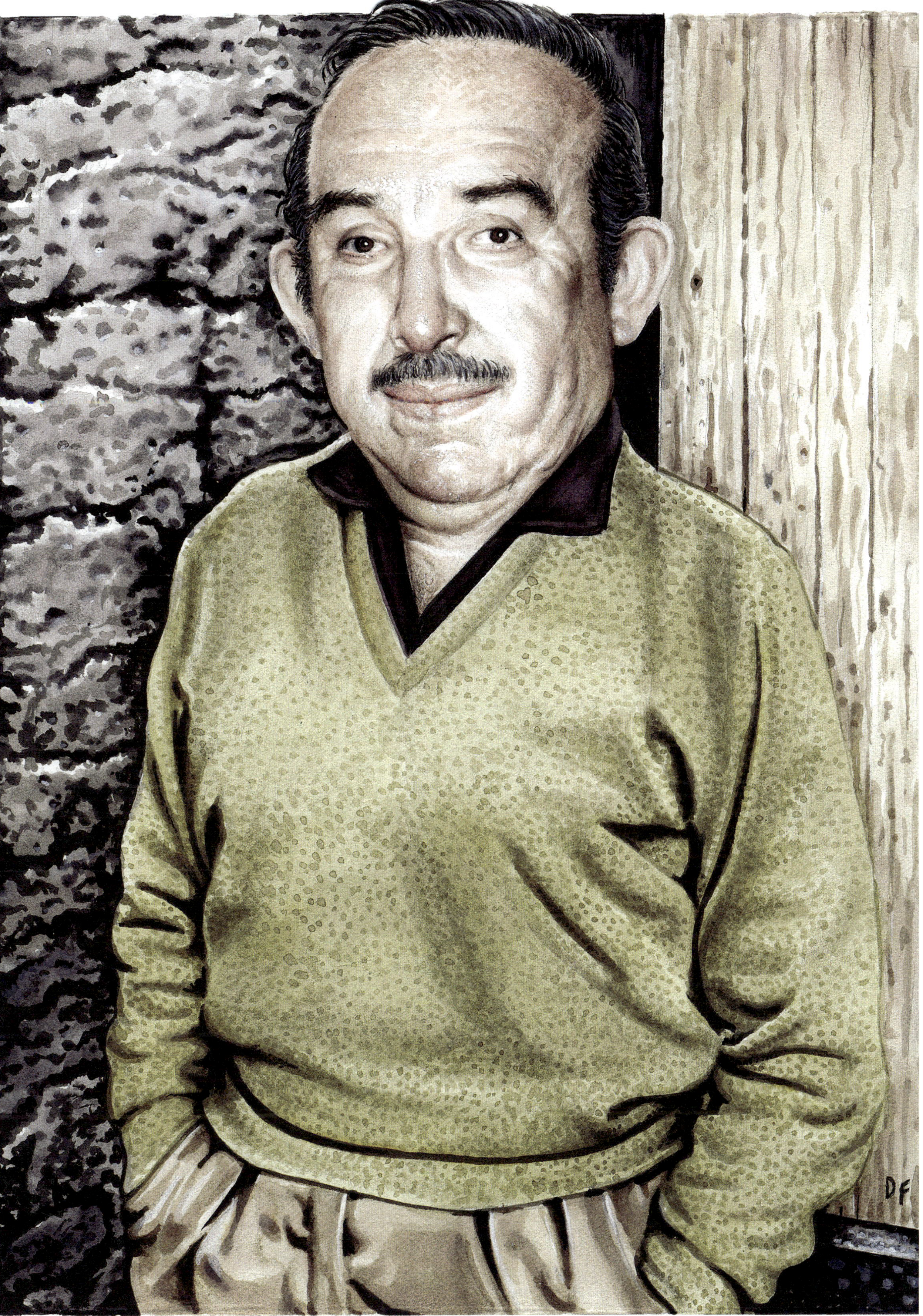
DF

GEORGE TUSKA

1916-2009

plate 92

George Tuska was born in Hartford, Connecticut. As a teenager, he moved to New York to study at the National Academy of Design, before taking a position at Eisner & Iger's comic book production shop.

Tuska's earliest confirmed work was a three-page story, "Skullduggery on Smoky Mountain," starring Wing Turner. It was published in *Mystery Men Comics* #1 in 1939. By 1940, Tuska had left Eisner & Iger for a staff position at Fiction House, where he stayed for the next six years, drawing characters like Kaänga in *Jungle Comics*, and Greasemonkey Griffin in *Wings Comics*. After Eisner and Iger dissolved their partnership, Tuska rejoined Eisner to pencil *The Spirit* and *Uncle Sam*. He also worked on Fawcett's *Captain Marvel* for a brief period. He was drafted in 1942 and was honorably discharged a year later and rejoined Fiction House. As the popularity of superheroes waned in the postwar years, he made his way to Lev Gleason's *Crime Does Not Pay*, where he spent several years as a featured artist, as well as working on the comics strips *Scorchy Smith and Buck Rogers.*

Tuska had freelanced on war and horror titles for Marvel Comic editor Stan Lee when the company was still operating as Atlas in the mid- to late '50s. Tuska returned to the company at Lee's invitation in 1964, penciling a *Tales of Suspense* story. Tuska became a formidable presence at Marvel, working as a penciler and inker on best-sellers *Iron Man*, *Daredevil*, and *the X-Men.* In 1972, Tuska helped create *Luke Cage: Hero for Hire* and adapted *Planet of the Apes* into comic books and black-and-white magazines. Tuska later worked for DC Comics on several titles, and for five years drew the syndicated comic strip *The World's Greatest Superheroes,* featuring Batman, Superman, and Wonder Woman.

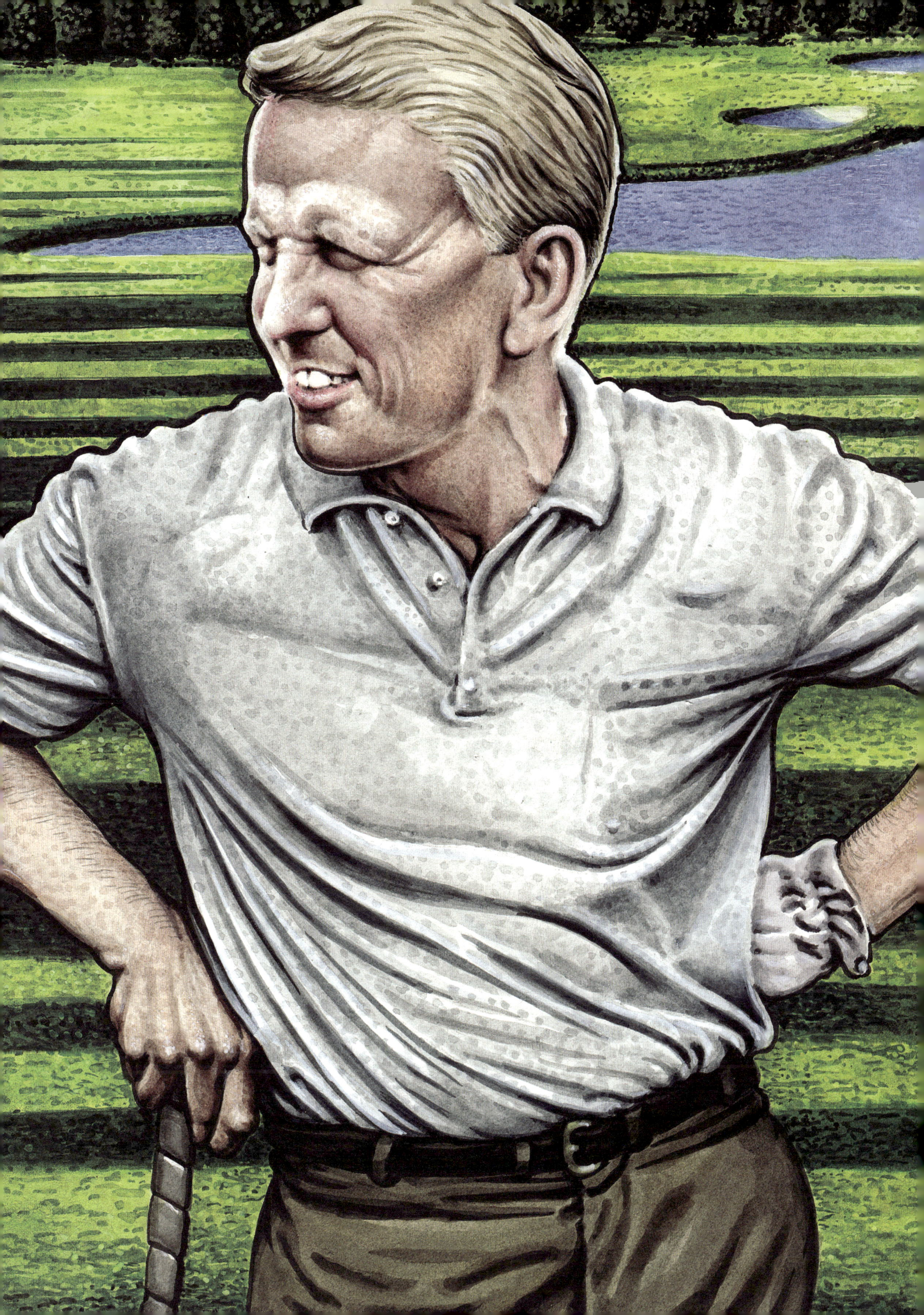

BILL VIGODA

1920-1973

plate
93

William "Bill" Vigodah (the original family name, later shortened to "Vigoda") was born in Brooklyn. He was the oldest of the three Vigoda brothers, who were raised by Jewish Russian immigrant parents. His younger brother, Herman, ("Hy"), became a comic book writer, and his older brother, Abraham ("Abe"), born in 1921, became a celebrated actor, known for his roles as Tessio in The *Godfather* and as Fish on TV's *Barney Miller.*

Bill attended the Commercial Art Studios in New York, before started his career as a staff artist for Lloyd Jacquet's comic book production shop, Funnies Inc., where he worked alongside his brother Hy. Joe Edwards, creator of *Li'l Jinx,* says he recruited him to join Archie during the early days of World War II. Vigoda had an unspecified medical condition that left him ineligible for the military, and several artists had left the company to join the service. His earliest signed work for the company was a six-page superhero story, "Roy the Super-Boy," that appeared in *Shield-Wizard Comics* #12 in 1943. He made his debut drawing Archie and friends in 1944, with a five-page Betty and Veronica story in *Archie Comics* #10, and continued to draw for Archie until his death in 1973.

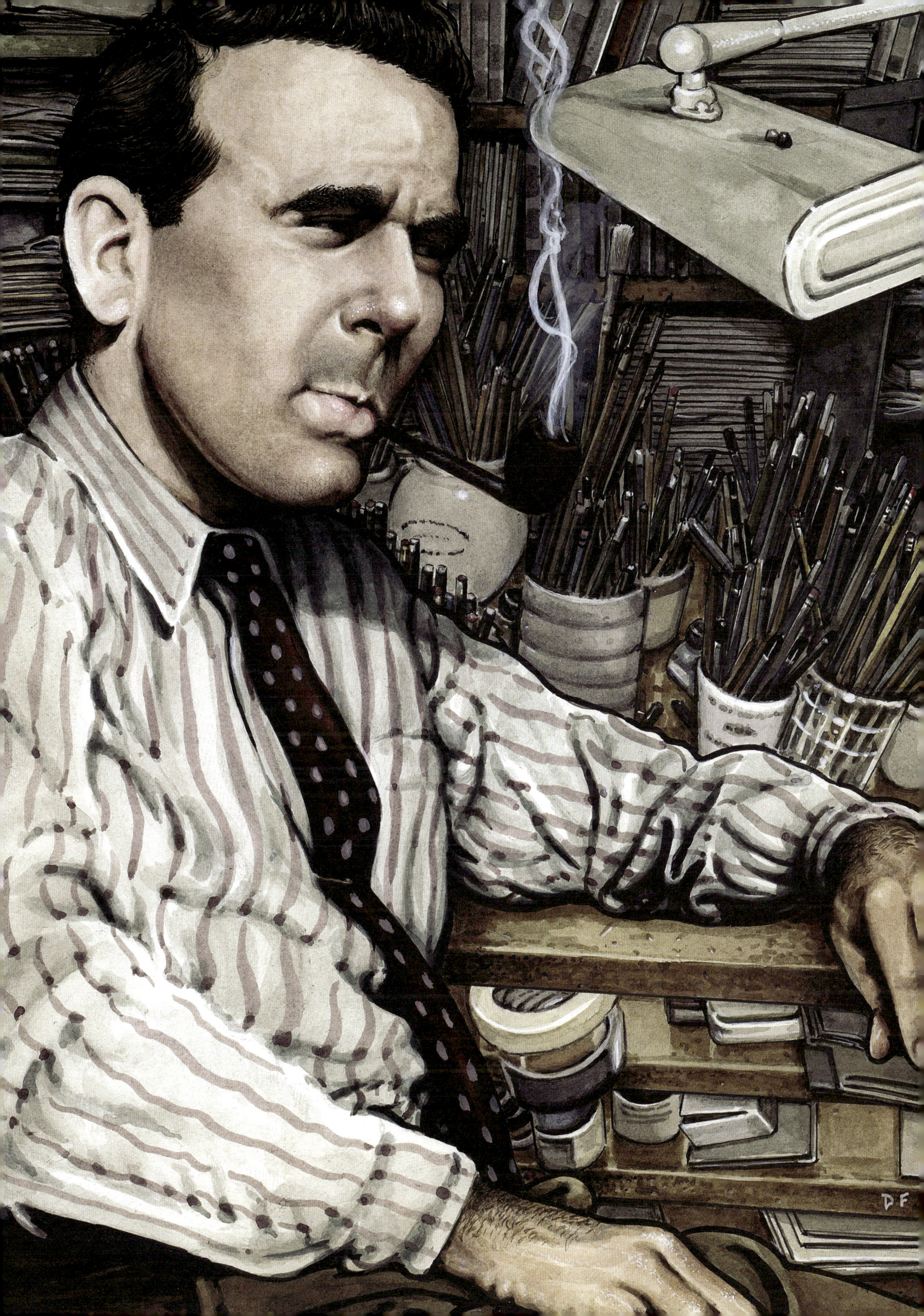
DF

HY VIGODA

1924-1993

plate 94

Herman "Hy" Vigoda, the youngest of the three Vigoda brothers, was born in Brooklyn, and attended the Art Students League in New York.

Hy started his career as a staff writer for Lloyd Jacquet's comic book production shop, Funnies Inc., where he worked alongside his artist brother Bill. He worked for Timely Comics, uncredited, on Sub-Mariner and the Human Torch stories, before joining Bill at Archie Comics. During the '40s, he scripted stories for DC's *Flash* and Fox Comic's *Blue Beetle*. In the '50s, he worked as an uncredited writer for syndicated comic strips *Aggie Mack* and *Bibs 'N' Tucker.* He continued to write for Archie Comics for several decades, while he also working as an art director and magazine editor.

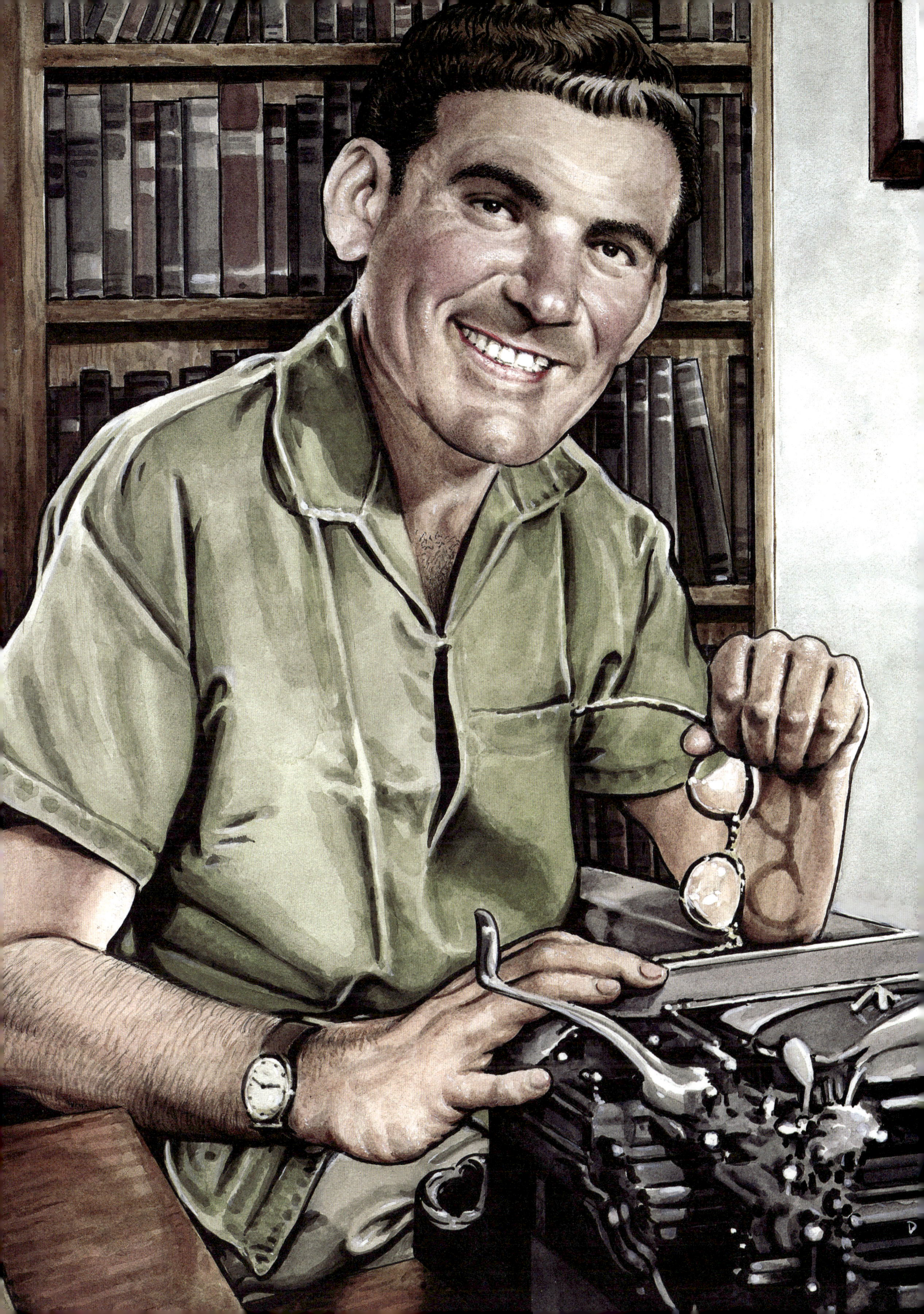

BILL WARD

1919–1998

plate
95

Born in Brooklyn and raised in Ridgewood, New Jersey, Bill Ward graduated from Brooklyn's Pratt Institute in 1941. He first found work as an art assistant in a Manhattan advertising agency. Ward entered the comic book business drawing backgrounds and inking panel borders as an assistant in Jack Binder's studio.

His earliest published work was in 1941, writing and drawing a two-page military humor story, "Private Ward," in Fawcett's *Spy Smasher* #2. In 1944, Ward's work caught the attention of Quality Comics, who hired him to replace Reed Crandall on the popular aviation adventure *Blackhawk*.

"Introducing Torchy," a five-page backup feature Ward wrote and drew for *Dollman* #8, featured a sexy, blonde-bombshell type that would earn him a reputation as a "good girl" artist. *Torchy* was also a backup feature in *Modern Comics* and was given her own title in 1949. In 1953, he scaled back his comic book work to concentrate on illustrations and gag panels for magazines.

His racy gag panels were right at home among the pinup girls in Martin Goodman's *Humorama* digest line, an array of titles like *Breezy*, *Joker*, *Romp*, and *Stare*. In the mid-'60s, he contributed to *The Adventures of Pussycat*, which featured a buxom secret agent, for various men's adventure magazines at Goodman's Magazine Management company.

His post–comic book work became more explicit in later years, where it could be found in magazines like *Leg Show* and *Juggs*.

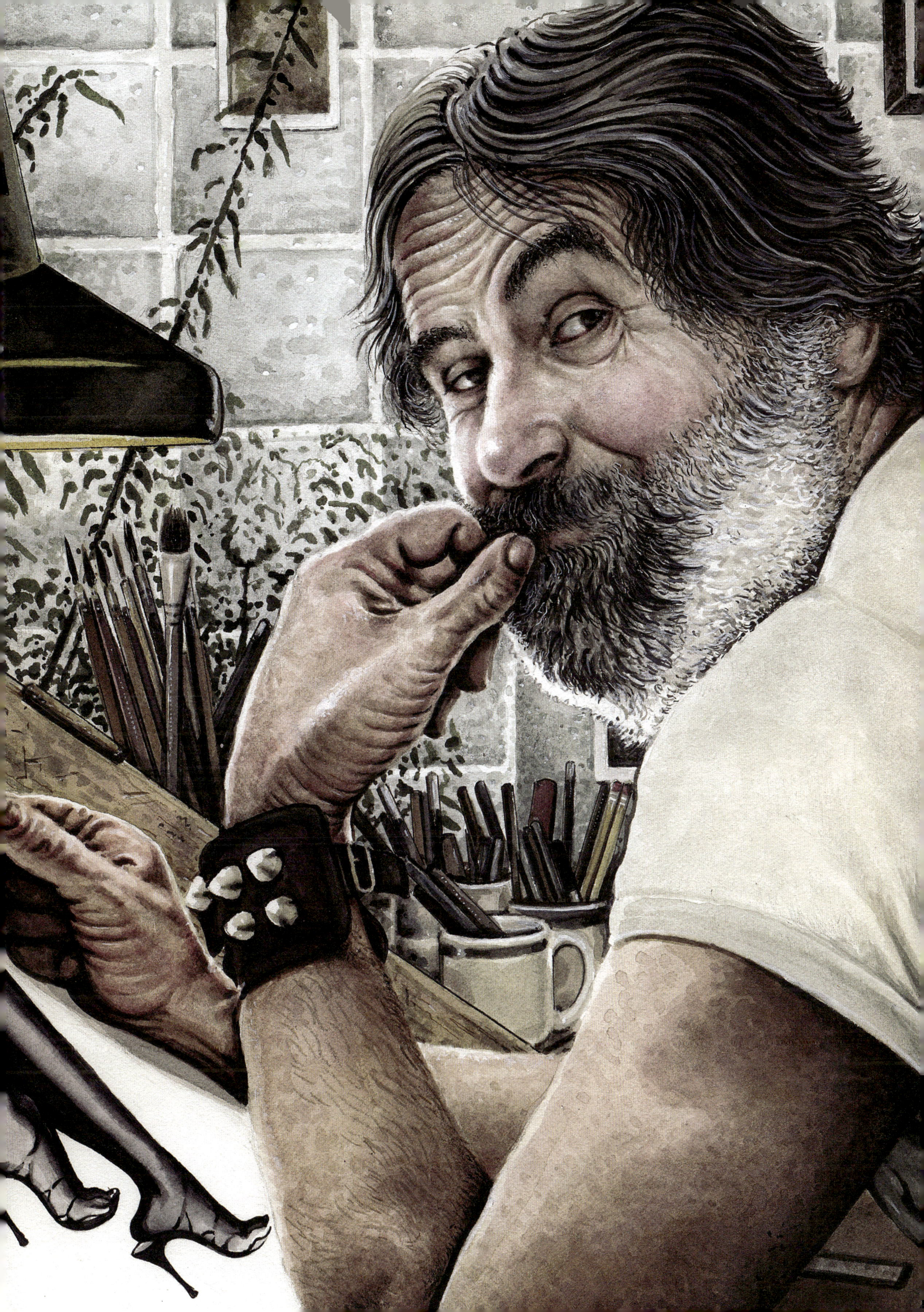

JAMES WARREN

b. 1930

plate 96

James Warren Taubman began his career at age eleven, hawking a self-published, mimeographed newspaper to neighbors in his hometown of Philadelphia. After graduating high school, Warren enrolled in the University of Pennsylvania to study architecture.

Warren's education was interrupted by his service in the Korean War. A close encounter with a machine gun left him with severe hearing loss. Warren received a medical discharge and returned to Philadelphia. In 1957, after a series of advertising jobs, Warren was inspired by Hugh Hefner's *Playboy* to launch his own men's magazine, *After Hours*. Financial problems and an overzealous district attorney's obscenity charge resulted in *After Hours* lasting only four issues. Literary agent and legendary science fiction fan Forrest J Ackerman's *After Hours* contribution, *Girls from Science-Fiction Movies*, helped inspire the creation of Warren's next magazine, *Famous Monsters of Filmland* (1958). Edited by Ackerman, it helped usher in Monster Mania in the 1960s. In this, it was aided and abetted by Warren's mail order merch business, Captain Company, which advertised in the back of the magazines.

After the success of *Famous Monsters*, Warren joined forces with former *Mad* editor Harvey Kurtzman. Kurtzman first edited *Wildest Westerns* for Warren, but soon launched *Help!*, a satirical magazine that often featured the work of Jack Davis and Will Elder. Kurtzman and Elder's modern-day Candide, Goodman Beaver, made his debut in *Help!*. *Help!* also helped to launch the careers of artists Robert Crumb, Jay Lynch, and Gilbert Shelton. Future Monty Python member Terry Gilliam and future feminist author Gloria Steinem were Kurtzman's assistants at *Help!*. *Help!* lasted for five years.

In 1964, Warren published the first issue of *Creepy*, a black-and-white comics magazine that presented beautifully rendered horror stories by many of the original EC artists, including Johnny Craig, Joe Orlando, and Reed Crandall, with scripts by Archie Goodwin and memorable covers by Frank Frazetta. The success of *Creepy* was soon followed by its sister publication *Eerie*; a war comics magazine, *Blazing Combat*; and later, *Vampirella*. In 1974, Warren published a series featuring reprints of Will Eisner's *The Spirit*. Warren left publishing in the late 1980s. His publications left an indelible imprint on millions of grateful fans.

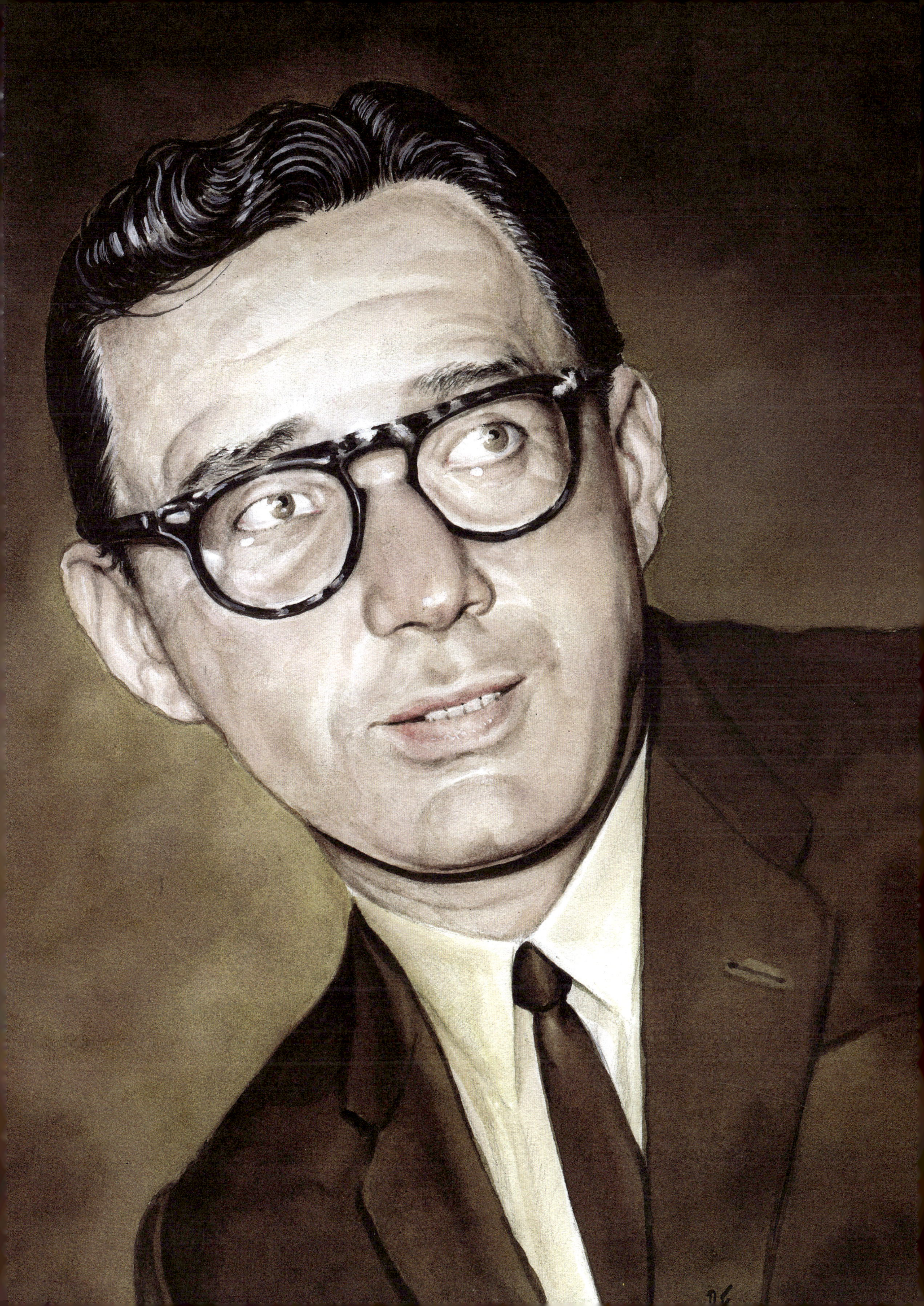

MORT WEISINGER

1915–1978

plate
97

Mortimer Weisinger was born in the Bronx. He sold his first published work to *Amazing Stories* while still in high school. A year later, he was firmly entrenched in the world of science fiction, publishing one of the earliest fanzines, *The Time Traveler*, with his friends Julius "Julie" Schwartz and Forrest J. Ackerman.

After graduating high school, Weisinger briefly attended New York University, where he served as the editor of the school newspaper. He and Schwartz formed Solar Sales Service, a literary agency dedicated to science fiction authors. Their client list included Ray Bradbury and H. P. Lovecraft. By 1940, he had left the agency to work for pulp magazine publisher Ned Pines's Standard Magazines, where he oversaw *Thrilling Detective*, *Thrilling Western*, and *Thrilling Wonder Stories*.

In 1941, Weisinger joined National Periodicals as an editor. His primary focus was capitalizing on the success of Batman and Superman titles and expanding the roster of DC superheroes, a task he performed for the next three decades, eventually demanding an appealing-yet-bland, static, sanitized Comics-Code friendly style of art from his artists. Weisinger also worked as story editor on the '50s TV series *The Adventures of Superman*. His paperback best-seller, *1,001 Valuable Things You Can Get Free*, was sold through comic book advertisements and went through eleven editions. He lived in Great Neck, New York.

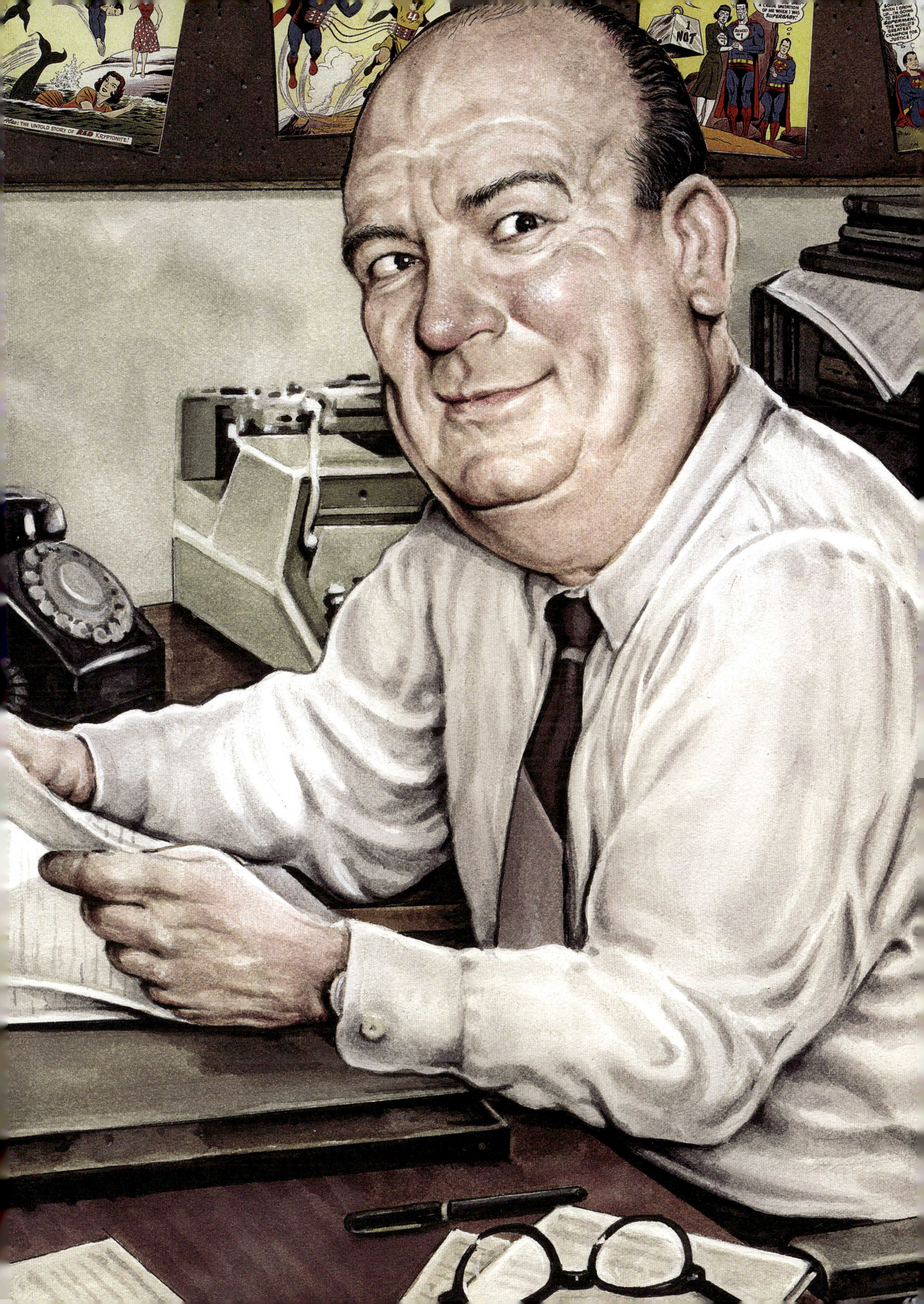
Also: THE UNTOLD STORY OF RED KRYPTONITE!
1 NOT
BIZARRO No 1
A CRUDE IMITATION OF ME WHEN I WAS SUPERBABY!
WHEN I GROW UP...I'M GOING TO BECOME SUPERMAN, THE WORLD'S GREATEST CHAMPION FOR JUSTICE!

ED WHEELAN

1888–1966

plate 98

Born in San Francisco, Edgar S. Wheelan attended New Hampshire's Phillips Exeter Academy and graduated in 1911 from Cornell University in Ithaca, New York. His earliest published work was a sports-oriented comic strip for the *New York America.*

In 1918, working for William Randolph Hearst, he created *Midget Movies,* a parody of contemporary films and stars. By 1920, he had parted ways with the publishing tycoon. Hearst replaced *Midget Movies* with the new *Thimble Theater* by E.C. Segar.

His next strip, *Minute Movies,* continued on the same theme as *Midget Movies* and ran until 1935. In 1939, National/DC reprinted the comic strip as an occasional backup feature in *Movie Comics* before making it a regular feature for the first fifty-nine issues of *Flash Comics.* By 1941, he had left newspaper work to try his hand at creating original work for comic books, like his biography of General George Marshall in *True Comics* #4.

Edgar Wheelan's Joke Book was published by DC in 1944. When Max Gaines launched EC Comics, the title characters were spun off into their own title, *Fat and Slat*, published in 1947. *Fat and Slat* also featured *Comics McCormick,* a parody of contemporary comic books. Wheelan left comics in 1947 after Gaines's death.

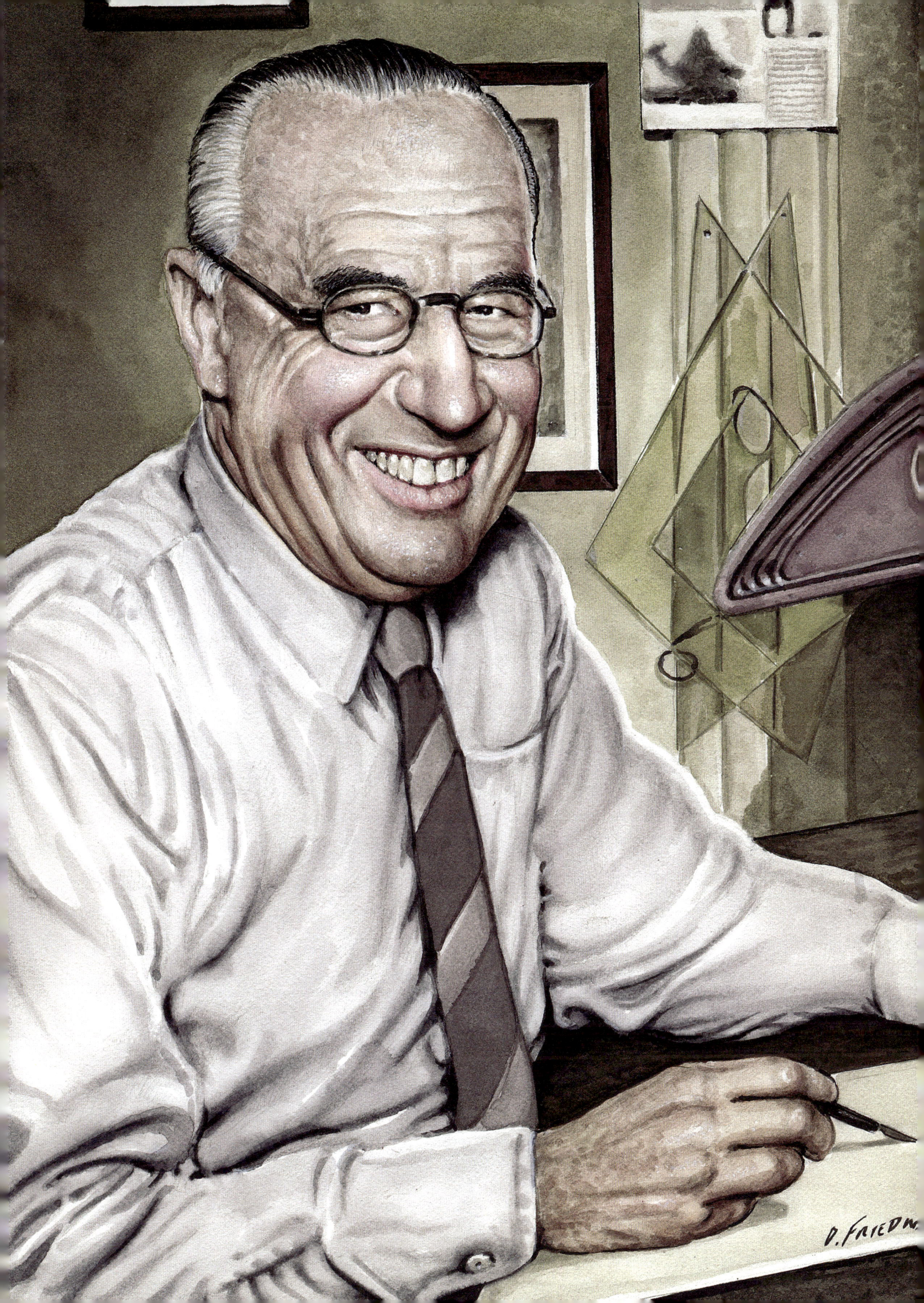

DOUG WILDEY

1922–1994

plate 99

Douglas S. Wildey was born in Yonkers, New York. He taught himself to draw and began his career drawing comics for a military newspaper, while stationed in Hawaii during World War II. His first professional work was a ten-page western, "Queen of Jeopardy," in *Top Secrets* #9, published by Street & Smith in 1949.

Wildey specialized in westerns over the next few years, like St. John's *The Texan,* with an occasional appearance in horror comics, such as Story Comics' *Fight Against Crime.* In 1954, he arrived at Atlas Comics, where he drew even more westerns, and spent time on the monster titles that were a mainstay of the publisher's output. His most significant work at the time started in 1954, when he introduced The Outlaw Kid, and drew nineteen issues of the popular western book over the next three years. When Atlas faltered toward the end of the decade, he freelanced for publishers Harvey and DC. For Dell Comics' *Four Color,* he drew an adaptation of the TV series *Dr. Kildare* in 1962. He also took over art duties on the long-running comic strip version of *The Saint.* Around the same time, he spent a short time as a fill-in artist on Milton Caniff's *Steve Canyon* newspaper strip.

Wildey went to Los Angeles in 1962 to work alongside artist Alex Toth on the primitive animated adventure series for TV, *Space Angel.* A few months later, he met producer Joe Barbera, who was looking to create an animated adventure series of his own. Wildey put together a presentation that was a mélange of *Terry and the Pirates*, *James Bond*, and futuristic gadgets cribbed from the pages of *Popular Science*. *Jonny Quest* premiered as a prime-time series on the ABC network in 1964.

Over the next two decades, Wildey worked on animated television shows like *Return to the Planet of the Apes*, *The Godzilla Power Hour*, and *Chuck Norris: Karate Commandos*. He also continued drawing comics, notably Gold Key's *Tarzan*, and stories for Skywald's black-and-white horror magazines *Psycho* and *Nightmare*.

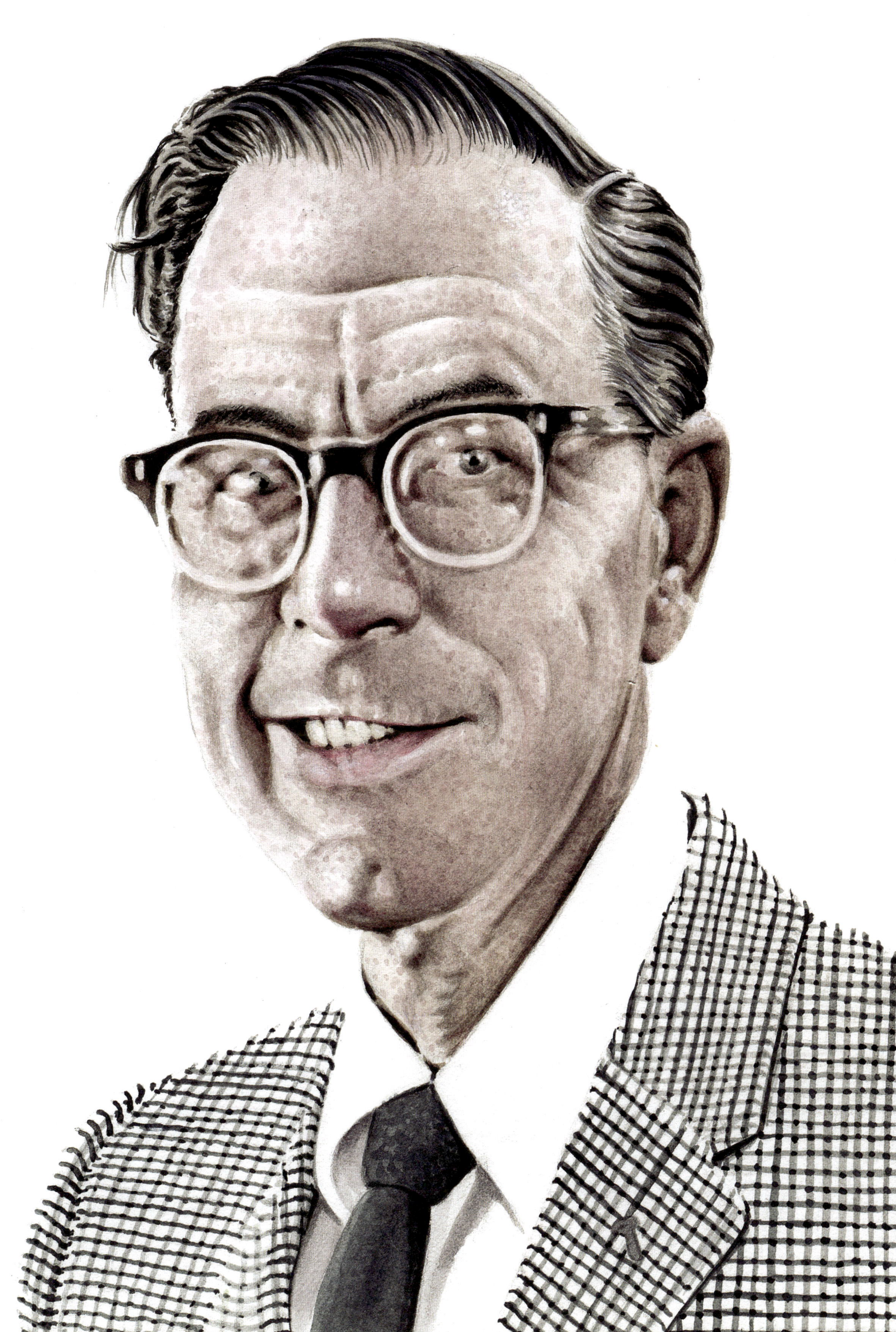

BOB WOOD

1918-1962

plate 100

Boston-born Robert Wood was a talented athlete and artist in high school. Wood brushed aside a chance at a major league baseball tryout to pursue a career as an artist.

Inspired by *Popeye* cartoons, he made his way to New York in 1935 and landed a job at the Fleischer cartoon studio, working on *Popeye* and *Betty Boop* cartoons. Soon, he returned to Boston, determined to make his fortune on his own as an animator.

Wood soon tired of the laborious animation process, and headed back to New York to break into the booming comic book business. He joined Harry "A" Chesler's shop, (alongside former Fleischer colleague Charles Biro), and began creating comics for publishers like Novelty Press, Dell, and MLJ.

Wood and Biro were reunited at the end of the decade, writing and drawing *Daredevil* and *Blue Bolt* comics at Lev Gleason Publications. Over drinks one night in a seedy, downtown bar, Wood and Biro hatched a plan for a gritty "true crime" comic book. The next day they approached Gleason and pitched their idea.

Crime Does Not Pay hit the newsstands in November 1942 and was a runaway success. Wood and Biro had negotiated a generous royalty agreement with Gleason, and the duo prospered over the next decade. But by 1955, things changed drastically. Comic books were under siege for depicting the very violence that made *Crime Does Not Pay* a huge success. Lev Gleason was forced to shut down the comic after one-hundred-and-forty-seven issues. Biro got a job as a graphic artist at NBC, but Wood drifted from job to job, in a haze of booze and substantial gambling debts.

On August 27, 1958, Wood flagged down a taxi on Irving Place and told the driver "I'm going to get a couple of hours of sleep and jump in the river. I killed a woman in Room 91 of the Irving Hotel." After dropping Wood off at a Greenwich Village hotel, the cabbie called the police.

At the Irving Hotel, police found the body of Wood's "girlfriend," clad only in a bloody negligee, surrounded by empty whiskey bottles. Wood had capped off an eleven-day drinking binge by crushing Violette Phillips' skull with an electric iron.

Wood pleaded guilty to first-degree manslaughter, yet served only three years in Sing Sing prison. A year after his release, Wood went missing from his job as a short-order cook in a New Jersey diner. His body was found alongside the New Jersey Turnpike, murdered by former prison acquaintances over unpaid loans. Crime, indeed, does not pay.

CRIME

10¢ DOES NOT PAY

No. 46

LEV GLEASON, PUBLISHER • CHARLES BIRO AND BOB WOOD, EDITORS

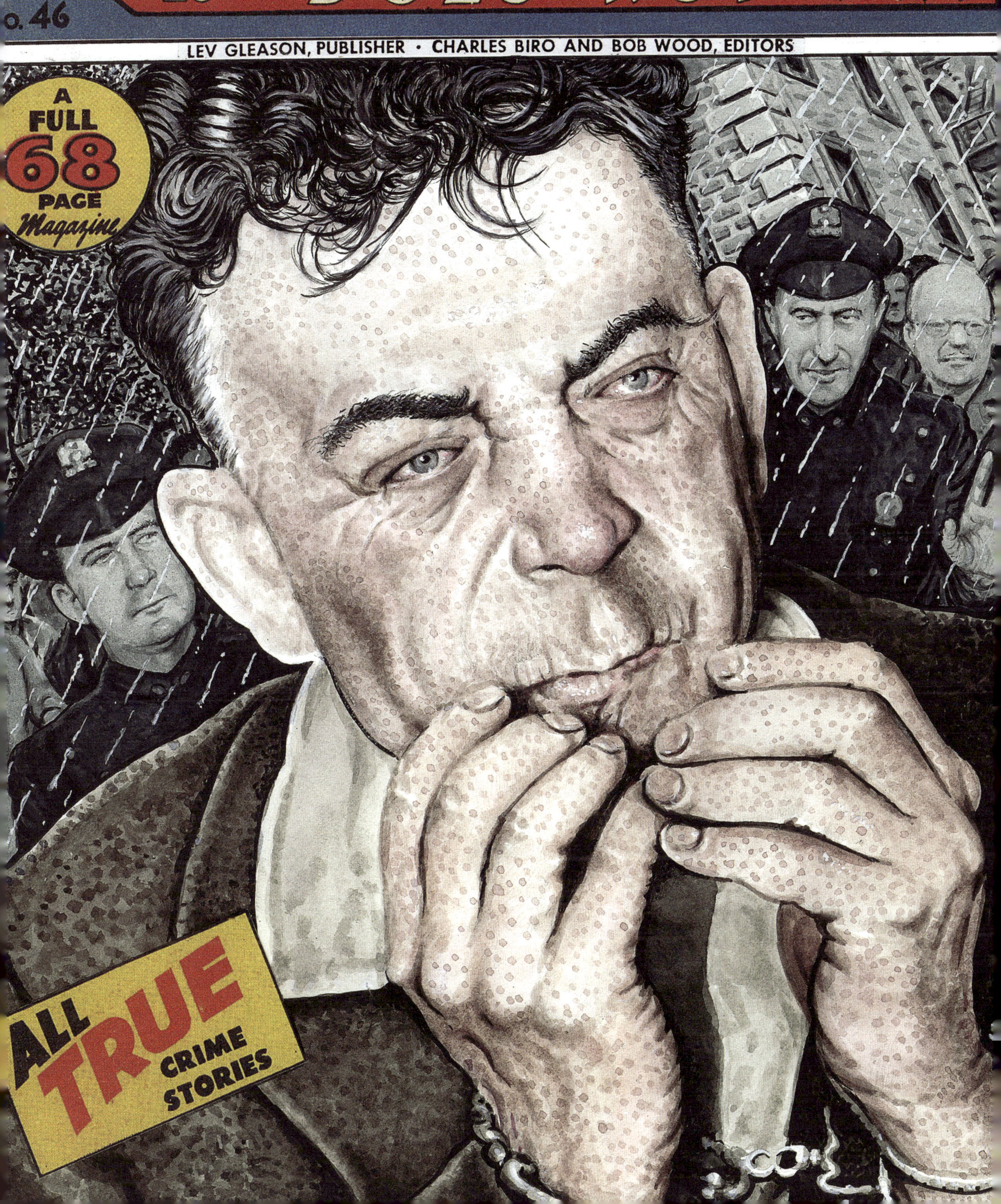

HONORABLE MENTIONS

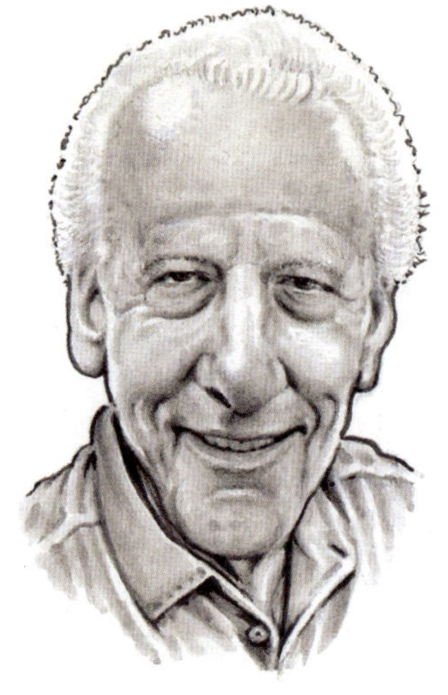

JOE GIELLA (b. 1928), a Silver Age comic book artist, is best known as an inker for DC Comics in the '50s and '60s, including inking Gil Kane's *Green Lantern* pencils.

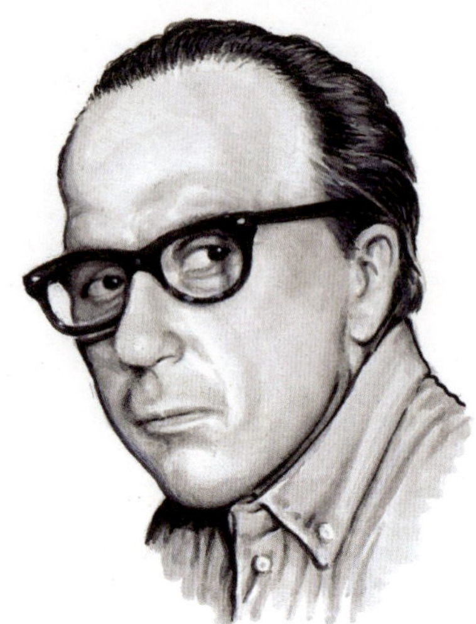

JERRY GRANDENETTI (1926–2010), was an innovative comics artist who worked on Will Eisner's *The Spirit*, and, later, war comics for DC. He was also an advertising art director.

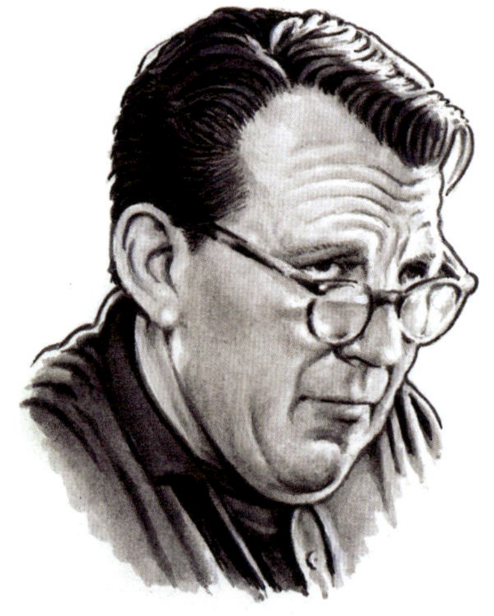

GILL FOX (1915–2004), was an editor, writer, and artist during the Golden Age of comics. He created covers for *Dollman*, and edited *Police Comics*, which featured Jack Cole's Plastic Man. He would later become a prominent political cartoonist.

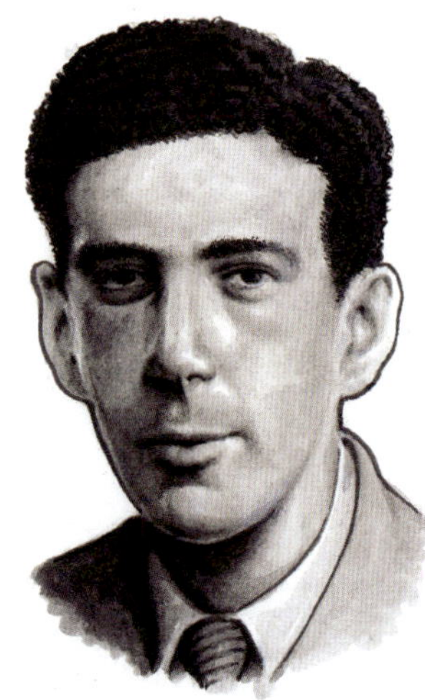

RUBEN MOREIRA (1922–1984), was a Puerto Rican comics artist and writer who penciled for various comics companies in the '40s, before, most prominently, working for DC Comics.

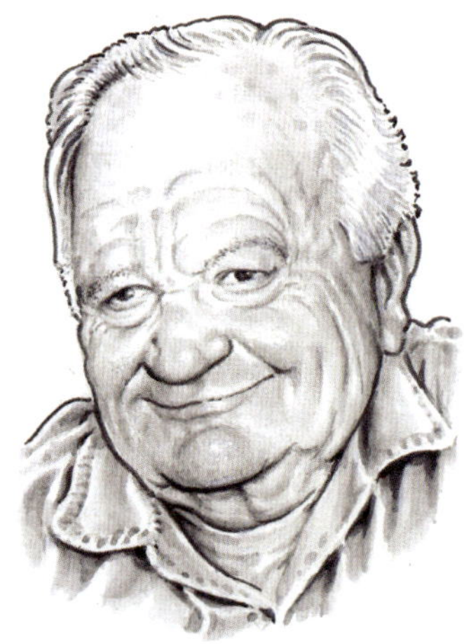

CHUCK CUIDERA (1915–2001), was a Golden Age comic book artist who co-created and drew the popular aviator character, Blackhawk, for Quality's Military Comics. He later worked as an art director for Quality.

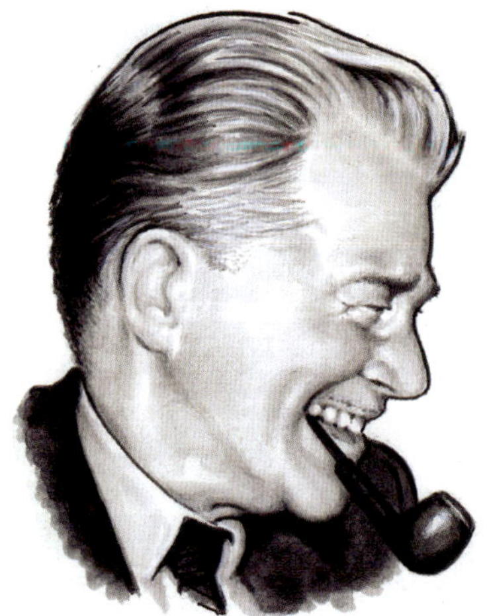

KLAUS NORDLING (1910–1986), was a Finnish-born Golden Age comics writer/artist. He worked on Lady Luck for Will Eisner's *Spirit* newspaper supplement, and co-created the comics character Thin Man.

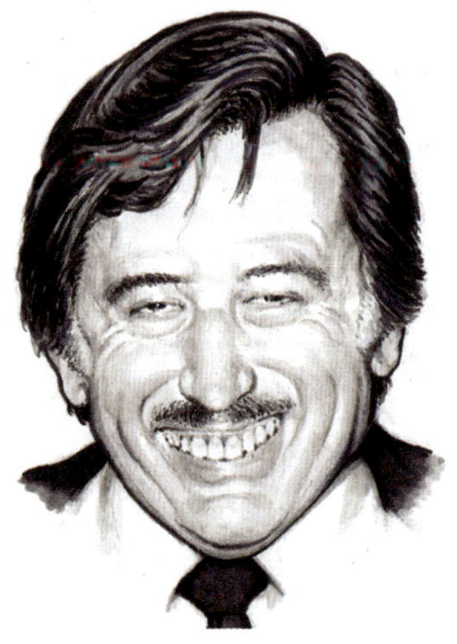

DICK GIORDANO (1932–2010), began his career in the early 1950s as an artist—and then an editor—for Charlton comics. He rose to become executive editor at DC Comics.

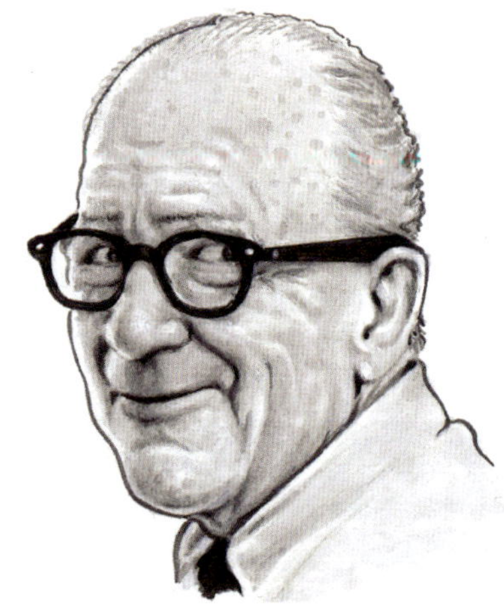

DAN GORDON (1897–1970), was a versatile funny animal and teen humor comic book artist in the '40s for ACG and DC Comics. He was also a storyboard artist/writer, and a director at the Fleischer Studios, Famous Studios, and Hanna-Barbera.

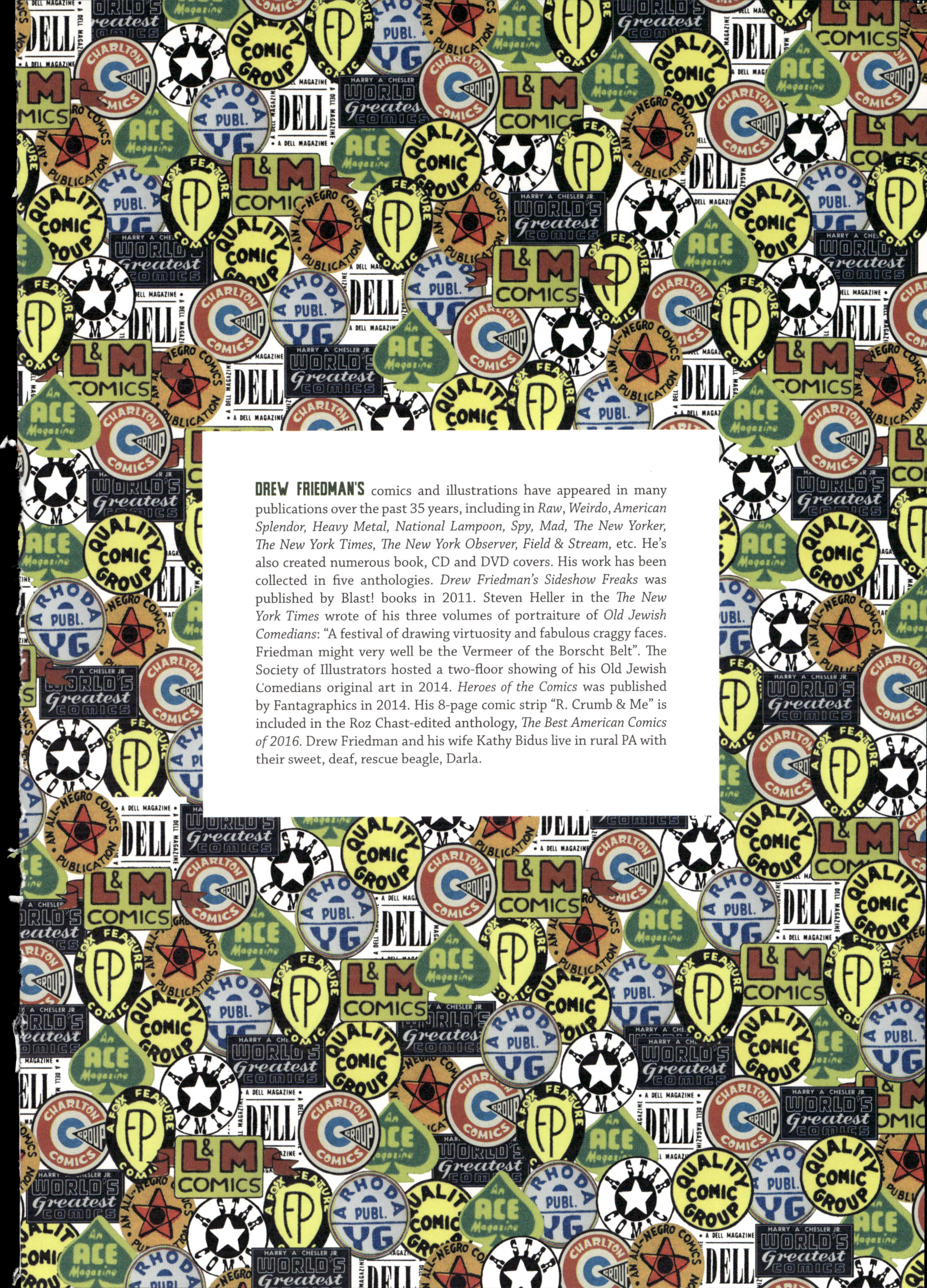

DREW FRIEDMAN'S comics and illustrations have appeared in many publications over the past 35 years, including in *Raw*, *Weirdo*, *American Splendor*, *Heavy Metal*, *National Lampoon*, *Spy*, *Mad*, *The New Yorker*, *The New York Times*, *The New York Observer*, *Field & Stream*, etc. He's also created numerous book, CD and DVD covers. His work has been collected in five anthologies. *Drew Friedman's Sideshow Freaks* was published by Blast! books in 2011. Steven Heller in the *The New York Times* wrote of his three volumes of portraiture of *Old Jewish Comedians*: "A festival of drawing virtuosity and fabulous craggy faces. Friedman might very well be the Vermeer of the Borscht Belt". The Society of Illustrators hosted a two-floor showing of his Old Jewish Comedians original art in 2014. *Heroes of the Comics* was published by Fantagraphics in 2014. His 8-page comic strip "R. Crumb & Me" is included in the Roz Chast-edited anthology, *The Best American Comics of 2016*. Drew Friedman and his wife Kathy Bidus live in rural PA with their sweet, deaf, rescue beagle, Darla.

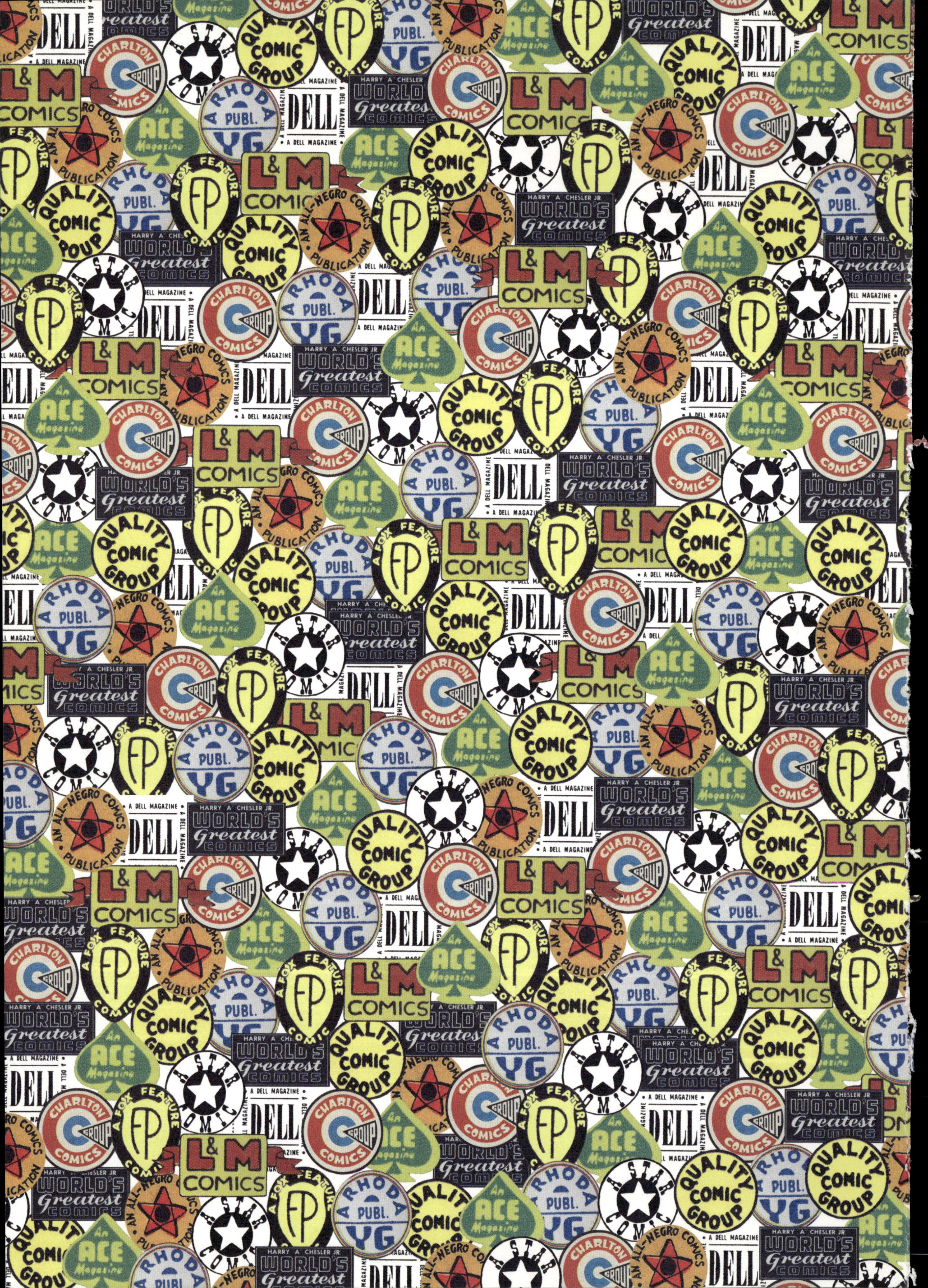

DELL
A DELL MAGAZINE
L&M COMICS
CHARLTON COMICS GROUP
QUALITY COMIC GROUP
A FOX FEATURE FP COMIC
A STAR COMIC
ARHODA PUBL. YG
An ACE Magazine
HARRY A CHESLER JR. WORLD'S Greatest COMICS
AN ALL-NEGRO COMICS PUBLICATION